Those of Little Note

THOSE
OF LITTLE NOTE

Gender, Race, and Class in Historical
Archaeology

edited by *Elizabeth M. Scott*

The University of Arizona Press
Tucson & London

The University of Arizona Press
Copyright © 1994
Arizona Board of Regents
All rights reserved

⊛ This book is printed on acid-free, archival-quality paper.
Manufactured in the United States of America

99 98 97 96 95 94   6 5 4 3 2 1

Library of Congress Cataloging-in-Publication Data
Those of little note : gender, race, and class in historical
archaeology / edited by Elizabeth M. Scott.
p.   cm.
Includes bibliographical references and index.
ISBN 0-8165-1411-9 (acid-free paper). — ISBN 0-8165-1499-2
(pbk. : acid-free paper)
    1. Archaeology and history—North America.   2. North
America—Antiquities.   3. Sex role—North America—History.
4. Social classes—North America—History.   I. Scott,
Elizabeth M.
CC79.H5T48   1994
070.01—dc20   94-12165
                                                        CIP

British Library Cataloguing-in-Publication Data
A catalogue record for this book is available from the British
Library.

in memory of Eugenia May Scott (1898–1993),
my grandmother on my father's side

Contents

viii

Contents

Contributors

EVERETT BASSETT is currently manager of cultural resources for Dames and Moore's Salt Lake City office. He has an A.B. in history from James Madison University and is currently completing his Ph.D. in anthropology at the University of Utah. Bassett's research includes the development and use of storage technology, prehistoric and historic land use, and contact-period Native American culture change. He has conducted fieldwork in the Sudan, in Egypt, and throughout the American Intermountain West.

DONALD L. HARDESTY is professor of anthropology at the University of Nevada, Reno. He was educated at the University of Kentucky and the University of Oregon (Ph.D., 1972). Hardesty has been president of the Society for Historical Archaeology, and his research interests include historical archaeology of the American West, mining history, and ecological anthropology. His recent publications include *The Archaeology of Mining and Miners*, "The Miner's Domestic Household: Perspectives from the American West" (in *Sozialgeschichte des Bergbau im 19. und 20. Jahrhundert*), and *Others Knowing Others* (with D. Fowler).

LOUISE M. JACKSON holds a joint appointment at the University of British Columbia's Department of Anthropology and Museum of Anthropology. She received a B.A. Hons. in art history, University College, London, 1979; a Graduate Certificate in museum practice and an M.A. in art history, University of Michigan, 1982; and a Ph.D. in anthropology, University of California—Los Angeles, 1991. Her dissertation, *Nineteenth Century British Ceramics: A Key to Cultural Dynamics in Southwestern Alaska*, was awarded an Honorable Mention in the Society for American Archaeology's 1991 Dissertation Prize Competition. Her research interests include Russian American material culture, Native Alaskan cultural centers, and museology.

ELIZABETH KRYDER-REID received her doctorate in anthropology at Brown University. Her publications include several articles on the interpretation of eighteenth-century landscapes and a coedited special issue, *Site and Sight*, of the *Journal of Garden History*. Her interest in the symbolic analysis of space has led to a study of California mission landscapes as a locus of contact. Supported by a fellowship from the Huntington Library, she is also examining the historiography and reconstruction of the mission gardens. Kryder-Reid is a research associate for an early American landscape vocabulary project at the Center for Advanced Study in the Visual Arts, National Gallery of Art.

NANCY LADD MULLER is currently a Ph.D. candidate in anthropology at the University of Massachusetts at Amherst. Her recent publications include an article on DuBois's pragmatic philosophy as he addressed the construction of the race concept and its predicated action, racism. Muller considers herself an activist scholar and was a consultant for the Women's International League for Peace and Freedom as they created a "Women's Treaty" in 1992 uniting the concerns of women in the Americas. She recently spent a year "behind the color line," in an urban area in the Northeast, working with peoples of African descent as they continued to resist racism.

DONNA J. SEIFERT graduated from Lawrence University and earned a Ph.D. in anthropology from the University of Iowa. She is a principal archaeologist and project manager with John Milner Associates, Inc.

Her current research interests include the historical archaeology of Washington, D.C., and understanding the role of gender in historical archaeology. Her recent publications on these topics are a contribution to *The Historical Archaeology of the Chesapeake* (coauthored with Charles D. Creek) and the volume of *Historical Archaeology* she edited, *Gender in Historical Archaeology*. Seifert has been elected to serve as president of the Society for Historical Archaeology in 1995.

SUZANNE M. SPENCER-WOOD, Associate of the Peabody Museum, Harvard University, wrote the first feminist article published in the leading journal *Historical Archaeology* (1987). She organized the first two gender symposia in American historical archaeology at the 1989 Society for Historical Archaeology Conference and at the 1989 Chacmool Conference (the latter published in *The Archaeology of Gender*). Spencer-Wood developed a feminist theoretical approach, most fully explicated in a contribution to *Quandaries and Quests: Visions of Archaeology's Future*. She presented related research on nonlinear systems theory at the 1989 Joint Archaeological Congress and the 1993 Chacmool Conference (published proceedings forthcoming). Previously she edited *Consumer Choice in Historical Archaeology*.

DAVID R. STARBUCK received his Ph.D. in anthropology from Yale University in 1975 and currently teaches at Plymouth State College and Adirondack Community College. He is the editor of *IA: The Journal of the Society for Industrial Archeology* and is also the staff archaeologist at Saratoga National Historical Park. His recent publications include several articles in *Archaeology* magazine, and he is currently directing excavations at the Revolutionary War fortress of Mount Independence on Lake Champlain and at the French and Indian War encampment on Rogers Island in Fort Edward, New York. He is the recipient of the 1988 Norton Prize of the Society for Industrial Archeology and the 1987 Chester B. Price Award of the New Hampshire Archeological Society.

Preface

This book began as a symposium at the annual meeting of the Society for Historical and Underwater Archaeology, held in 1992 in Kingston, Jamaica. All of the contributors to the book presented papers in the symposium, as did several scholars who, for a variety of reasons, could not be included here: Ellen-Rose Savulis, Margaret Purser, and Laura F. Klein. My thanks to all of the participants for an engaging, thought-provoking, and enlightening symposium.

The present volume contains substantially revised and expanded versions of those original conference papers. The conversions from oral presentation to book chapter were greatly facilitated by two anonymous reviewers and by Christine R. Szuter, Acquiring Editor for Social Sciences at the University of Arizona Press. I thank all of the authors for taking seriously the reviewers', Christine Szuter's, and my comments, for rethinking and reworking their chapters, and for meeting what must have seemed like an endless series of deadlines. This book exists because these (and other) scholars have been actively engaged in historical archaeological research concerning gender. Editing the volume has been a gratifying experience precisely because the research presented by the contributors is of the highest caliber.

Several persons and organizations have provided invaluable assistance in this endeavor. One could not ask for better editors than Christine Szuter and Judith Wesley Allen. I am grateful to them for their excellent guidance and to Jennifer Comeau for her thoughtful copyediting. Caroline G. Banks generously provided encouragement and assistance in numerous ways. Finally, Donald Heldman provided unfailing professional, personal, and financial support, and undertook much more than his fair share of housework; I am grateful, as always, for his clear insights and sound reckoning.

Those of Little Note

1 Introduction

1

Through the Lens of Gender

Archaeology, Inequality, and Those "of Little Note"

Elizabeth M. Scott

In 1779, at the fort and trading post of Michilimackinac in what is now northern Michigan, commanding officer Patrick Sinclair described a group of Native Americans visiting from Montreal: "some of them of little note, & other[s] dispicable" (*Michigan Pioneer and Historical Collections* 9:526–27). His description reveals a stereotypical British racist attitude toward Native Americans, of which abundant examples may be cited for colonial North America.

I use the phrase "those 'of little note'" in three ways, and they broadly describe the contents of this book. First, I use it in the sense that Sinclair did, meaning those considered of little importance, not worthy of "notice," by the dominant social, political, and economic group in a past society. Second, and following from the first, I use it to mean those considered not worth "noting" or writing about, those who therefore are not as visible to us in the written records we study. And thirdly, I use it to refer to those written about less frequently, or little "noted," by historical archaeologists.

This volume attempts to redress this by presenting case studies of historical and archaeological research on various ethnic, racial, gender, and socioeconomic groups in colonial and postcolonial North America. The authors use evidence from diverse past societies in eighteenth-, nineteenth-, and early twentieth-century North America to explore ways of making more visible Native Americans, African Americans, and Euro-Americans of differing ethnic groups and economic classes. The Euro-Americans examined here are those who were marginalized or out of the mainstream (monastic communities and predominantly male mining towns and military camps) and those who have been "little noted" by historical archaeologists (prostitutes and domestic reformers).

How does a focus on gender help make these groups more visible? What other aspects of social and economic relations in past societies are brought into sharper relief when viewed through the lens of gender? Scholars concerned with revealing inequalities in past societies have examined the less visible in those societies, and some have examined gender inequality specifically (e.g., Zinn 1980; McGuire and Paynter 1991; Ferguson 1991, 1992; Spencer-Wood 1991b; Yentsch 1991b; McDonald et al. 1991; Orser 1990, 1991; Heldman 1986; Harrison 1991c; Wolf 1982; Stone and MacKenzie 1990; Worsley 1981). However, the collection here examines the *interconnectedness* of gender, class, race, and ethnicity in past societies and the ways in which this can be made visible through historical archaeology.

Since publication of Margaret Conkey and Janet Spector's 1984 groundbreaking article "Archaeology and the Study of Gender," archaeological research on gender has steadily increased. Numerous journal articles and conference papers in both prehistoric and historical archaeology have resulted, and 1991 saw the publication of three volumes of research about gender and archaeology: *Engendering Archaeology*, edited by Joan Gero and Margaret Conkey; *The Archaeology of Gender*, edited by Dale Walde and Noreen Willows; and *Gender in Historical Archaeology*, edited by Donna Seifert. In addition, detailed reviews of feminist approaches in archaeology have been published by Janet Spector and Mary Whelan (1989) and Alison Wylie (1991, 1992).

Archaeologists concerned with gender in past societies are fortunate to be able to draw on a rich and varied array of feminist scholarship in several fields: cultural and biological anthropology, social history, and literary and social criticism.[1] The research presented in this book directly benefits from the work of these and other scholars during the last twenty or so years — that is, from the "second wave of feminism" in North America (Wylie 1992, 17; Gordon 1986, 21). Thus, the scholars included in this collection are writing at a time when cultural diversity is a prominent buzzword in academia;

when feminist scholars are concerned with the interrelatedness of gender, class, ethnicity, race, and sexuality; and when white Western feminisms (as well as other schools of white Western academic thought) are being criticized by scholars of color. It is no accident, then, that themes of colonialism/domination and resistance, of gender, class, and race, and of gender and sexuality appear throughout the book.

However, although we are entering the larger field of gender studies at a time of some maturity, historical archaeological research concerning gender is not nearly so advanced. For the majority of practitioners in the discipline, gender still is not considered a significant topic of research, or even a significant aspect of peoples' lives in the past societies being studied. Also, despite the fact that several different theoretical approaches to the historical archaeology of gender have been put forth (Yentsch 1991a, 1991b; Scott 1991b; Spencer-Wood 1991a,1991c; Spector 1991, 1993), the minority of practitioners who do address gender in their research often find themselves still asking questions of a rather fundamental nature: How can we see the archaeological evidence of gender operating in past societies? What material remains can be associated with men, women, and children in the particular contexts we have available to us archaeologically? How do we move from men's and women's artifacts to interpretations about the role gender played in the structure of life in past societies, whether at the level of the household, community, or region? How do we link the material evidence of gender with (and separate it from) that of socioeconomic position, ethnicity, and race in our interpretations of the past? How does paying attention to gender enable us to say more than we otherwise could about the societies we study?

In the essays presented here, archaeologists grapple with these questions in a variety of contexts and using a variety of material and archival records. Others recently have pointed out that by looking at gender archaeologically, or by trying to make women visible archaeologically, we can find ways to make other nonelite, disenfranchised, or less-powerful groups in past societies more visible as well (Conkey 1991; Yentsch 1991a, 254, 259; Wylie 1991, 22). Kathleen Deagan (1991) has observed that historical archaeology has "a major obligation and opportunity" (108–9) to make the pasts of these groups more visible.

Some but not all of the contributors here focus on women in the societies they study. Some but not all use explicitly feminist approaches in their research. Some place more emphasis than do others on gender as an analytical category. However, the archaeology presented here cannot be disengaged from sociopolitical conditions in the United States in the late

1980s and early 1990s. That is, regardless of political leanings, and whether or not feminist ideas per se are mentioned, these archaeologists, like many others, have likely come to this research in a way similar to the scenario so elegantly related by Alison Wylie (1992, 17): issues about women's rights or pay equity raised in their own lives, or the lives of those they know, call into question the "naturalness" of gender relations in the present, which then calls into question interpretations about gender relations in the past. The sociopolitics of archaeology in general (Trigger 1980; Gero et al. 1983; Fowler 1987) and the gendered politics of archaeology in particular (Gero 1983, 1985, 1991) have been addressed in detail elsewhere.

Although the essays in this book concern quite different societies, many of them address similar themes and issues. I discuss these below, placing the essays in the context of recent feminist scholarship in anthropology and related fields. This is followed by a discussion of "food for thought" for historical archaeologists, raised by recent critiques of feminist theory. I close with a discussion of the implications this scholarship has for future approaches to archaeology.

Colonialism, Domination, and Resistance

Resistance to domination is a topic increasingly addressed by historical archaeologists (Deagan 1991, 109) (e.g., McGuire and Paynter 1991; Ferguson 1991, 1992; McDonald et al. 1991; Orser 1990, 1991; Handsman 1990). By looking at the specific political, economic, and social contexts in which domination and resistance occurred in daily life, it is possible to see different kinds of power being used by various groups in a past society. "To be less powerful is not to be power-less, or even to lose all the time" (Gordon 1986, 24).

In her essay here, Louise Jackson reveals much more resistance than domination among Native Alaskans during Russian colonization, seen especially in women's roles in trading and in the ways they put Russian cloth and clothing items to their own uses. Everett Bassett delineates late nineteenth- and early twentieth-century U.S. policies of domination over the Western Apache and the ways in which Apache families used those constraints to revive traditional kin relations and ties among themselves. Nancy Muller details the political, economic, and social domination of African Americans by white Americans in one community in Massachusetts, and then reveals the way several generations of women in one family, that of W. E. B. DuBois, managed to retain ownership of family land during a time when racial segregation forced African American men to migrate out of that community to gain employment. Donald Hardesty discusses the sense of class identity that emerged among working-class women and men in mining towns as a means of resisting and opposing the interests of corporate capitalists there. Finally, Suzanne Spencer-Wood reveals how working-class and minority women successfully requested changes in some of the programs of middle- and upper-class reformers.

Feminist scholarship has always concerned colonialism and/or domination (be it sexual, racial, or class domination, or some combination thereof) and resistance to it, often employing a dualism of domination/resistance and oppressor/oppressed. Recent scholarship has revealed the necessity of going beyond this dualism when studying colonial and postcolonial societies to understand the complexity and variety of interactions that took place in specific historical contexts (Gordon 1986; Mohanty 1991a; hooks 1989; Stoler 1991). Dorothy Smith's (1987, 2) term *relations of ruling*, discussed by Chandra Mohanty (1991a, 13-14), provides a useful way to think about the processes of ruling—the processes of domination and resistance at a variety of levels and interstices—among peoples in colonial and postcolonial societies. This approach makes it not only possible but imperative to analyze the particular form of colonialism that existed in a specific time and place. Ann Stoler (1991) has shown that both gender and racial inequalities were necessary for establishing imperial authority.

Much feminist scholarship emphasizes ways in which women have been, and are, dominated by men, and peoples of color by whites, in various societies. However, bell hooks (1989, 20) notes the importance of challenging the idea that men have always been the oppressors and women always the victims by examining the role that women have played and do play "in the perpetuation and maintenance of systems of domination." Not only do both women and men have the capacity to be dominated or dominating, but "in many places in the world oppressed and oppressor share the same color." Simplistic, binary, and ahistorical categories do injustice to the complex relations in colonial and postcolonial communities. And however difficult it may be, it is necessary, as Linda Gordon (1986, 23) points out, to include both domination *and* resistance in interpretations of the past.

The Triumvirate: Gender-Race-Class

As a result primarily of criticism by women of color, feminist scholarship recently has begun to address the interrelatedness of gender with class and race, and, most recently, with sexual preference. Scholars have begun to pay attention to the ways in which these factors affect each other, and therefore cannot be studied in isolation.

However, scholars also have warned against reification of these analytical categories, pointing out that these terms are not universally defined but must be tied to specific historical contexts (Berger 1992, 284–85; Mohanty 1991a, 14). There is some skepticism that mere lip service is being paid to differences of class, gender, race, and ethnicity, especially when buzzwords such as "cultural diversity" often are used as a smoke screen "behind which power disparities and economic polarizations lie unaddressed or inadequately treated" (Harrison 1991a, 3–4). Nancy Hewitt (1992) has noted that even those scholars who accept the use of gender-race-class "worry that it will only be applied to women, Blacks, and workers and not to men, whites, and owners"; there is still the sense that "women have more gender than other groups, that Blacks have more race, and that men have more class" (315–16).

Several scholars have pointed out that neither anthropology nor history has contributed a great deal toward an understanding of racism and the cultural construction of race in the United States (Harrison 1991a, 3; Brown 1992). Elsa Brown (1992) believes this is related to "the failure to construct race as a significant factor in white [people's] experiences" (303). Although she is writing about women's history, her ideas can be extended to both men and women in past societies: white middle- and upper-class women and men were able to live the lives they did precisely because working-class, African American, Asian American, Latino, and Native American men and women were performing certain kinds of labor. Thus, it is important to analyze the ways in which white peoples' lives were shaped by race also. The differences that race made in the lives of people in past societies were *relational* differences, having to do with relations (and often hierarchies) between races, genders, and classes (Brown 1992, 298–99; Mohanty 1991a, 12–13).

Therefore, much recent feminist scholarship stresses the complexity of relations among people in past societies, even going beyond race, gender, and class. Micaela di Leonardo (1991a, 30) notes that in any society, the meanings of gender division will cross-cut and influenced by additional social divisions, such as religion, age, sexual preference, and nationality. When historical archaeologists interpret past societies, it is important to keep in mind how some of these factors combined to shape the lives of the men, women, and children who made, used, and discarded the material and/or documentary records we uncover. For example, Donald Hardesty describes in his essay here how class and ethnicity affected residence and business patterns in mining towns in the western United States, and how class affected the political strategies and ideologies adopted by different groups of women.

Gender and Sexuality

It may seem a bit unusual for archaeologists to be discussing, or even contemplating, sexual activity in their interpretations of the past. After all, how can one "see" that in archaeological remains?

First of all, archaeologists have discovered artifacts related to sexual activity in their excavations of prostitutes' workplace-residences (e.g., Seifert 1991a). Secondly, historical archaeologists analyze not only material records but also archival records—written, pictorial, and oral historical—for the cultures they study. These archival records often contain evidence not only of sexual activities but also of gender roles and ideologies. Finally, given the kinds of data available to historical archaeologists, and given that such researchers subscribe to interpreting as much as possible about past societies from those data, it should not be surprising that their interpretations include sexual activity just as they do other aspects of daily life.

In North America, different colonizing groups varied in their racial attitudes toward Native Americans and African Americans and in their attitudes toward interracial marriages, unions, and sexual relations (Zuckerman 1987; Van Kirk 1980; Sheehan 1980; Etienne and Leacock 1980; Peterson 1981; Brown 1980; Ekberg 1985; Scott 1991a). And in spite of what government regulations might have proscribed, sexual activity certainly varied with the individuals involved (however, see Stoler 1991, 52–57, for an argument to the contrary). In her essay here, Louise Jackson examines documentary references to sexual relations between Native Alaskan women and Russian men, and discusses what this suggests about women's roles in overall interaction between the two groups.

Several other contributors here also consider sexual relations between women and men in past societies. In her essay, Donna Seifert looks at change through time in the profession of prostitution in a working-class neighborhood in Washington, D.C., and shows how living conditions changed for women engaged in the profession and for their neighbors between the 1860s and the early 1900s. Donald Hardesty discusses both Chinese and Euro-American prostitutes in mining communities as well as gender ideologies among different groups of women in those communities, particularly as they relate to acceptance (or lack of it) of the widespread Victorian ideal of women's domesticity. In his essay, David Starbuck brings to light documentary evidence for the presence of large numbers of women and children in the military camps of the French and Indian War and the Revolutionary War in northeastern colonial America. These included families of enlisted men and officers, girlfriends and companions, and prostitutes, all of whom performed work such as cooking, sewing, and laundering in return for provisions and permission to live in camp.

Elizabeth Kryder-Reid looks at a very different kind of society, a nineteenth-century religious order in Annapolis, Maryland. Her discussion demands that we consider what it means to examine gender in single-sex celibate communities. Other archaeologists have dealt with the ways in which gender shaped activities in Shaker communities, which also were celibate (e.g., Starbuck 1984; Savulis 1992). However, while Shakers included both men and women, Kryder-Reid reveals a community inhabited only by men, in which we nonetheless see enacted the roles of both genders.

Feminist scholars often have stressed that gender is not a biological given but a cultural construction, the product, as Michelle Rosaldo (1980) states, "of social relationships in concrete (and changeable) societies" (393). As a concept, it is not ahistorical and universally defined but rather is culturally specific, one to be investigated rather than assumed. Margaret Conkey and Janet Spector (1984, 15) provide concise and useful definitions of gender role, identity, and ideology: "gender roles describe what people do and what activities and behaviors are deemed appropriate for the gender category"; gender identity is "an individual's own feeling of whether she or he is a woman or a man"; and gender ideology is "the meaning, in given social and cultural contexts, of *male, female, sex,* and *reproduction.* The system of meaning includes the prescriptions and proscriptions" for the behavior of persons in particular culturally defined gender categories.

Thus gender (man, woman, gender-crossers such as the *berdache*) is not the same as sex (biological assignation of male or female) and not the same as sexuality (sexual preference, sexual practice, sexual relations). The differences between these terms are real and can affect our interpretations.

Clearly, then, studying gender does not mean studying only women. Scholars in several fields have shown that one cannot examine women's lives in the past or present without also examining men's lives and the ways in which they are interrelated (Moraga 1986, 187; di Leonardo 1991a, 30–31; hooks 1989, 127–30; Rosaldo 1980, 396). As Cherríe Moraga (1986) points out, "women do not usually grow up in women-only environments. Culture is sexually-mixed" (187). One might argue that denying or not paying attention to the ways in which gender shaped men's as well as women's lives is very similar to denying or not paying attention to the ways in which race shaped white people's lives. There is the general sense, to paraphrase Nancy Hewitt (1992, 315–16), that women have more gender than men, and African Americans have more race than white Americans. On reflection, the flaw in the logic is apparent; what remains then is for feminist scholars to conduct more research about men, as well as men *and* women, in past and present societies.

Critiques of White Western Feminisms

Although archaeologists do not have twenty years' worth of feminist approaches to the archaeology of gender on which to reflect, some of the issues brought to light by recent critiques of Western feminist theories can prove helpful as we develop an archaeology that pays attention to gender as well as other aspects of daily life.

Current thinking in anthropology and other disciplines encourages scholars to be self-reflexive about their research and the ways they write about it. Joan Scott (1986) recently noted that "we must find ways (however imperfect) to continually subject our categories to criticism, our analyses to self-criticism" (1065). Some of the most thought-provoking and potentially transforming criticism of feminist theories has come from non-Western feminists and feminist scholars of color (e.g., di Leonardo 1991a, 1991b; hooks 1989; Moraga 1986; Brown 1992; Mohanty 1991a, 1991b; Lazreg 1990; O'Neale 1986; Mohanty et al. 1991).

Briefly, these critiques reveal that many white, predominantly middle-class Western feminists have fashioned feminist theories using their own experiences and lives as the standard "from which all others must (negatively) deviate" (O'Neale 1986, 145). These critiques note particularly that the differences that race, class, sexual preference, and religion make in the lives of working-class men and women and people of color cannot be understood within the framework of much of contemporary feminist theory.

One concept that has come under increasing scrutiny in both feminist anthropology and women's history is that of public/private spheres or a public/domestic dichotomy in men's and women's lives. The concept of separate spheres was tied to the rise of industrial capitalism, beginning about 1780 but prominent in the nineteenth century, in Britain and the United States (Kerber 1988; Cott 1977; Ryan 1990); it is not necessarily applicable to societies in other time periods or locations (Rosaldo 1980; Moore 1988; Mohanty 1991a; di Leonardo 1991a). Even in nineteenth-century Britain and the United States, women's suffrage, reform, and other activist movements "made use of domestic, feminine, 'moral mother-

hood' rhetoric to argue for women's rights to enter the public sphere" (di Leonardo 1991a, 16), as Suzanne Spencer-Wood reveals in her essay here concerning the domestic reform movement. She discusses as well the ways in which relations between classes and ethnic groups affected both the roles of women in the movement and the programs they undertook. Elsa Brown (1992) also stresses the importance of race and class in analyzing these reform movements. She notes that white middle-class women began to become involved in voluntary associations "when they were able to have their homes and children cared for by the services — be they direct or indirect — of other women" (299).

African American and Latina feminists have emphasized the importance of race in analyses of the people we study. Faye Harrison (1991a) points out that anthropology has "effectively peripheralized or erased significant contributions made by peoples of color and women from the canon" (6). Chandra Mohanty (1991a) notes that "third world women have very different histories with respect to the particular inheritance of post-fifteenth-century Euro-American hegemony" (10). And, as Elsa Brown (1992) points out, although scholars are likely to acknowledge these different experiences, "the relation, the fact that these histories exist simultaneously, in dialogue with each other, is seldom apparent in the studies we do" (300).

Although Cherríe Moraga (1986) writes about feminist theories of sexuality, her ideas could apply to other aspects of people's lives as well when she notes that "the boundaries white feminists confine themselves to in describing sexuality are based in white-rooted interpretations of dominance, submission, power-exchange, etc." She gives an eloquent example of the ways in which these interpretations affect her as a Latina feminist: "Although they are certainly *part* of the psychosexual lives of women of color, these boundaries would have to be expanded and translated to fit my people, in particular, the women in my family. And I am tired, always, of these acts of translation" (186).

This current of criticism has led to scholarship that relies on models other than those rooted in white, Western gender relations (e.g., Smith 1983; Lorde 1984; hooks 1989, 1990; Lazreg 1990). An assumption that has come under increased scrutiny because of its implications for the study of non-Western groups is that "women" and "men" are universally homogeneous and unchanging categories (Mohanty 1991b, 64). When an analysis of women, or men, takes them out of their local political and cultural contexts, "it ultimately robs them of their historical and political agency" (71–72). In their essays here, Everett Bassett and Louise Jackson examine the role gender played in relations between Native American and Euro-American groups in specific political and historical contexts. They bring to bear not Western feminist theoretical models but archaeological, written, oral, and photographic evidence from the specific peoples they are studying. Nancy Muller uses similar kinds of evidence in her study of African Americans in the specific context of nineteenth- and early twentieth-century Massachusetts.

Although it is necessary to acknowledge "different experiences" by people of various groups in past societies, that alone is not enough (Gordon 1986, 28; Brown 1992, 300). This knowledge needs to be integrated into and change the ways we approach the study of the past—through the questions we ask, the data we examine, the methods we devise, the perspectives we employ throughout, and the criteria by which we evaluate the findings.

Gender, Cultural Diversity, and Visibility in Historical Archaeology

The essays in this volume exemplify a variety of approaches being taken by historical archaeologists as they attempt to come to grips with the social complexity of the past communities they study. By placing the themes and issues addressed by these archaeologists in the context of recent feminist scholarship in related fields, I hope to have shown that archaeological research concerned with gender necessitates as well a concern with other aspects of social inequality. As Nancy Hewitt (1992) has noted, we need to capture "both the messy multiplicity of lived experience and the power relations within which those lived experiences [were] played out" (317). Historical archaeologists recently have insisted that we strive to deal with all races, genders, and ages in our interpretations of past societies (Yentsch 1991a, 259; Deagan 1991, 110), and to do so successfully will demand reflection about the discipline at present and the possibilities for change within it.

To create more inclusive archaeologies requires change of at least two kinds: in the visibility of nonelite and disenfranchised groups in the past and in the incorporation of non-Western perspectives in our interpretations of the past.

We need to continue trying to make more visible those who were less powerful in past societies, those little noted in written records and illiterate themselves, and those marginalized economically, politically, and socially in the past. The contributors to this volume take on this task, utilizing both archival and material records and confronting the difficulties involved with those data, what historian Linda Gordon (1986) has called "the finite, capricious, mottled nature of the evidence" (22).

Historical archaeologists deal with biases not only in the archival records but in the material records as well. Yet by combining the information gained from these varied sources, however incomplete they might be, archaeologists in this volume succeed not only in making women more visible, but in so doing make Native American groups and African Americans more visible, revealing the complexity of social relations in predominantly white, male communities and in white working-class and middle-class women's lives. These contributions reveal new possibilities for increasing the visibility of all of these groups, and we hope they will lead others to conduct additional research along similar lines.

Historical archaeologists also should be aware of both the positive and negative impacts that their research might have on nonelite, disenfranchised, and largely excluded groups in our own society. After all, it is their pasts we are investigating, as well as the dominant, white past, and there is enormous public interest in archaeology. We need to remember that for minority and excluded groups today, making the past visible can be a means of empowerment, an affirmation that they in fact do have "a history," that there are specific historical reasons for the inequities we see around us today, and that these are not the result of "natural" or "biological" differences. The questions we ask about the past are rooted in the present, and it cannot be otherwise; we therefore have the responsibility to be aware of whom our research serves (e.g., see Blakey 1983).

The second kind of change in our discipline requires the inclusion of the perspectives of these underrepresented groups in our research. Alison Wylie (1991) recently noted that "archaeology as a whole should celebrate the emergence of diverse perspectives," and that "we should do everything we can to expand the range of standpoints from which we, collectively, as a discipline, approach the archaeological record" (22). Just as the questions women felt should be asked about the past are now beginning to guide research by men *and* women archaeologists, so should the questions of Native Americans, African Americans, Latinos/as, and Asian Americans be part and parcel of our research.

Admittedly, there are very few historical archaeologists from these groups; it is no surprise that all of the contributors to this volume are white. While we recognize the need to increase minority student enrollment in anthropology as a whole, this does not mean that white historical archaeologists cannot change their approaches as well. Indeed, the works of Leland Ferguson (1992), Janet Spector (1993), and Russell Handsman (1990) provide vivid examples of more inclusive archaeology. We can work to increase our interaction with those minority communities whose sites we dig by involving them in all stages of the research, from research design through analysis and interpretation (e.g., Cowan-Ricks 1993; McGuire 1992).

We have only the slightest inkling, perhaps, of the kinds of questions different members of minority groups might have about their history in the New World, and the kinds of things they would like to see investigated by archaeologists and historians. White, often privileged archaeologists, must begin trying to see how, for example, Latinos and Latinas in North America "find their roots in a four-hundred-year-long Mexican history and mythology" (Moraga 1986, 174), and realize that this affects the questions they ask about and the way they view the past.

Ultimately, one might hope that these perspectives could be brought to bear also on the pasts of Euro-Americans. How, for instance, might an African American archaeologist approach the archaeology of a seventeenth-century Dutch settlement in the Northeast? What might an Asian American archaeologist want to know about sixteenth-century Spanish colonies in Florida? How would a Native American archaeologist approach the archaeology of nineteenth-century plantations in the South? Recognizing, of course, that there is variability within any group, whether minority or majority, it should be clear that the inclusion of what Faye Harrison (1991b) has called "alternative sets of priorities, visions, and understandings" (89) will make for more detailed, richer, and, one might hope, better, historical archaeology.

The essays in this volume provide several windows through which the North American past might be seen. There are, of course, other windows unopened, other aspects of that past not revealed here. But building on what has gone before, these authors demonstrate movement toward the kinds of complex analyses that will be required of historical archaeologists if we are to continue to bring the past to our present.

Acknowledgments

This essay benefited from careful readings by Donald Heldman, Janet Spector, Mary Whelan, Christine Szuter, and Suzanne Spencer-Wood. Although their advice was not always heeded, I thank them nonetheless for offering it. The responsibility for any remaining errors, in logic or in fact, rests with me alone.

Notes

1. For cultural and biological anthropology, see Morgen 1989b; Ortner and White-head 1981; Etienne and Leacock 1980; di Leonardo 1991b; Albers and Medicine 1983; Rosaldo 1980; Harrison 1991a; D'Amico-Samuels 1991; Silverblatt 1980, 1991; Stoler 1991; Lazreg 1990; and Mascia-Lees et al. 1989. For social history, see Cott and Pleck 1979; DuBois and Ruiz 1992; Freedman 1982; Jeffrey 1975; Pomata 1993; Orleck 1993; Ulrich 1980; Calvi 1990; Ryan 1981, 1990; Evans 1988; Gordon 1986; Scott 1986; Brown 1992; Berger 1992; Hewitt 1992; Ruggiero 1990; Kerber 1988; and Davis 1981. For literary and social criticism, see Hirsch and Keller 1990; Moraga 1986; O'Neale 1986; hooks 1989, 1990; Mohanty 1991a, 1991b; Childers and hooks 1990; de Lauretis 1986b; and Mohanty et al., 1991.

A history of feminist approaches in anthropology can be found in Rosaldo 1980; Moore 1988; di Leonardo 1991a; Morgen 1989a; and Jacobs and Roberts 1989. A history of feminist approaches in social history and related fields may be found in de Lauretis 1986a; Gordon 1986; Hewitt 1992; Scott 1986; and Kerber 1988.

References

Albers, Patricia, and Beatrice Medicine, eds.
1983   *The Hidden Half: Studies of Plains Indian Women.* Washington, D.C.: University Press of America.
Berger, Iris
1992   Categories and Contexts: Reflections on the Politics of Identity in South Africa. *Feminist Studies* 18 (2): 284–94.
Blakey, Michael
1983   Socio-Political Bias and Ideological Production in Historical Archaeology. In *The Socio-Politics of Archaeology*, ed. Joan M. Gero et al., 5–16. Research Reports, 23. Amherst: University of Massachusetts, Department of Anthropology.
Brown, Elsa Barkley
1992   "What Has Happened Here": The Politics of Difference in Women's History and Feminist Politics. *Feminist Studies* 18 (2): 295–312.
Brown, Jennifer S. H.
1980   *Strangers in Blood: Fur Trade Company Families in Indian Country.* Vancouver: University of British Columbia Press.
Calvi, Giulia
1990   Women in the Factory: Women's Networks and Social Life in America (1900–1915). In *Sex and Gender in Historical Perspective*, ed. Edward Muir and Guido Ruggiero, 200–34. Baltimore: Johns Hopkins University Press.
Childers, Mary, and bell hooks
1990   A Conversation About Race and Class. In *Conflicts in Feminism*, ed. Marianne Hirsch and Evelyn Fox Keller, 60–81. New York: Routledge.

17

Through the Lens of Gender

Conkey, Margaret
1991   Does It Make a Difference? Feminist Thinking and Archaeologies of Gender. In *The Archaeology of Gender*, ed. Dale Walde and Noreen D. Willows, 24–33. Calgary: University of Calgary Archaeological Association.
Conkey, Margaret W., and Janet D. Spector
1984   Archaeology and the Study of Gender. In *Advances in Archaeological Method and Theory*, Vol.7, ed. Michael B. Schiffer, 1–38. Orlando, Fla.: Academic Press.
Cott, Nancy F.
1977   *The Bonds of Womanhood: "Woman's Sphere" in New England, 1780–1835.* New Haven: Yale University Press.
Cott, Nancy F., and Elizabeth H. Pleck, eds.
1979   *A Heritage of Her Own: Toward a New Social History of American Women.* New York: Simon and Schuster.
Cowan-Ricks, Carrel
1993   Historic Houses Archaeology Project: A Program for Inclusion of African Americans. Paper presented at the annual meeting of the Society for Historical Archaeology, January 6–10, Kansas City, Missouri.
D'Amico-Samuels, Deborah
1991   Undoing Fieldwork: Personal, Political, Theoretical and Methodological Implications. In *Decolonizing Anthropology: Moving Further Toward an Anthropology for Liberation*, ed. Faye V. Harrison, 68–87. Washington, D.C.: American Anthropological Association/Association of Black Anthropologists.
Davis, Angela Y.
1981   *Women, Race, and Class.* New York: Random House.
Deagan, Kathleen
1991   Historical Archaeology's Contributions to Our Understanding of Early America. In *Historical Archaeology in Global Perspective*, ed. Lisa Falk, 97–112. Washington, D.C.: Smithsonian Institution Press.
de Lauretis, Teresa
1986a   Feminist Studies/Critical Studies: Issues, Terms, and Contexts. In *Feminist Studies, Critical Studies*, ed. Teresa de Lauretis, 1–19. Bloomington: Indiana University Press.
de Lauretis, Teresa, ed.
1986b   *Feminist Studies, Critical Studies.* Bloomington: Indiana University Press.
di Leonardo, Micaela
1991a   Gender, Culture, and Political Economy: Feminist Anthropology in Historical Perspective. Introduction to *Gender at the Crossroads of Knowledge: Feminist Anthropology in the Postmodern Era*, ed. Micaela di Leonardo, 1–48. Berkeley and Los Angeles: University of California Press.

di Leonardo, Micaela, ed.

1991b   *Gender at the Crossroads of Knowledge: Feminist Anthropology in the Postmodern Era.* Berkeley and Los Angeles: University of California Press.

DuBois, Ellen Carol, and Vicki L. Ruiz, eds.

1992   *Unequal Sisters: A Multicultural Reader in U.S. Women's History.* New York: Routledge.

Ekberg, Carl J.

1985   *Colonial Ste. Genevieve: An Adventure on the Mississippi Frontier.* Gerald, Mo.: Patrice Press.

Etienne, Mona, and Eleanor Leacock, eds.

1980   *Women and Colonization: Anthropological Perspectives.* New York: Praeger.

Evans, Sara M.

1988   *Born for Liberty: A History of Women in America.* New York: Free Press.

Ferguson, Leland

1991   Struggling with Pots in Colonial South Carolina. In *The Archaeology of Inequality*, ed. Randall H. McGuire and Robert Paynter, 28-39. Oxford: Basil Blackwell.

1992   *Uncommon Ground: Archaeology and Early African America, 1650-1800.* Washington, D.C.: Smithsonian Institution Press.

Fowler, Don D.

1987   Uses of the Past: Archaeology in the Service of the State. *American Antiquity* 52 (2): 229-48.

Freedman, Estelle B.

1982   Sexuality in Nineteenth-Century America: Behavior, Ideology, and Politics. *Reviews in American History* December: 196-215.

Gero, Joan M.

1983   Gender Bias in Archaeology: A Cross-Cultural Perspective. In *The Socio-Politics of Archaeology*, ed. Joan M. Gero et al., 51-57. Research Reports, 23. Amherst: University of Massachusetts, Department of Anthropology.

1985   Socio-Politics and the Woman-at-Home Ideology. *American Antiquity* 50 (2): 342-350.

1991   Gender Divisions of Labor in the Construction of Archaeological Knowledge. In *The Archaeology of Gender*, ed. Dale Walde and Noreen D. Willows, 96-102. Calgary: University of Calgary Archaeological Association.

Gero, Joan M., and Margaret W. Conkey, eds.

1991   *Engendering Archaeology: Women and Prehistory.* Oxford: Basil Blackwell.

Gero, Joan M., David M. Lacy, and Michael L. Blakey, eds.

1983   *The Socio-Politics of Archaeology.* Research Reports, 23. Amherst: University of Massachusetts, Department of Anthropology.

Gordon, Linda

1986   What's New in Women's History. In *Feminist Studies, Critical Studies*, ed. Teresa de Lauretis, 20-30. Bloomington: Indiana University Press.

Handsman, Russell G.
1990   Corn and Culture, Pots and Politics: How to Listen to the Voices of Mohegan Women. Paper presented at the annual meeting of the Society for Historical Archaeology, Tucson, Arizona, January 11.
Harrison, Faye V.
1991a   Anthropology as an Agent of Transformation: Introductory Comments and Queries. In *Decolonizing Anthropology: Moving Further Toward an Anthropology for Liberation*, ed. Faye V. Harrison, 1-14. Washington, D.C.: American Anthropological Association/Association of Black Anthropologists.
1991b   Ethnography as Politics. In *Decolonizing Anthropology: Moving Further Toward an Anthropology for Liberation*, ed. Faye V. Harrison, 88-109. Washington, D.C.: American Anthropological Association/Association of Black Anthropologists.
Harrison, Faye V., ed.
1991c   *Decolonizing Anthropology: Moving Further Toward an Anthropology for Liberation*. Washington, D.C.: American Anthropological Association/Association of Black Anthropologists.
Heldman, Donald P.
1986   Michigan's First Jewish Settlers: A View from the Solomon-Levy Trading House at Fort Michilimackinac, 1765-1781. *Journal of New World Archaeology* 6 (4): 21-34.
Hewitt, Nancy A.
1992   Compounding Differences. *Feminist Studies* 18 (2): 313-26.
Hirsch, Marianne, and Evelyn Fox Keller, eds.
1990   *Conflicts in Feminism*. New York: Routledge.
hooks, bell
1989   *Talking Back: Thinking Feminist, Thinking Black*. Boston: South End Press.
1990   *Yearning: Race, Gender, and Cultural Politics*. Boston: South End Press.
Jacobs, Sue-Ellen, and Christine Roberts
1989   Sex, Sexuality, Gender, and Gender Variance. In *Gender and Anthropology: Critical Reviews for Research and Teaching*, ed. Sandra Morgen, 438-62. Washington, D.C.: American Anthropological Association.
Jeffrey, Julie Roy
1975   Women in the Southern Farmers' Alliance: A Reconsideration of the Role and Status of Women in the Late Nineteenth-Century South. *Feminist Studies* 2 (2/3): 72-91.
Kerber, Linda K.
1988   Separate Spheres, Female Worlds, Woman's Place: The Rhetoric of Women's History. *Journal of American History* 75 (1): 9-39.
Lazreg, Marnia
1990   Feminism and Difference: The Perils of Writing as a Woman on Women

in Algeria. In *Conflicts in Feminism*, ed. Marianne Hirsch and Evelyn Fox Keller, 326–48. New York: Routledge.

Lorde, Audre
1984   *Sister Outsider.* Trumansburg, N.Y.: Crossing Press.

Mascia-Lees, Frances E., Patricia Sharpe, and Colleen Ballerina Cohen
1989   The Postmodernist Turn in Anthropology: Cautions from a Feminist Perspective. *Signs: Journal of Women in Culture and Society* 15 (1): 7–33.

McDonald, J. Douglas, Larry J. Zimmerman, A. L. McDonald, William Tall Bull, and Ted Rising Sun
1991   The Northern Cheyenne Outbreak of 1879: Using Oral History and Archaeology as Tools of Resistance. In *The Archaeology of Inequality*, ed. Randall H. McGuire and Robert Paynter, 64–78. Oxford: Basil Blackwell.

McGuire, Randall H.
1992   Archaeology and the Columbus Quincentennial. Paper presented at the annual meeting of the American Anthropological Association, San Francisco, California.

McGuire, Randall H., and Robert Paynter, eds.
1991   *The Archaeology of Inequality.* Oxford: Basil Blackwell.

Michigan Pioneer and Historical Collections
1874–1929 Collections of the Pioneer and Historical Society of Michigan, Vol. 9. Lansing: Pioneer and Historical Society of Michigan.

Mohanty, Chandra Talpade
1991a   Introduction: Cartographies of Struggle—Third World Women and the Politics of Feminism. In *Third World Women and the Politics of Feminism*, ed. Chandra Talpade Mohanty, Ann Russo, and Lourdes Torres, 1–47. Bloomington and Indianapolis: Indiana University Press.

1991b   Under Western Eyes: Feminist Scholarship and Colonial Discourses. In *Third World Women and the Politics of Feminism*, ed. Chandra Talpade Mohanty, Ann Russo, and Lourdes Torres, 51–80. Bloomington and Indianapolis: Indiana University Press.

Mohanty, Chandra Talpade, Ann Russo, and Lourdes Torres, eds.
1991   *Third World Women and the Politics of Feminism.* Bloomington and Indianapolis: Indiana University Press.

Moore, Henrietta L.
1988   *Feminism and Anthropology.* Minneapolis: University of Minnesota Press.

Moraga, Cherríe
1986   From a Long Line of Vendidas: Chicanas and Feminism. In *Feminist Studies, Critical Studies*, ed. Teresa de Lauretis, 173–90. Bloomington: Indiana University Press.

Morgen, Sandra
1989a   Gender and Anthropology: Introductory Essay. In *Gender and Anthropology: Critical Reviews for Research and Teaching*, ed. Sandra Morgen, 1–20. Washington, D.C.: American Anthropological Association.

Morgen, Sandra, ed.
1989b   *Gender and Anthropology: Critical Reviews for Research and Teaching.* Washington, D.C.: American Anthropological Association.
O'Neale, Sondra
1986   Inhibiting Midwives, Usurping Creators: The Struggling Emergence of Black Women in American Fiction. In *Feminist Studies, Critical Studies,* ed. Teresa de Lauretis, 139–56. Bloomington: Indiana University Press.
Orleck, Annelise
1993   "We Are That Mythical Thing Called the Public": Militant Housewives during the Great Depression. *Feminist Studies* 19 (1): 147–72.
Orser, Charles E., Jr.
1991   The Continued Pattern of Dominance: Landlord and Tenant of the Postbellum Cotton Plantation. In *The Archaeology of Inequality,* ed. Randall H. McGuire and Robert Paynter, 40–54. Oxford: Basil Blackwell.
Orser, Charles E., Jr., ed.
1990   *Historical Archaeology on Southern Plantations and Farms.* Special issue of *Historical Archaeology* 24 (4): 1–126.
Ortner, Sherry B., and Harriet Whitehead, eds.
1981   *Sexual Meanings: The Cultural Construction of Gender and Sexuality.* Cambridge: Cambridge University Press.
Peterson, Jacqueline L.
1981   The People in Between: Indian-White Marriage and Genesis of a Metis Society and Culture in the Great Lakes Region, 1680–1830. Ph.D. diss., University of Illinois, Chicago Circle.
Pomata, Gianna
1993   History, Particular and Universal: On Reading Some Recent Women's History Textbooks. *Feminist Studies* 19 (1): 7–50.
Rosaldo, Michelle Z.
1980   The Use and Abuse of Anthropology: Reflections on Feminism and Cross-cultural Understanding. *Signs: Journal of Women in Culture and Society* 5 (3): 389–417.
Ruggiero, Guido
1990   Introduction. In *Sex and Gender in Historical Perspective,* ed. Edward Muir and Guido Ruggiero, vii–xxii. Baltimore: Johns Hopkins University Press.
Ryan, Mary P.
1981   *Cradle of the Middle Class: The Family in Oneida County, New York, 1790–1865.* Cambridge: Cambridge University Press.
1990   *Women in Public: Between Banners and Ballots, 1825–1880.* Baltimore: Johns Hopkins University Press.
Savulis, Ellen-Rose
1992   Alternative Visions: Shaker Gender Ideology and the Built Environment. Paper presented at the annual meeting of the Society for Historical Archaeology, January 8–12, Kingston, Jamaica.

Scott, Elizabeth M.

1991a   *"Such Diet As Befitted His Station As Clerk"*: *The Archaeology of Subsistence and Cultural Diversity at Fort Michilimackinac, 1761–1781*. Ph.D. diss., University of Minnesota, Minneapolis. Ann Arbor, Mich.: University Microfilms.

1991b   A Marxist-Feminist Perspective in Historical Archaeology: How We Can Get There from Here. Paper presented at the annual meeting of the Society for Historical Archaeology, Richmond, Virginia, January 10.

Scott, Joan W.

1986   Gender: A Useful Category of Historical Analysis. *The American Historical Review* 91 (5): 1053–75.

Seifert, Donna J.

1991a   Within Sight of the White House: The Archaeology of Working Women. *Historical Archaeology* 25 (4): 82–108.

Seifert, Donna J., ed.

1991b   *Gender in Historical Archaeology*. Special issue of *Historical Archaeology* 25 (4): 1–155.

Sheehan, Bernard W.

1980   *Savagism and Civility: Indians and Englishmen in Colonial Virginia*. Cambridge: Cambridge University Press.

Silverblatt, Irene

1980   "The Universe has turned inside out . . . There is no justice for us here": Andean Women Under Spanish Rule. In *Women and Colonization: Anthropological Perspectives*, ed. Mona Etienne and Eleanor Leacock, 149–85. New York: Praeger.

1991   Interpreting Women in States: New Feminist Ethnohistories. In *Gender at the Crossroads of Knowledge: Feminist Anthropology in the Postmodern Era*, ed. Micaela di Leonardo, 140–71. Berkeley and Los Angeles: University of California Press.

Smith, Barbara, ed.

1983   *Home Girls*. New York: Kitchen Table/Women of Color Press.

Smith, Dorothy

1987   *The Everyday World As Problematic: A Feminist Sociology*. Boston: Northeastern University Press.

Spector, Janet D.

1991   What This Awl Means: Toward a Feminist Archaeology. In *Engendering Archaeology: Women and Prehistory*, ed. Joan M. Gero and Margaret W. Conkey, 388–406. Oxford: Basil Blackwell.

1993   *What This Awl Means: Feminist Archaeology at a Wahpeton Dakota Village*. St. Paul: Minnesota Historical Society Press.

Spector, Janet D., and Mary K. Whelan

1989   Incorporating Gender into Archaeology Courses. In *Gender and Anthro-*

pology: Critical Reviews for Research and Teaching, ed. Sandra Morgen, 65-94. Washington, D.C.: American Anthropological Association.

Spencer-Wood, Suzanne M.

1991a   Toward a Feminist Historical Archaeology of the Construction of Gender. In *The Archaeology of Gender*, ed. Dale Walde and Noreen D. Willows, 234-44. Calgary: University of Calgary Archaeological Association.

1991b   Toward an Historical Archaeology of Domestic Reform. In *The Archaeology of Inequality*, ed. Randall H. McGuire and Robert Paynter, 231-86. Oxford: Basil Blackwell.

1991c   Feminist Empiricism: A More Holistic Theoretical Approach. Paper presented at the annual meeting of the Society for Historical Archaeology, Richmond, Virginia, January 10.

Starbuck, David R.

1984   The Shaker Concept of Household. *Man in the Northeast* 8:73-86.

Stoler, Ann Laura

1991   Carnal Knowledge and Imperial Power: Gender, Race, and Morality in Colonial Asia. In *Gender at the Crossroads of Knowledge: Feminist Anthropology in the Postmodern Era*, ed. Micaela di Leonardo, 51-101. Berkeley and Los Angeles: University of California Press.

Stone, Peter, and Robert MacKenzie, eds.

1990   *The Excluded Past: Archaeology in Education*. London: Unwin Hyman.

Trigger, Bruce

1980   Archaeology and the Image of the American Indian. *American Antiquity* 45: 662-76.

Ulrich, Laurel Thatcher

1980   "A Friendly Neighbor": Social Dimensions of Daily Work in Northern Colonial New England. *Feminist Studies* 6 (2): 392-405.

Van Kirk, Sylvia

1980   *Many Tender Ties: Women in Fur-Trade Society, 1670-1870*. Norman: University of Oklahoma Press.

Walde, Dale, and Noreen D. Willows, eds.

1991   *The Archaeology of Gender*. Calgary: University of Calgary Archaeological Association.

Wolf, Eric

1982   *Europe and the People Without History*. Berkeley and Los Angeles: University of California Press.

Worsley, Peter

1981   Marxism and Culture: The Missing Concept. *Dialectical Anthropology* 6: 103-21.

Wylie, Alison

1991   Feminist Critiques and Archaeological Challenges. In *The Archaeology of Gender*, ed. Dale Walde and Noreen D. Willows, 17-23. Calgary: University of Calgary Archaeological Association.

24

SCOTT

1992   The Interplay of Evidential Constraints and Political Interests: Recent Archaeological Research on Gender. *American Antiquity* 57 (1): 15–35.

Yentsch, Anne

1991a   Access and Space, Symbolic and Material, in Historical Archaeology. In *The Archaeology of Gender*, ed. Dale Walde and Noreen D. Willows, 252–62. Calgary: University of Calgary Archaeological Association.

1991b   The Symbolic Divisions of Pottery: Sex-Related Attributes of English and Anglo-American Household Pots. In *The Archaeology of Inequality*, ed. Randall H. McGuire and Robert Paynter, 192–230. Oxford: Basil Blackwell.

Zinn, Howard

1980   *A People's History of the United States*. New York: Harper & Row.

Zuckerman, Michael

1987   Identity in British America: Unease in Eden. In *Colonial Identity in the Atlantic World, 1500–1800*, ed. Nicholas Canny and Anthony Pagden, 115–57. Princeton, New Jersey: Princeton University Press.

II Native American and African American Communities

2

Cloth, Clothing, and Related Paraphernalia

A Key to Gender Visibility in the Archaeological Record of Russian America

Louise M. Jackson

A systematic study of the contact period in southwestern Alaska was initiated by Wendell Oswalt and James VanStone in the early 1950s. Their goal was a comparative analysis of culture change from the Yukon River to Bristol Bay from the time of earliest historic contact to the present (VanStone 1970b, 53). Focusing their investigations on the Kuskokwim and Nushagak river systems, they excavated six sites intimately associated with the nineteenth-century fur trade (see fig. 2.1). These sites were Nushagak, a Yup'ik village adjacent to the Russian trading post Aleksandrovskiy Redoubt at the mouth of the Nushagak River (VanStone 1968); Tikchik and Akulivikchuk, Yup'ik Eskimo villages in the Nushagak River drainage (VanStone 1970a, 1972); Crow Village, also a Yup'ik settlement, on the Kuskokwim River (Oswalt and VanStone 1967); the Russian trading post Kolmakovskiy Redoubt, upriver from Crow Village and containing Russian, Creole, Eskimo, and Ingalik Athapaskan dwellings (Oswalt 1980); and Kijik, the Dena'ina Athapaskan village at Lake Clark, which VanStone dug with Joan Townsend (VanStone and Townsend 1970).

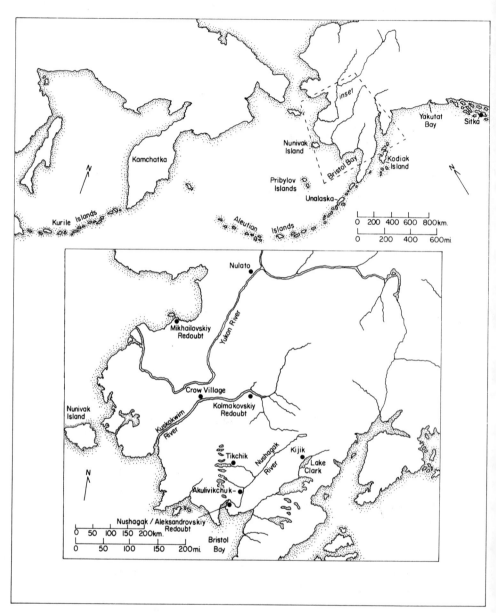

Figure 2.1. Map of Russian America showing places mentioned in text, with detail of southwestern Alaskan sites. Map by Susan Matson.

Although excavated with an ethnoarchaeological approach in mind (clearly articulated in Oswalt and VanStone 1967), these sites nevertheless constitute the first serious attempts at Alaskan historical archaeology. Along with assemblage data and discussion, all the reports contain detailed historical information concerning Native Alaskan populations and the timeline of contact events, thus placing the sites within the larger framework of Russian colonial endeavors. Indeed, much of the historical material was published for the first time in these reports. Today, the six monographs still constitute the most thorough published historical archaeological survey of any single region in Alaska, and their data are frequently used for comparative purposes by many currently engaged in Russian American archaeology. For these reasons, data in the six southwestern Alaskan site reports (hereinafter referred to as the study sites or study reports) provide a useful starting point from which to explore contemporary issues in historical archaeology as these pertain to Russian America.

To date, little attention has been paid to women in the Russian American literature. The present study focuses on gender visibility—specifically, how we can identify Native Alaskan women in the archaeological record, and what we can learn about their participation in the nineteenth-century Russian American fur trade. In what follows, my goals are as follows: (1) to outline the information pertaining to Native women in southwestern Alaska that is presented in the study reports; (2) to locate in the archaeological and historical records the complex of Western trade goods that I consider to be the most promising for articulating women's involvement in the fur trade—Western cloth, clothing, and associated paraphernalia; (3) to present a brief narrative of incorporation for this exogenous complex into Native Alaskan lifeways; (4) to demonstrate how documentary evidence pertaining to this class of trade goods cogently illuminates women's activities in the fur trade; and finally, (5) to discuss the implications of this research for archaeological assemblages elsewhere in Russian America.

Native Women in the Southwestern Alaskan Archaeological Record

Little information is given in the study reports about women's activities at the various sites, either in the accompanying historical background material or, in the case of Crow Village, through Oswalt and VanStone's reconstruction of life at that settlement from the 1840s to about 1900. When women are mentioned, it is usually in conjunction with discussions of population estimates or in the context of occasional sightings by outsiders visiting the region; their presence also can be inferred when numbers of families are listed for a settlement. For example, when Lavrentiy Zagoskin (author of the first ethnography of the Yukon and Kuskokwim valleys, Zagoskin 1967) visited Crow Village in 1843, he noted that all of the people, with the exception of one man and three women, were attending a feast of the dead at a nearby village, and that one of the women gave him fish for dog food (Oswalt and VanStone 1967, 4). In a less visible vein, population estimates at Kijik refer only to gross numbers of people, but we can assume that women were present because several marriages are recorded (VanStone and Townsend 1970, 21). However, at Aleksandrovskiy Redoubt (the trading post to which the Native Alaskan village of Nushagak was attached), we know that 74 men and 94 women were living there in 1849; ten years later there were 76 men and 103 women (Documents Relative to the History of Alaska [DRHA] 1936-1938, 2: 3). Given their numerical superiority, it is not unreasonable to presume that they would have left some markers in the archaeological record.

Thus, even though they are difficult to count, we know beyond a doubt that women were present at the study sites. The key question is, how then can they be identified in the archaeological record? I am proposing two approaches that can be used to distinguish male and female domains of material culture in Russian America. The first is somewhat general. Relying on ethnographic analogy and snippets of documentary evidence, this approach assumes, for example, that men do the hunting and engage in trade negotiations with the Russians, while women prepare food, make garments, and look after children. Thus, items associated with hunting constitute part of the male domain, whereas those involved with food preparation and garment making belong to the female domain. The second approach is more specific. It focuses on stylistic attributes distinguishing male- from female-associated items and thus leaves us with no question about ownership or use. Interestingly, the only artifacts that can be so identified for women in the study reports are a few articles of clothing, shoes, and boots (see table 2.1). Furthermore, this differentiation applies not only to locally made traditional garments but also to imported manufactured items, i.e., exogenous items received in trade. To go one step further, if both approaches are utilized, the corpus of artifacts that can be assigned to women increases. Otherwise, artifacts remain in a disconcertingly gender-free environment.

Table 2.1: Western Cloth and Clothing Items in Six Southwestern Alaskan Archaeological Assemblages

	Kijik	Nushagak	Tikchik	Akuli-vikchuk	Crow Village	Kolmakovskiy Redoubt
I. CLOTH TYPES						
Cotton fabric fragments[1]	2					5
Woolen fabric fragments[2]	19					33
Broadcloth	2 (black)			1		
Backed cloth with wool face and cotton backing	8					
Felt fragments	2 (1 may be a patch)					5
Burlap fragments						6
Silk fragment						1
Oil cloth fragment			1			
Leather fragments[3]	16	12	3	7	3	85
Fragments of rubberized material	3					
Misc. textile scraps	2				4	
II. CLOTHING						
Wool felt hat fragments	12				1 (wide brim)	
Rainhat fragments		3				
Raincoat fragments		6				

Table 2.1, continued

	Kijik	Nushagak	Tikchik	Akuli-vikchuk	Crow Village	Kolmakovskiy Redoubt
Jacket fragment		1				
Woman's dress fragment		4				
Silk kerchief		1			1	
Pants fragment		1				
Knit wool stockings					1	2
Overshoe section					1	
Leather women's shoes and boots		1		2	1	
High laced shoes						5
Men's leather shoe fragments		2		1	1	
Shoe or boot fragments					1	95
III. ADORNMENT AND GARMENT PARAPHERNALIA						
Necklace			5 (round pieces of can metal)			
Copper Russian Orthodox cross	2					
Brass crucifix		1		1		
Pendants	1 (from brass or copper button)		3	1 (metal)	1 (metal)	1 (painted porcelain)
Glass beads[4]	1,229	465[5]	407	944	415	2,431
Cartridge case bead separators	2		1	4	5	

Brooch						1 (brass set with lavendar stone)
Watch parts	2					6
Finger rings[6]	7					4
Bracelets			1	1	1 (copper)	1 (brass, inscribed BABY)
Labret non-Eskimo pottery				1		
Sherd non-Eskimo pottery with drilled hole	2			1	1 (ironstone)	
Ceramic buttons[7]	50		7	7	5	82
Glass buttons four-hole type[8]		1	7			
Metal buttons[9]	35	3		7		11
Rubber button[10]		1				4
Mold for fabric-covered button			2			
Fiber button						1
Horn button						3
Buckles/fasteners/snaps/clasps[11]	21	2			2	21
Strap or belt rings	2					
Mirror fragment	1					
IV. SEWING PARAPHERNALIA						
Thimbles	2 (copper)		1			
Whole scissors	1			1		

Table 2.1, continued

	Kijik	Nushagak	Tikchik	Akuli-vikchuk	Crow Village	Kolmakovskiy Redoubt
Scissor fragments	3	1	3	1		3
Needle case						1 (Ivory)
Metal awls				1		2
Thread spools						3 (wooden)
Steel safety pin	1					
Bent wire safety pin	1					
Shoe lasts						2

1 Longcloth, corded, drawstring, edging, satine.
2 Simple weave, basket weave, twill weave, serge, gabardine, monk's cloth, black worsted.
3 Braided, knotted, strap, patch or reinforcing pieces, and miscellaneous.
4 Seed and pound beads, opaque and translucent: white, pale blue, dark blue, dark red with black centers, black, green, yellow, pink, brown-lined red, white-lined red, green-lined red, blue-lined white, polychrome, blue faceted, yellow hexagonal, clear, painted.
5 458 seed beads were attached to a single garment fragment.
6 Copper, wire, lead, brass, iron, stone settings.
7 White four-holed: plain, calico, molded face, molded and painted face, painted; white two-holed: plain; brown four-holed; gray two-holed; pearl two-holed, four-holed; ivory four-holed.
8 White, colored.
9 Zinc-base two-holed; stamped; gold cuff button; self shank; four-holed.
10 Two-holed molded face design, one backmarked "GOODYEAR'S P=T 1851 N.R.C. CO"; four-holed plain, one face mark "GOODYEAR 1851 I.R.C. CO."
11 Suspender, vest, overall, belt.

The Cloth and Clothing Complex in the Historical and Archaeological Records

Ideally, one would like to be able to consult inventories for all three Russian-American Company posts serving southwestern Alaska: Aleksandrovskiy, Mikhailovskiy, and Kolmakovskiy Redoubts. Together these would provide the full range of items made available to Native Alaskans by way of trade. Unfortunately, such detailed information does not exist. However, a listing of goods compiled after the 1867 sale of Russian America to the United States is available; it details the goods and chattels that were being sold from the principal Russian-American Company warehouse at Sitka (Sitka Customs House, Property Records, Book B, in Oswalt 1980, 152–54). While it is unlikely that all of these items were available in the more remote posts such as Kolmakovskiy Redoubt, the listing nevertheless gives us an idea of the range of goods that might have been available.

From the 479 articles listed, almost one-fourth can be extracted and placed into four categories pertaining to the cloth and clothing complex: cloth types, clothing and other cloth items, items of personal adornment and garment paraphernalia, and sewing paraphernalia (table 2.2). This categorization of artifacts differs from that used in either the Native Alaskan site reports or at Kolmakovskiy Redoubt. For the Native villages, Oswalt and VanStone either listed artifacts in order of their text description, or, at Crow Village, divided them into two principal categories—locally manufactured and imported manufactured (see Oswalt and VanStone 1967, 115–20). Locally manufactured items include those made from exotic materials introduced by Europeans. Some of these are attempts to render traditional forms in new materials, such as labrets made from British ceramics, while other forms are direct products of the contact situation, such as cartridge case bead separators for necklaces (VanStone and Townsend 1970, 59). The latter are found at Akulivikchuk and Kijik and are described as follows: "Two 44 caliber cartridge cases, one centerfire and one rimfire, have been drilled at the proximal end and have small sections of twine knotted on the inside and protruding through the holes. These and similar cases have been strung at intervals with beads as bead separators to form a necklace" (71). Imported manufactured items include buttons, buckles, suspender fasteners, Russian Orthodox crosses and other metallic pendants, scissors, beads, and fragments of clothing, including a woman's dress at Nushagak. Items from the Western cloth and clothing complex are thus scattered throughout the various trait lists.

For Kolmakovskiy Redoubt, Oswalt (1980) chose to present artifacts

Table 2.2: Items from the Western Cloth and Clothing Complex Extracted from the Inventory of the Russian-American Company Goods and Chattels at Sitka Sold to Hayward M. Hutchinson and Abraham Hirsch of San Francisco in 1867 (from Oswalt 1980: 152–54)

Cloth Types	Clothing and Other Cloth Items	Items of Adornment and Garment Paraphernalia	Sewing Paraphernalia
Cotton	Hats	Brooches	Thimbles
Cotton drill	Southwesters	Bracelets	Pins
Cotton prints	Scotch caps	Rings	Scissors
Cambric	Ladies' caps	Earrings	Needles
Nankeen	Tufts	Stones for earrings	Sewing machine needles
Gray coarse calico	Silk scarfs	Glass beads	Sail needles
White coarse calico	Wool scarfs	Wire buckles	Awl
Blue coarse calico	Colored scarfs	Hooks and eyes	Thread
Camlet	Collars	Boot front hooks	Shoemakers thread
Fustian	Neck cloths	Pintles	Artificial thread
Worsted	Epaulets	Buttons	Threading leather
Baize	Braces (suspenders)	Hairbrushes	Smoothing irons
Shalloon	Great coats	Cloth brushes	
Drape de dame	Wool coats (Missus)	Boot brushes	
Tricot (woolen fabric)	Jackets	Combs	
Doeskin (satin weave wool fabric)	Waistcoats	Watches	
Flannel	Shirts	Looking glasses	
Packing flannel	Trousers	Amber shaving cases	
Wadding	Mittens		
Irish linen	Gloves		
Dutch linen	Handkerchiefs		
Thin sail linen	Drawers		
White linen	Belts		

Cloth Types	Clothing and Other Cloth Items	Items of Adornment and Garment Paraphernalia	Sewing Paraphernalia
Satin	Stockings		
Ribbon	Gaiters		
Galloon (trimming)	Socks		
Velvet	Shoes		
Border	Pumps		
Tapestry with border	Boots		
Stuff	Soles		
Silkstuff	Leather soles		
Velvet stuff (plush)	Blankets		
Moleskin stuff	Tablecloths		
Moscova stuff	Napkins		
Furniture stuff (plush)	Towels		
Purnell stuff			
Figured stuff			
Batin stuff			
Regatt stuff			
Embroidery canvas			
Net			
Taffeta			
Bunting			
Coarse cloth			
Drapp (cloth)			
Cowhair felt			
Horsehair			
Sail cloth			
Oilcloth for table			
Carpet			
Skins			

according to three usage networks: protective, procurement, and maintenance. Two of these networks are of relevance here. The protective network
includes apparel (subdivided into garment materials, garments, and buttons), while that of maintenance includes tools such as thimbles, needles,
and scissors, as well as items of personal adornment. Since these tools were
needed to transform traded raw fabric into wearable garments, and since
personal adornment includes necklaces and pendants as well as beads used
both for jewelry and to decorate clothing, it makes sense to include them
in one complex as I have done (see also table 2.1). Moreover, it will become
clear later that *all* the items from the Western cloth and clothing complex
play a part in rendering women as visible, active participants in the conduct of the fur trade.

Yet despite their preponderance in the inventory listing (table 2.2), items
of cloth and clothing are among the most sparsely represented Western
trade goods in the archaeological record. Because of this, little significance was attached to Western garments or their related paraphernalia in
the study reports. The archaeological absence of cloth and clothing itself
in southwestern Alaska is perhaps not surprising, since the annual freeze/
thaw and permafrost conditions would not allow fabric to survive well in
the ground. However, associated sewing paraphernalia such as needles and
thimbles are also sparsely represented. A possible explanation for this will
be offered later.

Disconcertingly, at first glance the site reports suggest that the few fabric remnants found in southwestern Alaska are associated with trade in the
American era after the 1867 sale of Alaska. Nevertheless, despite the fact
there may be no pieces of cloth or clothing dating to the Russian era sur-
viving in the archaeological record, its presence in Russian America before
1867 can be determined from two independent sets of evidence: linguistic
and historical.

Linguistic evidence is found in the large number of Russian loan words
currently used in the Yup'ik language. Among them are several specific
garments of female attire. They include shoes, boots, shirts, vests, jackets,
overcoats, hats, women's bonnets (hair nets), shawls, scarves, suspenders,
stockings, and petticoats (slips), as well as buttons, pins, and safety pins
and cotton cloth, silk, and ticking. Also, in contrast to the archaeological
record, historical accounts are replete with information about this artifact complex. Inventory listings in the historical record already have been
touched upon. Additional documentary evidence indicates that trade of
items in this complex began with the onset of Russian interaction in this
region. Expedition inventory lists invariably include some items from this

complex or include reasons for their omission. For example, blankets, which were highly desired by Native Alaskan populations, were occasionally left at the trading posts because they were heavy and awkward to transport. It was hoped that when Native people learned they could get them by trading at the redoubts in person, they would journey there, making the logistics of trading easier for the Russians (Russian American Company, vol. 11, no. 273, 9 May 1834, fol. 256; vol. 20, no. 43, February 1841, fol. 54). Thus, blankets are not always listed on expedition inventories.

That my grouping of artifacts differs from Oswalt and VanStone's reflects a fundamental difference between our respective views of trade goods as analytical tools for investigating culture contact. Oswalt and VanStone were primarily interested in using trade goods as chronological tools for assessing changes in Native Alaskan technology occurring in response first to Russian and later to American influence; my interest in the southwestern Alaskan data has focused instead on the trade goods themselves (see, e.g., Jackson 1990a, 1990b, 1991b, 1991c).

In fact, a considerable amount of information pertaining to the cloth and clothing complex does not appear in the study reports. To rectify this omission, I have returned to the historical records (including some of the same sources used by Oswalt and VanStone), but instead of focusing on the operation of the fur trade, I have mined colonial accounts for all the information they contain about cloth and clothing-related Western trade goods. Based on this information, a narrative of the incorporation of these goods into Native Alaskan lifeways can be constructed. Likewise, other topics suitable for exploration can be identified using this reconfigured data (see, e.g., Jackson 1990a and 1991c for similar discussions concerning tea-related ceramics, and Jackson 1991b for an overview of topics that can be accessed through an examination of cloth and clothing items).

To reconstruct the incorporation of cloth and clothing into southwestern Alaskan Eskimo and Athapaskan lifeways, I adopted a method similar to that used by Oscar Lewis (1942) in his classic study of Blackfoot culture change. I sifted through accounts written by fur traders, explorers, missionaries, naturalists, teachers, military and government personnel, and other visitors to southwestern Alaska, extracting as many references as possible to cloth and clothing and its paraphernalia. Recurring themes were identified and references were grouped chronologically so that the process of the adoption and incorporation of these items could be examined.

Toward this end, I consulted sources that describe a variety of cultural groups encountered by the Russians in southeastern and southwestern Alaska as well as the Aleutians, Kodiak, Nunivak, and the Pribylov

Islands. My intention is not to suggest that Alaskan peoples encountered by the Russians were culturally homogeneous, because they certainly were not. Rather, my purpose is to show, through an introductory overview, that the topic of gender can be examined throughout Russian America, and to suggest that in the future, it may well be possible to construct similar narratives for specific Alaskan peoples.

Narrative of Incorporation

Along with beads (the most significant Western trade item with respect to adornment), cloth, clothing, needles, scissors, and other sewing paraphernalia feature prominently in colonial accounts of the Russian American fur trade. Articles from this complex were standard items of Russian foreign trade by 1739, when they are mentioned in the report of Bering's second Kamchatka expedition (Müller 1986, 90). They were among the first items traded by Europeans to Native Alaskans when firsthand contact was established. Throughout the nineteenth century they continue to be included in lists of the most desired trade goods in Alaska (see, e.g., William Weinland's 1887 comments cited in Oswalt 1963, 110).

Moreover, travelers commented on what they saw, and accounts invariably mention dress. Indeed, Russian-American Company agents were specifically instructed to comment on clothing in their reports. Throughout the period, Native Alaskan clothing is described (usually men's and women's separately), often in considerable detail. In early accounts writers mention whether exclusively Native Alaskan attire is observed, such as in the mid-1780s on Andreianov Island in the Aleutian chain (Shelikhov 1981, 69), or when Native dress is supplemented by items of Western adornment. Indeed, it is usually with reference to adornment that we first encounter Russian influence on Native Alaskan dress. Grigorii Shelikhov (1981), for example, includes descriptions of glass beads on the Fox Islands (74) and also on Kodiak, where he says that strings of beads "were obtained by barter from the Russians" (77). Other late eighteenth-century accounts also note the occasions when European cloth was used for its decorative effects as an addition to traditional fur clothing (e.g., Merck 1980), a practice that continued for over a hundred years. A number of examples from southwestern Alaska can be seen in Adolf Etholén's ethnographic collection compiled in the 1840s (Varjola 1990, 250–54, 256–57; for Kodiak and the Aleutian Islands see Varjola 1990, 140–65, 177–91, 224–25, 229–35). Henry Elliott stated in 1886 that "garments are made of skins of ground squirrels, ornamented with pieces of red cloth" (411) and this practice of ornamentation is reiterated by H. M. W. Edmonds (1966) at the end of the century: "Here and there, small bits of bright cloths . . . are sewn into the seams to brighten the effect" (64).

We also learn from historic accounts when Western garments themselves were worn, either in conjunction with Native Alaskan clothing or on their own. In 1790, Carl Merck (1980, 102) described the elimination of furs such as sea otter from the repertoire of Kodiak dress. It became Russian-American Company policy in the early years of the nineteenth century to discourage the making and wearing of Native clothing from certain furs throughout Alaska. In some instances "civilizing" the savages was given as a reason, but the prevalent motivation in encouraging the adoption of Western dress was to maximize the number of furs that could be procured for Russian trade with China and Europe. However, several comments suggest that in some regions assimilation with regard to clothing went too far or too quickly even for Russian liking. In this vein Kyrill Khlebnikov (1976), in the first quarter of the nineteenth century, notes of Sitka Company headquarters that

> In other colonies Aleuts wear bird skin parkas, which are warm, comfortable and attractive. But on Sitka they want to have clothes made not of regular soldier cloth, but from good frieze or fine wool. Many of them wear frockcoats and dress coats. Their wives were formerly delighted to have parkas of rodent fur and cotton kamleis [shirts], but here they all want a printed cotton dress, a shawl etc. All of this represents a style of luxury which is harmful both to them and to the colony. (105)

When items of foreign clothing are first mentioned with reference to Native Alaskans, they are usually noted as being associated with headmen and "well-to-do" people. The foreign clothing Shelikhov noted on the Kurile Islands in the late eighteenth century was Chinese and Japanese, which is not surprising given the islands' location. However, while in Yakutat Bay he was visited by two *baidaras* (Native Alaskan boats) and he noted there that in addition to "clothing made of otter, sable, marten, wolverine and marmot, [t]hey also wore European clothing apparently bartered from foreign vessels, made from thin green serge and bright printed linen [naboika]" (Shelikhov 1981, 93). He further noted that they had been trading with Europeans since 1786, and that they had hats like grenadier caps with copper emblems, which they apparently received from European traders (Shelikhov 1981, 95–96).

Zagoskin gives us the most detailed mid-century descriptions of the differential distribution of Western dress throughout the colonies. Writing from Ilyulyuk [Iliuliuk] on Unalaska Island, he noted:

> In our more important settlements in the colonies, as in the capitals, the native type is less and less noticeable. The Aleuts go about in jackets and frock coats, their wives and daughters in calico dresses and kamleya [parka covers], which are long shirts made of ticking or nankeen [unbleached cotton] with red cloth trimming around the collar and hem. The married women, guarding against sin, keep their heads always covered while the girls wear their hair long, tied at the back of the neck with a ribbon. (Zagoskin 1967, 87)

Discussing the spread of these items into the Alaskan interior, he stated:

> In the period between 1838 and 1844 the chief export to the natives of the Nulato area were red and white beads, shells, pots, copper jugs, and different articles of iron. During the time we were at Nulato the rich traders who saw the advantages of our summer clothing began to ask for calico shirts, blankets, and cloth dresses and caps; some even wanted shoes. And the manager of the post, who saw definite advantages to the Company in the growing demand, spared himself nothing. We also helped out where we could, giving as rewards some of our own linen to those of the natives who had shown special devotion to the expedition. If this tendency continues, we may expect the time to arrive very soon when all the Yukon peoples will turn from the bagatelles they now find so fascinating and demand more useful articles. (Zagoskin 1967, 185)

In addition to clothing, sometimes specific types of cloth are singled out in texts (e.g., calico, muslin, drilling, and mosquito net) or their decoration is described (e.g., gaudy, striped, and flowered prints). At other times specific items of clothing are listed: gowns, shawls, calico and "Mother Hubbard" dresses, men's overalls, denim parkas, shirts, and caps; alternatively, they may be referred to simply as "white men's garments" (Anderson 1940, 47, 65, 66, 104; Dall 1870, 231; Edmonds 1966, 18, 34, 39, 94, 108; Elliott 1875, 41-42; Khlebnikov 1976, 105; Petroff 1884, 14; Zagoskin 1967, 87, 233).

The Cloth and Clothing Complex As a Key to Gender Visibility

In choosing how to present Russian American gender-related data, I could have presented a chronological account of the introduction of cloth, clothing, and adornment into the Native Alaskan women's material inventory and focused on what we can learn about this female domain of material culture. Such an account would have concentrated on changing styles and documented in detail the phasing out of traditional attire (alluded to briefly above). This narrative also would have commented on fashion, introducing us for example to smooth red copper bracelets weighing a quarter-pound per pair, which were, in the 1840s, "What is the mode at present, or as they say in the colonies, what is 'the go' " (Zagoskin 1967, 293).

I have chosen instead to concentrate on issues that concern the conduct of trade: who did the trading, for whom goods were traded, who handled the traded articles, and who used them. In this respect, cloth and clothing texts are surprisingly informative.

Turning first to the conduct of trade, of interest in southeastern Alaska is the active role that Tlingit women took in trading. In a comment directed at Tlingit men, Petr Tikhmenev (cited in Gsovski 1950, 66) notes that they "have aptitude for commerce and in this and their housework their women help them a great deal, never forgetting though to look out for their profit in trade transactions." Laura Klein has discussed Tlingit gender roles and cultural interaction in depth, highlighting the difficulties nineteenth-century European men experienced in being forced to deal with women as principal negotiators. She explores sex roles, noting, "The European colonizers, then, expected the people with whom they dealt to have the same, rather strict and limited sex-role pattern as they. Among the Tlingit this expectation was not valid" (Klein 1980, 93). A further insight into differing cultural attitudes about sexuality and sexual activity is contained in the following text, which also provides another example of how Western trade items were redistributed to communities at large:

> [T]he Kolosh have found yet another profit which they consider necessary for their manner of living. Many of them bring their slaves and young girls and invite the Russians to use them. The owner takes everything the girl receives. And this new branch of their industry also brings them every possession the promyshlenniks [Russian fur traders] have. Many promyshlenniks have lost everything trying to dress their notorious lovers. (Khlebnikov 1976, 71)

In other words, there appears to have been a lot more to intercultural sexual activity than meets the eye (cf. Klein 1980, 93). And one can profitably ask: who was using whom?

While not all Alaskan women may have participated in Western trade as overtly as the Tlingit, nevertheless their covert role in transactions is evident in items that often were designated specifically for them. On 24 July 1800, for example, Baranov requested "a large bolt of nankeen [kitaika]—or at least 1½ bolts for women" (Tikhmenev 1979, 121). A tantalizing secondary source (McNamara 1986, 71) states that toward the end of the century, women carried out their own exchange at Kolmakovskiy Redoubt while the men conducted their business with the trader. However, I have yet to locate a primary source that mentions such an activity.

In a similar vein, the wives of *toions* (Native Alaskan male leaders so designated by the Russians) were not infrequently singled out by Company managers to receive gifts. Gift giving was recognized as early as the 1760s as being essential to the establishment and maintenance of good trading relationships with Native Alaskans (see, e.g., Tikhmenev 1979, 121; Pierce 1984, 60; Zagoskin 1967, 149, 239). Drawing from the Vasiutinskii/Lazarev report, Lydia Black (1984) states that Andreaian Tolstykh "distributed rich presents to the island chiefs and their retinue, carefully grading his gifts by the recipient's rank. He even gave presents for the wives, to be taken home by the Aleuts visiting his camp" (90). Appropriate gifts for the wives of toions included nankeen and green baize for shirts and boots (Pierce 1984, 25–26). There are many similar accounts throughout the nineteenth century. For example, dress material was considered a suitable potlatch gift item (see, e.g., Anderson 1940, 109, 167; Edmonds 1966, 94–96; Elliott 1875, 42). It would be interesting to document whether the Russians chose to give these women presents voluntarily, or whether they were prompted because of existing Native Alaskan protocol.

Status was visibly measured by the quantity and rarity of jewelry worn by men and women alike. Men evidently went to a great deal of trouble to adorn their women. We are told that prior to the arrival of the Russians,

> Not infrequently, recklessly bold men with great difficulty and even with danger to their lives undertook journeys to far countries . . . only to obtain sukli [rock crystals] or something similar for their beloved. Of war's booty such ornaments were valued above everything and they were always the lot only of the bravest and of the leader. . . . [Moreover] All such women's ornaments and especially the necklaces were very costly. (Veniaminov 1984, 213)

Beads were thus highly desirable items when the Russians introduced them to trading networks. In a lecture delivered in 1854, Holmberg stated:

> In the lips and ears one wore what the surroundings made available, such as coral, shells, small polished bones, and colored stones, all of which were bored and suspended on a string. These were replaced with the arrival of the Russians by beads, which at first were used sparingly, but later were paid for with vast amounts of animal pelts so that even at the turn of this century the lips and ear jewelry of a rich Koniag woman or an adorned dandy might have weighed a whole pound. (Holmberg 1985, 37)

Sewing paraphernalia also was highly prized. Adelbert von Chamisso, the naturalist on Kotzebue's voyage of 1815-16, notes that on Unalaska Island

> The customary gift which you could present to a [visiting Russian] ship's captain here . . . consists of a finely worked kamlaika [or shirt], the ornamentation of which is truly admirable. The gift costs the directors only the labor of the poor Aleut girls, who get nothing for it except for a few sewing needles—considered as valuable as gold and jewels—and a piece of red frieze the size of a hand. Half of that however, has to be used on the kamlaika itself. (Fortuine 1986, 43)

Elsewhere he comments,

> Aleut girls were our paddlers. Poor creatures! Misery, sickness, dirt, vermin, and ugliness do not exclude a certain tender delicacy of manners; these girls have given me proof of it, and a gift that I possess from them and value touched me more than the signs of favor from kings could do. On the spot where we came ashore in the middle of the afternoon, we set up camp immediately. Lying under the baidar [boat] I was gazing at my cap which was torn and seizing the opportunity to repair the damage, I stuck three sewing needles into it and passed it thus to the girl who was lying next to me and made her to understand what I wanted. Three sewing needles! Such a treasure for nothing! An inexpressible joy shone wonderfully from her eyes. All the girls came close to admire the needles, to congratulate the favored one, and some seemed to remember their own misery with melancholy. Thereupon I made them all happy and presented each with three needles. We broke camp early next morning and were at Iliuliuk by three o'clock. Here Sanin presented me with the return gift of the grateful girls, which he was charged to hand over to me only after our arrival. A ball of sinew thread of their manufacture. (Fortuine 1986, 58)

In a telling comment that perhaps explains why so few garment-making tools are found in the archaeological record, Lavrentiy Zagoskin commented in the 1840s that

> The Company buildings at Ikogmyut [present-day Russian Mission] had been left at the mercy of the natives during the summer, and of course were not in shape. The doors had been removed and window frames taken out, and except for the framework of the walls not a single partition, not a single floorboard, was in place—all had been torn up and turned over for the sake of a stalk of tobacco or a needle that might have been lost in the dirt. (Zagoskin 1967, 199)

In other words, tools such as needles were highly prized and every effort would have been made to ensure that they stayed with their users.

Porter (1893) provides us with two similar insights concerning the value of these tools from Nunivak Island about 1890. At Koot he says, "A young man . . . who had left a pair of magnificent tusks with the trader in March, received in August 2 squares of matches (100 each), 1 pound of leaf tobacco (value 30 cents), and 2 needles" (115). At Kwigamiut he observes, "it was the mere accident of a woman coveting a small pair of scissors in a dressing case that induced her to sell her own rather dilapidated kayak" (112).

From cloth and clothing texts, insights can also be gained into women's education and expectations about the skills they should possess. Ivan Veniaminov (1984) notes in his 1840 account that

> Except for moral instruction the education of girls consisted in learning to sew all sorts of clothing, to embroider designs in wool and hair, to weave mats and baskets, to clean fish and prepare for eating everything that their husbands furnished them. . . . [Furthermore] Women are ashamed not to know how to sew, to dance, and to perform women's work; to caress one's husband and children in the presence of people, and even to speak before strangers. (192, 215)

He also makes a point of stressing sexual division of labor:

> A man never took up female tasks because it was considered a disgrace and a vice for a man to perform women's work such as: to sew, weave [that is make baskets], or to make thread and cordage [mauty, ropes], to prepare food, to pick grass for roofing and other uses, to gether [sic] berries and products of the tideflats, to look for roots, and so on. Even to clean up around [outside] the house was not considered a man's work. It is rare even now for one of them to undertake [such a task]. (211; square brackets in original)

Since we are told that only women did the sewing, we can surmise that regardless of whom the cloth in the inventory lists was given to or intended for, ultimately all the traded raw cloth passed into and through the hands of women. It was they who then manufactured the fabric into garments for both sexes. This is not an insignificant point to make, since the quantities of cloth traded were large (see, e.g., Khlebnikov 1976, 13, 19, 63-64, 69, 72-73, 84; Pierce 1984, 29, 42, 153). Moreover, it speaks to the integral involvement of women in the colonial fur trade and to the additional skills they had to acquire in manufacturing a different order of garments from new materials, as well as to what was expected with regard to foreign fashions and styles.

The amount we can learn about these matters from colonial texts describing cloth and clothing is interesting. Veniaminov (1984), for example, states, "In general, Koloshi [Tlingit] women learn the Russian language very rapidly and speak it better than do the Aleuts. They also quickly acquire skills in various handicrafts. For instance, one Koloshi woman, within two years following her christening, spoke Russian, could sew and even cut women's dresses" (430). That women were capable of skill acquisition invariably seems to come as a surprise to Veniaminov, and his comments are replete with value judgments, usually not very sympathetic to women. A completely different picture is provided by Von Chamisso:

> I have seen Aleut girls examine closely a shirt button of fancy trim, consult about it among themselves, and finally imitate the decorative object in such a manner as that their handiwork was deemed worthy to be sewn in the captain's shirt. . . . Everywhere I have seen women apply themselves to ornamentation and with no little expenditure of time and effort, and thought, embellish their handicrafts in the most artistic manner, taking pains on the finery of men as well as their own. If I see it done abroad, however, I have always taken particular pleasure in it. (Fortuine 1986, 58)

Another topic that we can access through the cloth complex is the Russian-American Company's employment of Native Alaskan women in fur trade activities and what those workers were paid. On the Pribylov Islands in October 1818, instructions were given to the toions "that guts, throats [sea lion esophagus]" and other items were to be issued for their clothing, and that their wives were to receive payments "for sewing kamleikas for company use" (Pierce 1984, 137). In a later account from St. Paul Island in the Pribylovs, we are given an insight into wage differentials according to gender. Veniaminov (1984) states that "the Aleut wives, who work only during the fur seal season, receive from 25 to 35 rubles" (141). He does not tell us what work was entailed nor its duration, but he does note that the first or top category of year-round male workers were receiving 220 to 250 rubles annually, with the most diligent getting a bonus from 50 to 100 rubles; the sick and aged received about 150 rubles.

Women also were employed by the Russian-American Company as translators, for which they received clothing and subsistence allowances on account. Thus, "The interpreter of the Kolosh (Tlingit) Language, Domna, asks to be supplied as usual with various items of clothing, etc. As she was not assigned subsistence previously, the office will give her, from 1 January 1818, 60 rubles a year for clothing to be issued to her on account" (Pierce 1984, 42). Zagoskin (1967), writing about the Nulato post, provides us with a final example of the employment of Native Alaskan women by the Russian-American Company in the 1840s:

> During my time at the post the detachment included a woman of the Yukon people who was called Kuropatka [Russian for "partridge"] . . . and she was taken along by the manager to help the men with all kinds of women's work . . . and it is a pleasure to remember that we are indebted to her for keeping all

the clothing and the boots of the expedition in order. . . . Finally she took on the work of stringing beads and was in this way a help in our trading. This task will be appreciated if I explain that beads are handled in a string a *sazhen* [2.33 yards] long. One pound usually produces 12 *sazhens*. The yearly quantity of beads issued during 1843 was about 7 *puds* [or 280 Russian pounds of 0.90 lb, that is, 3,360 strings of beads 1 *sazhen* long]. (185)

So we see that by reconfiguring textual excerpts from a variety of historical sources pertaining to the Western cloth and clothing complex, a clear picture emerges of the integral role Native Alaskan women played in the nineteenth-century Russian American fur trade.

In the above discussion, my aim was to show how an in-depth analysis of colonial texts pertaining to the cloth and clothing complex can provide unexpected insights to the archaeological record and bring meaning to an artifact class previously considered to be somewhat intractable (see Oswalt 1980, 37). I have sought to demonstrate that women as well as gender roles are indeed visible in the Russian American documentary record — we simply need to reconsider where and how we look for this information and how to piece it together. For while the site reports in toto contain a useful compendium of locally produced and imported artifacts used in nineteenth-century southwestern Alaska, they provide little insight into what the role of the entire corpus, specific complex, or indeed any single Western item might have been. In other words, we learn little about when and why trade goods were incorporated into Native Alaskan lifeways; who owned or used them; whether they retained their original configuration or underwent changes in form, function, and/or meaning to fit the needs of the receiving culture; or what value was placed on these objects in their new setting.

Yet by looking at texts associated with the disbursement of cloth and clothing in Russian America, we can learn about Native Alaskan women's education, expectations of their skills, sexual division of labor, garment manufacture, the value of associated paraphernalia, and women's role in economic affairs, and, in more general terms, about the participation of Native women in cultural interactions with Westerners, including their employment by the Russian-American Company in fur trade activities ranging from sewing clothes to bead stringing to translating. In short, we see Native Alaskan women as recipients and consumers of goods, as manufacturers of items for both male and female use from raw materials procured in trade, as economic advisors, and as traders themselves. And we can also examine how their needs, wants and desires may have influenced or dictated trade negotiations and activities.

Implications for Archaeological Research

The above discussion illustrates how just a few items in the archaeological record, insignificant in terms of numbers, in fact provide us with a key to looking at larger issues in Alaskan colonial encounters. Cloth, clothing, and related paraphernalia are key in making Native Alaskan women visible in the colonial contact picture in a way that is not possible with other items of material culture. Thus, however few items there are in archaeological assemblages, this complex should not be shortchanged in future examinations of historical sites in Russian America. Attention should be paid to how these artifacts appear in the historical record, since this information is critical in explaining the presence of such items in the archaeological record; the historical data allow us to assess the impact of the items in their Native Alaskan setting and to address questions of current theoretical import.

The issues that have emerged from the present study are as follows. First, one can investigate the function, utility, value, and meaning of trade goods in their new context, but specifically from a Native Alaskan rather than Western perspective. Second, the cloth complex allows us to look at several aspects of the fur trade such as gender roles and economic values. Third, because textual references to cloth, clothing, and its paraphernalia begin with Bering's Kamchatka voyage in 1739 and are also found in accounts of Russian ventures in Japan, the Sandwich Islands (Hawaii), and Australia, we will in the future be able to use this artifact category to look at Russian colonial impact beyond the spatial and chronological boundaries of current artifact analyses (e.g., Jackson 1991c). Fourth, the accounts that document contact in Russian America and provide us with the first known descriptions of Native Alaskan groups indicate very clearly in their references to clothing and adornment the pervasiveness of Western influence considerably in advance of either firsthand Russian contact or sustained Western presence. Fifth, we can look not just at contact dynamics between the Russians and those Native Alaskans that they identified as "dependent" (e.g., the Aleut and Koniag) and "semidependent" (e.g., southwestern Alaskan Natives), but through historical accounts we can also look at the role of material culture in inter-ethnic dynamics among the "independent" Natives of southeastern Alaska, the Tlingit. Sixth, the relationship between provisionment items for Russian-American Company personnel (who included Creoles, Aleuts, and Kaiurs [slaves] in Company employment as well as the promyshlennik) can be considered with regard to the spread of these items to Native Alaskans. Seventh, we can look at Native Alaskan motivation for participation in the fur trade; isolate needed, sought after, and luxury trade items; and look at those that gave status to their acquisitors. Eighth and finally, information about this complex allows us to reveal the ideological as well as practical underpinnings of the fur trade from a Native Alaskan perspective.

Hence, by piecing together cloth and clothing texts that have been extracted from a variety of published ethnohistoric sources, we not only gain insights into the activities of Native Alaskan women but also can come to an understanding of their involvement in the fur trade and in intercultural relationships. Perhaps most importantly, we now know which items in the archaeological record will guide us to these topics.

References

Anderson, Eva

1940   *Dog Team Doctor: The Story of Dr. Romig.* Caldwell, Idaho: Caxton Press.

Black, Lydia T.

1984   *Atka: An Ethnohistory of the Western Aleutians.* Kingston, Ontario: Limestone Press.

Dall, William H.

1870   *Alaska and Its Resources.* Boston: Lee and Shepard.

Documents Relative to the History of Alaska (DRHA)

1936–1938 *Documents Relative to the History of Alaska.* Vol. 2. University of Alaska, Fairbanks. Mimeograph.

Edmonds, H. M. W.

1966   *Report on the Eskimos of St. Michael and Vicinity.* Ed. Dorothy Jean Ray. Anthropological Papers of the University of Alaska, 13 (2). Fairbanks: University of Alaska Press.

Elliott, Henry.

1875   *A Report upon the Condition of Affairs in the Territory of Alaska.* Washington, D.C.: U.S. Government Printing Office.

1886   *Our Arctic Province.* New York: Scribners.

Fortuine, Robert, trans.

1986   *The Alaska Diary of Adelbert von Chamisso, Naturalist on the Kotzebue Voyage, 1815–1818.* Anchorage: Cook Inlet Historical Society.

Gsovski, Vladimir

1950   *Russian Administration of Alaska and the Status of Alaska Natives.* U.S. Senate, 81st Congress, 2nd Session, Document 152. Washington, D.C.: U.S. Government Printing Office.

Holmberg, Heinrich J.
1985   *Holmberg's Ethnographic Sketches*. Ed. Marvin W. Falk, trans. Fritz Jaensch.
        The Rasmuson Library Historical Translation Series, 1. Fairbanks: Uni-
        versity of Alaska Press.
Jackson, Louise M.
1990a   *"Trade Goods for the Savages": A Study in Contact Archaeology*. Paper pre-
        sented at the 89th Annual Meeting of the American Anthropological
        Association, New Orleans, November 30.
1990b   Were Nineteenth Century Trade Goods "Things That the Natives Did
        Not in the Least Need"? In *Culture Contact and Change in Arctic and Sub-
        arctic Areas of Asia and North America: A Symposium*, 225-57. Anchorage:
        Alaska Anthropological Association.
1991a   "As Valuable as Gold and Jewels": Needles and Cloth in the Russian
        American Fur Trade. Paper presented at the Alaskan Anthropological
        Meetings, March 22, Anchorage.
1991b   Interethnic Contact and Nineteenth Century British Ceramic Distribu-
        tion. *Canadian Journal of Archaeology* 15: 129-42.
1991c   *Nineteenth Century British Ceramics: A Key to Cultural Dynamics in South-
        western Alaska*. Ph.D diss., Department of Anthropology, University of
        California, Los Angeles. Ann Arbor, Mich.: University Microfilms.
Khlebnikov, Kyrill T.
1976   *Colonial Russian America: Kyrill T. Khlebnikov's Reports 1817-1832*. Trans.
        and ed. Basil Dmytryshn and E. A. P. Crownhart-Vaughan. Portland:
        Oregon Historical Society.
Klein, Laura
1980   Contending with Colonization: Tlingit Men and Women in Change: In
        Women and Colonization: Anthropological Perspectives, ed. Mona Etienne and
        Eleanor Leacock, 88-108. New York: Praeger.
Lewis, Oscar
1942   *The Effects of White Contact upon Blackfoot Culture with Special Reference
        to the Role of the Fur Trade*. Monograph of the American Ethnological
        Society, 6. New York: American Ethnological Society.
McNamara, Katherine.
1986   Francis Demientieff. In *The Artists Behind the Work*, ed. Suzi Jones, 59-98.
        Fairbanks: University of Alaska Museum.
Merck, Carl H.
1980   *Siberia and Northwestern America 1788-1792: The Journal of Carl Hein-
        rich Merck, Naturalist with the Russian Scientific Expedition Led by Captains
        Joseph Billings and Gavril Sarychev*. Ed. Richard A. Pierce, trans. Fritz
        Jaensch. Materials for the Study of Alaska History, 17. Kingston, Ontario:
        Limestone Press.
Müller, Gerhard F.
1986   *Bering's Voyages: The Reports From Russia*. Trans. Carol Urness. The

Rasmuson Library Historical Translation Series, 3. Fairbanks: University of Alaska Press.

Oswalt, Wendell H.

1963   *Mission of Change in Alaska: Eskimos and the Moravians on the Kuskokwim.* San Marino, Calif.: Huntington Library.

1980   *Kolmakovskiy Redoubt: The Ethnoarchaeology of a Russian Fort in Alaska.* Monumenta Archaeologica, 8. Los Angeles: Institute of Archaeology, University of California, Los Angeles.

Oswalt, Wendell H., and James W. VanStone

1967   *The Ethnoarcheology of Crow Village Alaska.* Bureau of American Ethnology Bulletin, 199. Washington, D.C.: U.S. Government Printing Office.

Petroff, Ivan

1884   *Report on the Population, Industries and Resources of Alaska.* Department of the Interior, 10th Census Office, 1880. Washington, D.C.: U.S. Government Printing Office.

Pierce, Richard A., trans.

1984   *The Russian-American Company: Correspondence of the Governors Communications Sent 1818.* Materials for the Study of Alaska History, 25. Kingston, Ontario: Limestone Press.

Porter, Robert P., comp.

1893   *Report on Population and Resources of Alaska at the Eleventh Census: 1890.* Department of the Interior, Census Office. Washington, D.C.: U.S. Government Printing Office.

Russian American Company Communications Sent

1818–65 *Russian-American Company: Communications Sent.* Vols. 1–47. U.S. National Archives, Washington, D.C.

Shelikhov, Grigorii I.

1981   *A Voyage to America, 1783–1786.* Ed. Richard A. Pierce, trans. Marina Ramsay. Materials for the Study of Alaska History, 19. Kingston, Ontario: Limestone Press.

Tikhmenev, Petr

1979   *A History of the Russian American Company.* Vol. 2, *Documents.* Ed. Richard A. Pierce and Alton S. Donnelly, trans. Dmitri Krenov. Materials for the Study of Alaska History, 13. Kingston, Ontario: Limestone Press.

VanStone, James W.

1968   *Tikchik Village: A Nineteenth Century Riverine Community in Southwestern Alaska.* Fieldiana: Anthropology, 56 (3). Chicago: Field Museum of Natural History.

1970a   *Akulivikchuk: A Nineteenth Century Village on the Nushagak River, Alaska.* Fieldiana: Anthropology, 60.

1970b   Ethnohistorical Research in Southwestern Alaska: A Methodological Perspective. In *Ethnohistory in Southwestern Alaska and the Southern Yukon:*

Method and Content. Ed. Margaret Lantis, 49-69. Studies in Anthropology, 7. Lexington: University of Kentucky Press.

1972   *Nushagak: An Historic Trading Center in Southwestern Alaska.* Fieldiana: Anthropology, 61.

VanStone, James W., and Joan Townsend

1970   *Kijik: An Historic Tanaina Indian Settlement.* Fieldiana: Anthropology, 59.

Varjola, Pirjo

1990   *The Etholén Collection: The Ethnographic Alaskan Collection of Adolf Etholén and His Contemporaries in the National Museum of Finland.* Helsinki: National Board of Antiquities.

Veniaminov, Ivan.

1984   *Notes on the Islands of the Unalashka District.* Ed. R. A. Pierce, trans. Lydia T. Black and R. H. Geoghegan. Materials for the Study of Alaska History, 27. Kingston, Ontario: Limestone Press.

Zagoskin, Lavrentiy

1967   *Lieutenant Zagoskin's Travels in Russian America 1842–1844: The First Ethnographic and Geographic Investigations in the Yukon and Kuskokwim Valleys of Alaska.* Ed. Henry A. Michael. Anthropology of the North, Arctic Institute of America Translations from Russian Sources, 7. Toronto, Ontario: University of Toronto Press.

3

"We Took Care of Each Other Like Families Were Meant To"

Gender, Social Organization, and Wage Labor Among the Apache at Roosevelt

Everett Bassett

One of the great frustrations in archaeology has been our inability to extend levels of analysis to specific groups within a community. Ethnographers routinely attribute change to powerful or innovative individuals, to kin, clan, or age groups, and in many analyses gender also has been recognized as a subunit of society that can respond differentially to change. Although recent attempts at engendering archaeology are encouraging (Gero and Conkey 1991; Walde and Willows 1991), occasionally new and possibly naive generalizations have merely replaced older ones, especially where assumptions are made about prehistoric gender roles. One advantage offered by the historical archaeology of indigenous peoples is that it allows bridges to be constructed among ethnography, ethnohistory and the prehistoric past.

In this chapter, gender roles are used to help understand the lifeways of the Western Apache peoples during a critical period in their history. The original goal of this research was not specifically to make gender visible within the archaeological record, nor was it to analyze the situation of women within Apache society. Rather, it was merely to describe Apache lifeways in the early twentieth-century dam construction camps at Roosevelt, Arizona, and examine how these might have affected assimilation into the American capital economy. Several contradictions emerged from the study, however, that could only be resolved by defining Apache society in terms of gender and then observing how Apache women and men responded differently to a changing social environment.

The use of gender as an analytical focus might imply that gender is a central structuring principle in all societies. However, applying Western feminist analytical perspectives to non-Western cultures raises its own set of biases. For this reason, the experiences and perspectives of Apaches themselves take on added importance.

Historical documents that discuss the role of Apaches in the construction of Roosevelt Dam provide some insight into Apache assimilation, but they do not document the maintenance of Apache social structure and ideology, nor do they address the role that women or men may have played in this process. This research was made possible only by the simultaneous application of archival, oral historical, and archaeological approaches. Together, these provide a three-dimensional view of the past that is not possible in, for example, the analysis of prehistoric societies. The use of oral histories in the Apache language provided by elderly Apache women and men has been especially helpful in avoiding naive, Eurocentric, or androcentric assumptions about gender.

One problem with understanding Apache culture through archaeology has been that, to date, very little Apache archaeology has been done in central Arizona (e.g., Gladwin and Gladwin 1930; Peck 1956; Dittert 1976; Redman and Hohmann 1986; Ferg 1992), and few residential camps have even been identified (Longacre and Ayres 1968; Hohmann and Redman 1988). For the most part, identified Apache remains have been limited to roasting pits, accidentally broken pots, and burials. This relative invisibility of Apaches in the archaeological record can be attributed to three factors. First, the Western Apache are not indigenous to the Southwest and probably did not even appear in central Arizona until the seventeenth century (Ferg 1992). Thus, the archaeological record covers only a small number of bands living in the area for less than three hundred years (Perry 1991, 6–8). Second, Apache camps were generally used only seasonally; as a result they are extremely ephemeral. In addition, Apache material culture has, until recently, been little understood and poorly differentiated from that of the Yavapai, whose lands overlapped Apache territory from the west (Ferg 1992). Third, Apache territory is located in a region dominated by an earlier Puebloan culture; Apache camps were sometimes located near these impressive ruins so ground stone could be collected, and in the past the camps have not been considered a priority among archaeologists.

Because of their uniqueness, the 146 wickiup locations identified at Roosevelt and discussed here are an extremely important data set. Besides providing a detailed view of what these ephemeral camps look like archaeologically, they also may be useful in allowing us to recognize earlier, protohistoric Apache sites.

Traditional Apache Culture

The mythical view of the American West paints a distinctive picture of the Apache. However, their history is far more complex and dynamic than what these images portray. Historical records range from sensationalistic accounts of the noble savage to paternalistic statements implying that the natives needed Euro-American guidance and care. Unfortunately, few nineteenth- or early twentieth-century records document the "emic" perspective of Apache culture during this period of contact and assimilation. To better understand Apache culture, anthropologists must rely on post-reservation-period Apache accounts of traditional social organization, social structure, economics (Goodwin 1935, 1942; Basso 1971, 1983; Basso and Opler 1971; Cole 1981; Opler 1983; Buskirk 1986) and ideology (Goodwin 1942; Basso 1970). In addition, several books have been written by or about Apache women (Ball 1970; Ball et al. 1980; Buchanan 1986; Stockel 1991; Boyer and Gayton 1992). These can all be utilized in interpreting Apache archaeological sites. However, since such sites often exhibit a mélange of traditional and adaptive behaviors, oral histories used to complement the archaeological record are vital to resolving inherent contradictions in site interpretation. This is particularly true in cases such as at Roosevelt where the Apache consultants actually lived at known archaeological locations and the interviews were made on-site and in the Apache language.

The Indians that worked at Roosevelt were, for the most part, "San Carlos" Apaches, identified as such by the government since they had previously resided on the San Carlos Apache Reservation located approximately fifty miles southeast of the dam site (fig. 3.1). In reality they comprised an intermingling of distinct Western Apache groups including the Tonto, Pinal, White Mountain, Aravaipa, and San Carlos bands.

In pre-reservation times, prior to the late 1800s, these people had followed an unspecialized subsistence economy that included a limited amount

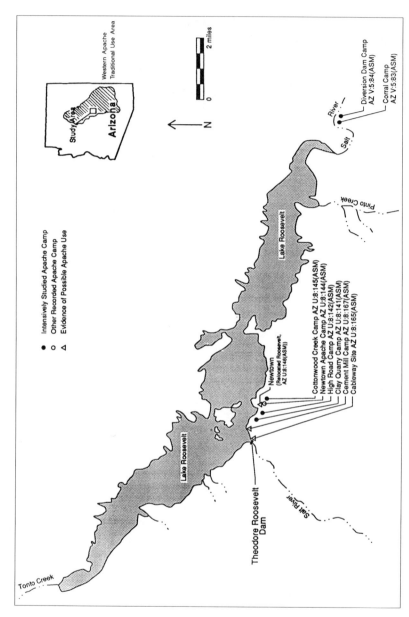

Figure 3.1. Location of Apache camp sites at Roosevelt.

of farming (Griffin et al. 1971, 69–76). Groups migrated seasonally between traditional hunting and harvesting grounds across much of east-central Arizona. The Tonto Basin, where the dam would be built, was rich in resources and especially favored, not only by the Tonto and Pinal Apache bands but also by Yavapai groups.

Because of this seminomadic existence, the Apache developed no real concept of surplus. Food production had always met immediate consumption needs, not long-term storage plans. Additionally, because all adults shared responsibility for food gathering, the Apache did not perceive the individual as a separate economic unit. Women from extended family groups accompanied each other during food gathering trips while men from the same family cluster hunted in twos and threes. Dividing resources among the entire local group encouraged cooperation between households: "Often the unfortunate were carried along by the fortunate, the unskilled by the skilled, and the lazy by the industrious" (Goodwin 1942, 123). Individuals who hunted or collected on their own were often condemned as being selfish.

Gender-differentiated tasks, however, were quite explicit for the Apache. A man was expected to make and care for his own clothing, to make and repair his tools, hunt and butcher the meat, raid enemy peoples, fight in times of war, and help watch the children. A woman was expected to make her own baskets, pots, tools, and clothing, as well as the clothing of the children; care for the children; plan, construct, maintain, strike, and move all elements of the camp, including all structures; gather and prepare wild plants used for food; store and prepare all meat; cook and clean up; and care for and saddle the horses and mules (Goodwin 1942, 284–320; Stockel 1991, 13–15).

This division of labor meant that women were more continuously occupied than men; it was said that a woman should never be still but should always be busy doing something (Stockel 1991, 14). Women socialized extensively while working and also engaged in recreation among themselves, usually through gambling. Men's work was at times more dangerous and occasionally entailed greater physical hardship, but it left more time for relaxation and recreation. Apaches believed that men were not able to survive for any extended time without the presence of women to gather and preserve food and maintain the camp. Women, however, could live for extended periods of time without the presence or assistance of men (Cole 1981, 123). In periods of extreme stress, some women also took on the roles of warrior and shaman (Buchanan 1986, 112).

Apache gender roles and behavior are different from those of Western cultures, and it is important that we not apply Western ideals to them. For example, Apaches have a deserved reputation for bravery and for living off the land. Even so, in pre-reservation society it would have been rare to find an adult male who had ever spent a night alone. Goodwin (1942, 560) described the loneliness and fear that resulted when a man was compelled, through some exigency, to live apart from others.

Girls were expected to take the lead in courtship, but they were also very shy; many would not allow their new husbands to watch them perform personal acts, such as chewing food, sometimes for months after marriage (Goodwin, 1942, 285–92). For a woman, divorce was easy; she merely put her husband's belongings outside of her wickiup, forcing him to return to his mother. However, if a widow did not show proper respect for her dead husband's family, retribution was permissible, including disfigurement.

A significant aspect of pre-reservation Apache culture was the role played by social groups in dictating and coordinating the rights and duties of the individual. The smallest of these groups, the household or *gowa*, included a woman, her husband, and their children. The family lived together in a wickiup, the physical manifestation of the gowa, a small dome-shaped structure framed with bent branches and covered with brush, blankets, or canvas (Clayton 1987). The extended family, or *gota*, consisted of three or four households (gowas) choosing to live together because of clan, marital, and economic ties. Finally, the local group or *itakowa* ("camps in a large cluster") included seven to twelve gotas, or twenty to forty-five gowas (wickiups). Each itakowa used specific farm sites and hunting localities, and each had a chief, often called the *nuxwagoya hi* ("our smart one") who directed collective enterprises (Goodwin 1942, 164–70).

While it is always difficult to retrodict past gender roles, in general men protected Apache society and women maintained it. However, for all Apaches the goal was to live close together in harmony, and to "have lots of relatives" (Goodwin 1935). The Apaches' strong sense of community cannot be overstated. Apache social structure was intricately tied to perceptions of group identity and personal value, and when these were eroded, the entire fabric of Apache culture was threatened.

U.S.—Apache Relations

As the non-Indian population of Arizona began to increase exponentially after the Civil War, dramatic changes occurred in the Apache way of life. New residents saw the native people as "the Indian problem" and initially sought to exterminate them. By 1871, the federal government had placed the Apaches on reservations and changed its policy from extermination to one of reducing the Indians to a "peaceful subordinate position" (U.S. Congress, Senate, 1871). In the 1880s, the Office of Indian Affairs began providing rations such as sugar, flour, and coffee to the Apaches. A growing dependence on manufactured goods echoed a contemporary trend in Anglo society and created a need for hard cash. In many cases Apaches turned to temporary wage labor in nearby Anglo communities to obtain money.

The concept of assimilation became widely accepted as the ultimate solution to "the Indian problem" and was especially popular among reform-minded Congressmen. For them, total assimilation matched their concern for native suffering with their faith in the promise of America. They saw Indian advancement as a model to hold before other minority communities, and the assimilated natives would be proof that America was indeed an open society where obedience and accommodation would be rewarded with social equality (Hoxie 1973, 160).

Implementation of this lofty philosophy was not easy. Initially, the ideal of the small Indian homesteader tilling his own private property led to an allotment system of land distribution and the subsequent breakup of reservation land. This was a hasty, ill-conceived policy, however, and even its supporters soon came to appreciate the abuses it engendered (Hoxie 1973, 165). Opportunities for small-scale wage labor for men in mining camps and at ranches near the San Carlos Apache Reservation included chopping wood, gathering hay, making adobes, herding cattle, and digging irrigation ditches. Often working only until their immediate needs were met, the Apache men would leave their jobs to meet family and clan obligations; they were considered by their employers to be hardworking but undependable (Adams 1971). By the 1890s, the image of the Indian as wage laborer had replaced the image of the Indian as a yeoman farmer in the minds of the reformers.

For the Indian Service (later the Bureau of Indian Affairs [BIA]), the vision of assimilation was an explicit one: the American Indian must be assimilated into a regional labor force and eventually into American society. "Our first duty to the Indian," the commissioner of the Indian Service wrote in 1906, "is to get him off the reservation and to teach him to work. The Indian's ancient habits must be destroyed for the benefit of a greater good" (Hoxie 1973, 168). These "ancient habits" included traditional gender roles, and in government-run boarding schools young Indian men and women were taught instead to be "proper" young men and women.

The Indian Service's job policy was carried out with calculated efficiency by Charles Dagnett, head of the Indian Employment Bureau. Dagnett's mandate was to "gather up all the able-bodied Indians [men] and plant them on ranches, on railroads, in mines—wherever in the outer world there is an opening for a dollar to be gotten for a day's work" (Hoxie 1973, 201). Often these projects were hundreds of miles from the reservation, and no accommodations were provided for the workers' families. Agents were instructed to have the Indian men cut their hair short and wear dungarees and hats instead of traditional clothing. Curiously, bareheaded workers were especially offensive to the Indian Service, which placed great stock in the civilizing influence of hats (U.S. Dept. of the Interior 1902).

Believing that forcing wage work on all the Apache men would further the goal of assimilation, the agent at San Carlos asked for and received permission to cancel deliveries of food rations in June of 1902 (Adams 1971). Dependent on consumer goods, the residents of the San Carlos Reservation had little recourse but to continue to seek employment off the reservation. Many adult men were transported by the Indian Employment Bureau away from the reservation to the beet fields in the Rocky Ford district of Colorado, to Yuma, Arizona, for levee construction, or to work in the copper mines of Arizona (U.S. Dept. of the Interior 1901, 158). Photographs from this period suggest that traditional residential patterning on the reservation had broken down. Much of the remaining population—the women, preschoolers, and elderly—lived in wickiups and army tents clustered close to the Indian Agency buildings, probably their only source of rations and protection. There is no indication that the gowa, gota, or itakowa, the basic elements of Apache social organization, were being maintained or that the family structure necessary to support these elements was even present.

For the Western Apache, these policies of breaking up families and separating men from women forced the abandonment of many traditional practices. There were likely few circumstances in which the Apache were free to maintain aspects of their traditional culture as they melded into Euro-American society. Ironically, one of the few instances where this was to become possible was on the Tonto (Roosevelt) Dam construction project.

Apaches at Roosevelt

The same week the Indian Commissioner in Washington was instructing his agent at San Carlos to cut Apache food rations, on the other side of town President Theodore Roosevelt was signing the Newlands Act into law. This law created the Reclamation Service (later the Bureau of Reclamation) and implemented a program to irrigate arid western lands and open them to settlement by homesteaders from the crowded East.

Five projects, including the Tonto Dam, were chosen as initial ventures.

The existence of the fledgling agency would depend on the success of these first projects, and President Roosevelt cautioned the Reclamation Service to move carefully to find out what "can and cannot be safely attempted" (Roosevelt 1902). The Tonto Dam, which Reclamation publicized heavily and which was to be their crowning jewel, was located in an isolated desert basin in central Arizona; the closest towns, Globe and Mesa, were far away over poor roads. Amenities were few and summer temperatures often exceeded 110°F.

The Tonto Dam Project would take nine years to complete and cost in excess of ten million dollars, nearly seven million dollars over budget (U.S. Congress, House, 1911). Although some of the overrun was attributed to inefficiency and fraud, the project was beset with a multitude of problems, not the least of which were the Reclamation Service's difficulties in attracting qualified laborers. Louis Hill, the supervising engineer, persistently stressed the critical nature of the labor shortage in his reports to Washington:

> The labor material is poor and there is very little of it. During the summer only those remain who have either good positions or are so worthless that they have not been able to get away and are too lazy to walk. During the winter, it seems to be a good place for the hobo to spend his vacation. The average length of service of a laborer on any job is about ten days. . . . The usual way is for a laborer to work until he has saved his "stake" and then he goes to Mesa or Globe and blows it. (Hill 1906)

Within a year, Hill had begun to hire Apache laborers. He explained to Congress in 1911:

> The Indians are pretty good people and have good heads. They had a hard time getting anything to do and they got awfully poor and hungry. They came down [from San Carlos] and wanted to have a powwow. One of them said, "We used to own all this land around here and then General Crook came down and took it all away. We think we ought to have a better right to work here than the Mexican and hobo whites." I told him I thought so too. (U.S. Congress, House, 1911)

The actual number of Apaches who moved to Roosevelt to work, and the timing of their move, is difficult to ascertain. Hill reported that he immediately hired "several hundred" Apache men and eventually "had nearly all of them working for us out there" (ibid.). Gustav Harders (1968), a Lutheran missionary at Roosevelt, claimed that about "1,000 red men" (22) appeared on the scene just to dig the nineteen-mile-long power canal, which was built between 1904 and 1906. Luther Kelly, the Indian agent at San Carlos, reported that "every Indian desiring work at the Tonto project has been supplied with work at good wages, so that now the reservation is pretty well depleted of able-bodied men and boys. Being nomadic by choice and tradition, or circumstances, they take their families with them" (U.S. Dept. of the Interior 1904, 152). Prior to 1903, the San Carlos Reservation had numbered 2,275 persons; most of these apparently moved to Roosevelt. Additionally, camps of Apaches from the White Mountain Reservation had moved to work on the dam. By 1905 Kelly was forced to import Mexicans just to maintain the San Carlos Reservation agency farm (U.S. Dept. of the Interior 1905, 176).

Hill rated the Apache workers above the Mexicans and Anglos and used them extensively for quarrying, road and canal building, and power line placement (Hill 1906). Apaches were found to be especially skillful at road construction, building the saw mill road into the Sierra Ancha, new roads into Globe and Payson, and eighty miles of the Apache Trail between Mesa and the dam site. On the Apache Trail project, they revealed their "inborn knack for employing dry masonry, choosing their material with such care and laying it with such skill that the result was a solid and enduring road bed" (Lockwood 1938, 335). Much of this work has lasted longer than the concrete work laid at the same time and can still be seen along the road. Smaller numbers of Apache men worked in the cement mill and the power house and on dam construction. However, there is no evidence that any Apache women were hired for the effort.

The Archaeological Record

The Apaches at Roosevelt lived in traditional camps in aboriginal wicki-ups or, as one observer described them, "their wretched teepees" (Harders 1968, 26). These small structures, about ten feet in diameter, were made from bent willow branches covered with brush or scraps of canvas (Clayton 1987; fig. 3.2). It should be noted that the wickiup and all of the items shown in figure 3.2 were produced, utilized, and maintained by the women. At least seven camps were established by Apaches during the construction period (1902–11), and two of these were inhabited intermittently into the 1920s (Ayres et al. 1991; fig. 3.1). These were built at a distance from the Anglo and Mexican settlements at locations of the Apaches' choosing, where "sitting rocks" were located and in close proximity to the water required for sweat lodges and cooking and cleaning purposes (Cutter 1987). Some camps established early in the construction phase were later abandoned for higher locations as the level of the reservoir rose.

The Apache camps identified archaeologically are of varying sizes and

Figure 3.2. Wickiup and Apache girl at Roosevelt, ca. 1909 (National Archives, Washington, D.C.).

composition. Despite the variability between camps, the characteristics of the material assemblages are a key to identifying them as Apache. These attributes are a polythetic set of traits (Clarke 1968, 37): that is, each camp assemblage exhibits many, but not necessarily all, of the attributes, and no single attribute is both necessary and sufficient to mark a site as an Apache camp.

Attributes that characterize Apache camps include ephemeral wickiup rings composed of cleared, leveled areas roughly ten to twelve feet in diameter that may or may not have rocks around their edges; small hand-sized cobbles with minimal use wear; reused manos and metates collected from nearby prehistoric sites; and mirror and glass fragments that may have been flaked. Other reused and altered Euro-American artifacts also are found on these sites, including cans and buckets punctured with numerous nail holes, sometimes in decorative patterns, which were used for straining *tulpai*, a mild corn beer. Also present are grills formed of woven and twisted wire used as ash bread cookers and a number of small cans with the lids folded back to form handles and create cups (Cutter 1987). These reused and altered Euro-American artifacts appear to reflect selective acculturation by the Apache.

More subtle than the presence of modified artifacts is the low frequency of food artifacts, architectural artifacts, and tools and hardware items. Artifacts associated with food are typically sparse when compared to Euro-American camps and do not display the same degree of variety. Food cans that originally contained fruits and vegetables were recovered from Apache camps as well as Anglo camps. However, spice, mayonnaise, vinegar, and fish containers are rarely represented at the Apache camps, but lard buckets, baking powder cans, and evaporated milk cans are common. The latter items were likely used by the women to make ash bread. Although the Apache diet initially appears bland, Apache consultants explain that their diet at Roosevelt included traditional foods such as acorn, yucca fruit, jackrabbit, and deer. Residents recall foraging trips to acorn gathering camps on Cherry Creek and deer hunting blinds along the flanks of Rockinstraw Mountain, a traditional resource area. Waterfowl were also hunted along the Salt River and on the newly formed Lake Roosevelt.

Perhaps the most striking artifacts we identified are the enamelware bowls, pans, and wash basins that had been "ritually killed," that is, intentionally slashed, punctured, or smashed. Oral histories and ethnographic accounts indicate that these artifacts represent a mortuary custom of destroying the personal belongings of a recently deceased individual, burning their wickiup, and relocating the remainder of the camp. This custom was practiced with the intent of dissuading the ghost of the deceased from returning to camp and causing mischief (Perry 1972). The specific gender of the deceased individual can usually be ascertained; our Apache consultants attribute killed cookware to women, and killed saddles, boots, and tools to men (Cutter 1987; Clayton 1987).

At one camp, ritually killed artifacts were found in association with a U-shaped rock alignment that may have been an uncovered windbreak for a workshop area. During excavation an ashen area was identified that contained over one hundred burned glass beads, tinklers, and nail plates as well as a belt buckle, shoe nails, decorative belt/jacket studs, and other clothing items. These artifact types continue to be used to decorate ceremonial garments worn by young Apache women during their *na ih es* puberty ceremonies (see Ferg and Kessel 1987, color illustration 21, for a picture of such a dress with tinkler and bead decoration). If the dress were burned, the reason is a mystery. Typically *na ih es* garments were quite valuable and passed on from one woman to another for reuse.

At another camp, excavation of a ritually burned wickiup produced over three hundred artifacts with both male and female associations. One possible explanation is that this was the wickiup of a couple who died during the particularly virulent flu epidemic that hit Roosevelt during this period. What they left may be a complete gowa assemblage.

Daagodigha, an Apache revitalization movement, was also apparently practiced at Roosevelt, as is evidenced by a photograph of the cross and crescent emblem worn by its adherents (Lubkin 1903–1911). This movement encouraged the belief that non-Indians would be removed from the earth, leaving their livestock and other possessions behind (Ferg and Kessel 1987, 144–49).

These features found at Roosevelt and their associated artifacts are significant because they represent a unique maintenance of Apache ideology and symbolic expression of cultural beliefs despite the reformation efforts of missionaries and government officials.

Apache Social Organization in the Archaeological Record

In an attempt to better understand Apache social organization at Roosevelt, the uses of cultural space within the camps were examined. Spaces are important since they possess special meaning to those who occupy them and become a focus of value, nurture, and support. One of the first things that a child learns in the maturational process is what the spaces around him or her mean. The child learns that distances between people and boundaries of the spaces they occupy are reflections of their relationships to each other. These relationships are significant in dictating and coordinating the rights and duties of the individual. Boundaries can result from shared principles of group formation and maintenance and create a sense of "belonging." For this reason, the study of boundedness and control over space, and especially the viewing of changes in spatial distribution over time, can be useful (Hastorf 1991, 153).

Oral histories indicate that the traditional social organization of these groups was based on matrilocal residence patterns. As discussed previously, Apache social units were composed of the nuclear family (*gowa*), extended family (*gota*), and local group (*itakowa*). Given the importance of Apache women in building and maintaining the wickiups (and thereby controlling social space), changes in the use of space through time help explain changing gender roles and responsibilities.

An initial task required defining and mapping individual wickiup rings. Because the wickiup platforms were ephemeral, lacking formal retaining walls and earthen platform bases, they were often difficult to identify archaeologically. Wickiups typically were simple and left few remnants in the archaeological record. We found that rocks sometimes outlined wickiup locations, but often the only evidence was a subtle, leveled clearing on a hillslope.

Artifact concentrations are not distributed in a precise relationship with regard to the wickiups, but several tentative patterns are evident. First, wickiups tend to be located in areas of low artifact density. Second, each artifact concentration suggesting extramural activity or trash deposition is within five to fifteen feet of a wickiup. Third, the location of these concentrations in relation to the wickiups is variable.

Based on archaeological evidence, the arrangements of wickiup rings at the Roosevelt camps dating between 1903 and 1915 demonstrate a clustering that appears to reflect traditional Apache residential patterns. The largest camp, at Cottonwood Creek, is comprised of eighty-seven wickiup platforms. These platforms are scattered across twelve hundred feet of ridge slope and cluster into nineteen gotas of two to nine wickiups each (fig. 3.3). In addition, three isolated wickiups were identified, possibly the homes of newlyweds or individuals who were, for some reason, mistrusted by the rest of the society. Assuming an average of 3 to 5 residents per wickiup (Clayton 1987), approximately 250 to 400 people may have resided at this camp, although perhaps not simultaneously. Wickiup clusters are also evident at the other Apache camps at Roosevelt. For example, five wickiup clusters (gotas) were recorded at the Clay Quarry camp, two at the Diversion Dam camp, and two at the High Road camp.

To improve on the initial intuitive approach to pattern recognition of social structure at the camps, nearest-neighbor distances for each wickiup were calculated. These measurements indicate that the distances between wickiup edges varied from 11 feet to 93 feet. However, this range forms a distinct bimodal distribution (fig. 3.4). Most wickiups were clustered within a range of between 11 and 35 feet of one another, and quite a few isolated wickiups had a nearest-neighbor distance of more than 50 feet. None, however, had a nearest-neighbor distance of between 40 and 50 feet. This distinct clustering appears to represent extended family groupings (gotas),

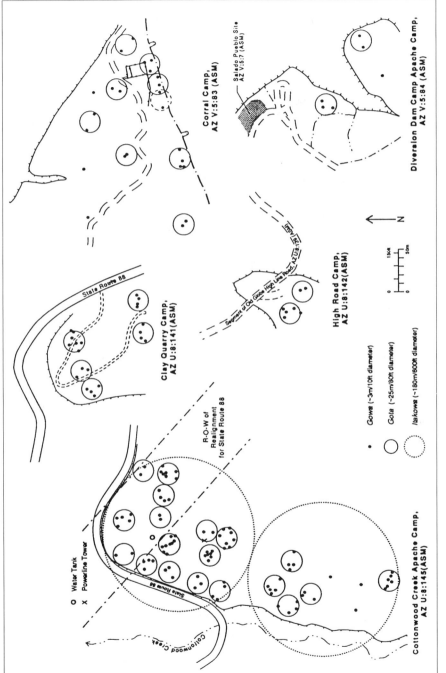

Figure 3.3: Spatial structure of the Roosevelt Apache camps.

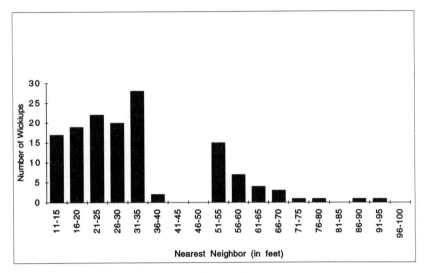

Figure 3.4. Apache wickiup spacing at Roosevelt, Arizona.

and the distance between them would have been socially important. Violating this distance may have been considered antisocial or even threatening.

Investigations at the larger Cottonwood Creek camp showed several large clusterings of wickiups that were separated by approximately 150 feet. These contain thirty-eight, twenty-eight, and twenty-five wickiups each and correspond quite well to Goodwin's (1942, 123–45) estimation of twenty to forty-five wickiups per itakowa. While these data are not sufficient to demonstrate that 150 feet represents the local group's, or itakowa's, social exclusion space, they are certainly suggestive.

This identification of social units within the archaeological record suggests specific future research questions: How were outdoor hearths shared? Can gota, as opposed to gowa, assemblages be discerned? Can pathways within and between gotas be recognized? Are larger gotas spaced farther apart than smaller ones, such as a gravity model might predict? How do these patterns compare to those at older, protohistoric camps?

In contrast, the later-era Apache camps at Roosevelt exhibit a gradual but distinct reduction in wickiup clustering, as had occurred at an earlier date among communities on the reservation. For example, at the Roosevelt Corral site, a predominantly 1920s-era camp, no gota clusterings were readily discernible, and the average nearest-neighbor distance between wickiups had increased by a factor of five. By 1940, Apaches were gone from Roosevelt and frame housing had mostly replaced wickiups across both the San Carlos and the White River Apache Reservations, where the average nearest-neighbor distance had increased to 300 feet. These trends were partially, but not entirely, influenced by BIA and WPA housing standards. During this period, housing construction responsibilities also shifted from the women to the men, many of whom had developed carpentry skills while working at Roosevelt and elsewhere.

The dissolution of the gota as a distinct spatial entity has had an immeasurable effect on the Apache lifestyle, one that has been well documented by ethnographers (Goodwin 1942, 124–26; Basso 1970, 25–26). The lack of danger from traditional enemies, coupled with the accessibility of nearby stores, reduced the necessity for economic cooperation. In addition, the development of wage labor, along with the encroachment of the Anglo ethic that profits are only for those who earn them, led to greatly reduced sharing among kin. This produced much contempt as well as stress within Apache society. One old man bitterly complained, "In the old times things were good, and we did not forget our relatives. Now we live as if we had no relatives" (Goodwin 1942, 125). It is possible that in an attempt to avoid traditional family responsibilities, or perhaps because of the shame involved in avoiding them, nuclear families tended to move away from the family cluster.

In sum, oral histories, complemented by archaeological evidence, indicate that at the turn of the century Apache social organization had been severely disrupted by federal policy. However, their experiences at Roosevelt provided an entire generation of Apaches with a refuge of sorts where traditional practices, including a residential patterning indicative of traditional social organization, could be and were maintained. Ironically, a federal policy aimed at assimilating Native Americans was turned on its head by the Apaches and utilized to their own purposes. By the 1920s, however, the Apache community at Roosevelt had diminished, as Apaches abandoned their traditional residential patterns and became more dispersed. This process was accelerated by the gradual acceptance of frame housing starting in the 1930s and 1940s.

Discussion and Conclusions

Certain obvious questions arise from an analysis of the Apache camps at Roosevelt. Why did the seeming contradiction arise between the Indian Service's goal of assimilation through labor and an apparent resurgence of traditional Apache culture? Also, why was the Reclamation Service so successful with Indian labor at Roosevelt when on their other projects Indian labor was considered a failure (Newell 1910)? Answers to both of these questions are intertwined and depend on understanding the overlapping, but different, spheres of Apache men and women. At Roosevelt, men were able to engage in long-term wage labor because women were able to maintain traditional camps close to the workplace. Conversely, women were able to maintain traditional camps because men were earning good wages at jobs protected by the Reclamation Service.

Two factors, the seriousness of the labor shortage at Roosevelt and the relative isolation of the project area, allowed Supervising Engineer Hill to deal with the Apaches on their own terms. By eschewing civil service procedures, which Hill felt were developed by "shoemakers and pumpkinrollers," many of the constraints normally placed on such projects were removed (Hill 1906). Hill's reaction to an edict proposed by George Corson, the San Carlos Indian agent, to round up and return to the reservation school-age children and individuals not gainfully employed at Roosevelt, illustrates his frustration. Corson's order resulted in many Apaches running away to the mountains to hide. Hill, recognizing the difficulties he would encounter if "the camps were broken up," wired Washington to complain and had the order rescinded and the agent replaced (U.S. Congress, House, 1911, 639–40).

Indeed, there is little evidence that the Apache children at Roosevelt had any formal schooling at all. In 1909 Reverend Harders attempted to establish a Lutheran Indian school there, but it lasted less than a year (Missionary Wisconsin Synodal-Bericht 1910). Instead, Apache children apparently received a traditional education at their homes.

From the Apache point of view, the single most important relaxation of civil service rules was the one that enabled them to share a single job among several individuals. As long as one man showed up for each job each day, supervisors turned a blind eye to the Apaches' different ideas of appropriate work schedules. The Reverend Harders (1968), among others, noted the efficiency of this system:

> (The Apache laborer) works perhaps two or three months and then demands four or five months vacation. So several good friends or relatives club together. One takes a job, and about three families share his income. When he tires of work, another takes his place. In this way they change off, so that one man's wages support about three families, the income being sufficient for their modest demands. With respect to food and living conditions, they are content with the least and simplest. (22)

Without really understanding it, Reverend Harders was describing the gota, the extended family. Louis Hill's relaxation of civil service procedures resulted in a resurgence of the Apaches' traditional sharing of tasks (formerly hunting and so forth) within the gota, releasing individuals to maintain the traditional family and clan obligations so important to Apache culture.

The Apache work crews at Roosevelt appear to have been comprised of twelve to fourteen men. For example, a typical road crew would include a foreman and four or five teamsters, with the rest manning shovels. These numbers correspond well to the number of gotas (extended families) within the itakowa, or camp, and it is possible that the social structure of the camp was transferred to the work crews. In addition, the Apache foremen appear to have been traditional clan leaders. Rosters of supervisors include such Apache leaders as Charlie Nontamenta, Isaac Cutter, and Henry Chilchuana (U.S. Congress, House, 1911, 702–6). These men earned an average of $80 per month, only slightly less than the Anglo foremen.

Wages for the Apaches at Roosevelt were initially $1.50 per day, somewhat less than for the Anglo employees. Hill reported that this was because they had been in wretched condition, and not having had enough to eat, were too weak to work much (ibid.). However, it was common practice to pay Mexicans and Indians less than Anglos. Eventually, as the Apaches became stronger and their work became recognized, they were paid the same as Anglos, averaging $1.75 to $2.50 per eight-hour day. Elsewhere in Arizona, Indian laborers averaged $1.25 for a longer ten-hour day. For a people with simple needs and an ethic that downplayed the importance of the individual, high wages and steady employment might have caused, quite literally, an embarrassment of riches.

This apparent contradiction also seemed to confuse the local press. Other than reporting crimes or amusing anecdotes, they largely ignored the Apaches, possibly because the reality of the Apache wage laborer conflicted with more powerful romantic or paternalistic images. For those impressed with bloodthirsty renegades or a Rousseauian image of noble savages, the idea of Apache men dressed in dungarees, operating heavy equipment, and working eight-hour shifts undoubtedly would have been disillusioning. A few references utilized popular images as in "Poor 'Lo' assisted on the Dam" and the slightly more romantic "Where Geronimo's blood-thirsty band once spilt blood, his followers now help the white man make the desert bloom" (*Arizona Republican*, 31 May 1905). In keeping with Frederick Turner's image of the West, the Indians may also have been considered by society as mere background noise, part of a "natural" environment in which a monument to a superior culture was being built.

It seems clear from historical and archaeological data that large numbers of Apaches from the San Carlos Reservation lived and worked at Roosevelt during the period 1902–11 and later. At least one contemporary writer suggested that the Tonto Dam could not have been completed without Apache labor (Steele 1918). Not only this dam but the Reclamation Service itself would probably have been in serious trouble without this convenient and efficient labor force.

Opler (1983) noted that while there is a "basic Apachean culture pattern . . . [in the past] basic ideas and content were reworked to harmonize with Apachean conceptions and purposes" (380). This reworking certainly seems to have been the case here. The Reclamation Service's regulations for employment on the Tonto Dam project seem, ironically, to have encouraged, rather than discouraged, continuation of Apache culture. The three most significant units of Apache society were all strengthened. The gowa (nuclear family) was strengthened because families were allowed to live together and to do so where they wanted and in traditional structures, and there was no compulsory education for the children. The gota (extended family) was strengthened by the encouragement of job sharing. And the usefulness of the itakowa (large camp) as a workforce under traditional leaders was legitimized and reinforced. Additionally, the Apache enjoyed less interference in their diet, religion, and lifestyle at Roosevelt than on the reservation. Obviously, the Indian Service's goal of assimilation through work off the reservation was not met in this case.

At Roosevelt, Apache men were blending efficiently into the American capital economy, at the same time that Apache women were reinforcing traditional Apache practices. As an accident of history, it worked well for the Apaches, at least for the short term. The Roosevelt experience reversed a trend of erosion of traditional Apache values and instilled a new sense of personal and cultural worth among them. Frank Cutter summarized his life at Roosevelt as follows: "We were happy. We were well fed. We took care of each other like families were meant to" (Cutter 1987).

Following the completion of the dam in 1911, many of the Apache residents of Roosevelt drifted out of the Tonto Basin, but a large number of families stayed on until well into the 1920s. Many of the men continued to perform maintenance work on the dam and power canal as well as work for local ranchers. Road building and maintenance became a major source of income during this period. Throughout the second and third decades of the twentieth century, crews of Apache graders could be seen along Arizona's roads utilizing skills learned at Roosevelt. However, by the mid-1920s, the advent of heavy equipment and macadamized roads had eliminated the need for Apache labor in road building jobs (Adams 1971).

The Depression years found most Apaches back on the reservation, where National Recovery Administration programs and a fledgling tribal cattle industry provided a small measure of security. Gender roles continued to change. The organization of women's production was a fundamental structuring element of Apache culture, and as this changed so did social interactions and the way in which the social landscape was perceived. During this period, a resurgence of resistance to the Anglo world took the form of an increasingly strong and articulate anti-Anglo sentiment, a withdrawal from the Anglo world, and rejection of Anglo values (Adams 1971, 122). A desire among many Apaches to maintain a separate economic and social existence continues to this day.

The period from 1880 to 1920 has been described as the "age of assimilation," the period of the most radical change in the culture of Native Americans (Hoxie 1973, 1). In Arizona and across the country, traditional Indian cultures were under attack on all fronts. However, at Roosevelt, a refuge of sorts from the twentieth century was provided in the shadow of the greatest engineering project of the day. For a while, Apaches were allowed to live as Apaches.

This research has shown the importance of thinking about the past with the assumption that gender is a fundamental element of culture. We should be prepared to examine those contexts where gender roles and engendered meaning are most likely to have been at work (Conkey 1991, 57). In this instance, examining Apache culture as a whole could not have addressed elements that appeared to be inherent contradictions. However, by teasing apart elements of the society (in this case, gender groups), we can see how they are differentially affected by a changing socioeconomic environment.

References

Adams, William Y.
1971   Wage Labor and the San Carlos Apache. In *Apachean Culture History and Ethnology*, ed. Keith Basso and Morris E. Opler, 115–28. Anthropological Papers of the University of Arizona, 21. Tucson: University of Arizona Press.
Arizona Republican
1905   Apaches Help Build Dam. 31 May 1905.

Ayers, J., A. E. Rogge, M. Keane, D. L. Douglas, E. J. Bassett, D. L. Fenicle, C. L. Myers, B. J. Clark, and K. Turnmire
1991   The Historical Archaeology of Dam Construction Camps in Central Arizona. Vol. 2A, Sites in the Roosevelt Dam Area. Draft report prepared for Dames & Moore, Phoenix. Photocopy.
Ball, Eve
1970   *In the Days of Victorio.* Tucson: University of Arizona Press.
Ball, Eve, Nora Henn, and Linda Sanchez.
1980   *Indeh: An Apache Odyssey.* Provo: Brigham Young University Press.
Basso, Keith H.
1983   Western Apache. In *Handbook of North American Indians,* Vol. X, Southwest, ed. Alfonso Ortiz, 462–88. Washington, D.C.: Smithsonian Institution Press.
1971   *Western Apache Raiding and Warfare: From the Notes of Grenville Goodwin.* Tucson: University of Arizona Press.
1970   *The Cibecue Apache.* New York: Holt, Rinehart and Winston.
Basso, Keith H., and Morris E. Opler, eds.
1971   *Apachean Culture History and Ethnology.* Anthropological Papers of the University of Arizona, 21. Tucson: University of Arizona Press.
Boyer, Ruth McDonald, and Narcissus Duffy Gayton
1992   *Apache Mothers and Daughters.* Norman: University of Oklahoma Press.
Buchanan, Kimberly Moore
1986   *Apache Women Warriors.* Southwestern Studies Series, 79. El Paso: Texas Western Press.
Buskirk, Winfred
1986   *The Western Apache: Living with the Land Before 1950.* Norman: University of Oklahoma Press.
Clarke, David L.
1968   *Analytical Archaeology.* London: Methuen.
Clayton, Louise
1987   Personal communication with Elizabeth Brandt. Interview recorded 19 March 1987, San Carlos, Ariz.
Cole, Donald C.
1981   An Ethnohistory of the Chiracahua Indian Reservation, 1872–1876. Ph.D. diss., Department of Anthropology, University of New Mexico, Albuquerque.
Conkey, Margaret W.
1991   Contexts of Action, Contexts for Power: Material Culture and Gender in the Magdalenian. In *Engendering Archaeology,* eds. Joan M. Gero and Margaret W. Conkey, 57–92. Oxford: Basil Blackwell.
Cutter, Frank
1987   Personal communication with Elizabeth Brandt. Interview recorded 16 February 1987, Roosevelt, Ariz.

Dittert, Alfred E., Jr.
1976   The 1976 Season: Archaeological Studies in the Payson Ranger District, Tonto National Forest, Arizona. Report on file with the Tonto National Forest, Phoenix. Photocopy.
Ferg, Alan
1992   Western Apache and Yavapai Pottery and Features from the Rye Creek Project. In *The Rye Creek Project: Archaeology in the Upper Tonto Basin*, Vol. 3, *Synthesis and Conclusions*, ed. Mark E. Elson and Douglas B. Craig, 3–27. Anthropological Papers, 11. Tucson: Center for Desert Archaeology.
Ferg, Alan, and B. Kessel
1987   *Western Apache Material Culture: The Goodwin and Guenther Collections.* Tucson: University of Arizona Press.
Gero, Joan M., and Margaret W. Conkey, eds.
1991   *Engendering Archaeology: Women and Prehistory.* Oxford: Basil Blackwell.
Gladwin, Winifred, and Harold S. Gladwin
1930   *An Archaeological Survey of the Verde Valley.* Medallion Papers, 6. Globe, Ariz.: Gila Pueblo.
Goodwin, Grenville
1935   Social Divisions and Economic Life of the Western Apache. *American Anthropologist* 73:55–65.
1942   *The Social Organization of the Western Apache.* Chicago: University of Chicago Press.
Griffin, P. Bion, Mark P. Leone, and Keith H. Basso
1971   Western Apache Ecology: From Horticulture to Agriculture. In *Apachean Culture History and Ethnology*, ed. Keith Basso and Morris E. Opler, 69–76. Anthropological Papers of the University of Arizona, 21. Tucson: University of Arizona Press.
Harders, Gustav
1968   *La Paloma.* Milwaukee: Northwestern Publishing House.
Hastorf, Christine A.
1991   Gender, Space, and Food in Prehistory. In *Engendering Archaeology*, eds. Joan M. Gero and Margaret W. Conkey, 132–62. Oxford: Basil Blackwell.
Hill, Louis C.
1906   Letter to F. H. Newell, Chief Engineer, U.S. Reclamation Service, 30 August 1906. Record Group 115, National Archives, Washington, D.C.
Hohmann, John W., and Charles L. Redman, eds.
1988   *Continuing Studies in Payson Prehistory.* Anthropological Field Studies, 21. Tempe, Ariz.: Office of Cultural Resource Management, Department of Anthropology, Arizona State University.
Hoxie, Norman
1973   *Broken Promises: Indian Assimilation in the Twentieth Century.* Norman: University of Oklahoma Press.

Lockwood, Frank
1938   *The Apaches*. Chicago: Macmillan.
Longacre, W. A., and J. E. Ayres
1968   Archaeological Lessons from an Apache Wikiup. In *New Perspectives in Archaeology*, ed. S. R. Binford and L. R. Binford, 151–59. Chicago: Aldine.
Lubkin, Walter J.
1903–1911 Collection of photographs of Apaches at Roosevelt taken by Walter J. Lubkin, the Reclamation Service photographer. Copies of many of these are in the National Anthropological Archives, Washington, D.C., and at the Arizona State Museum, Tucson.
Missionary Wisconsin Synodal-Bericht
1910   *Inhresbericht des Comitees fur die Mission unterden Apachen-Indianen in Arizona*. Milwaukee: Northwestern Publishing House.
Newell, Fredrick
1910   Letter to R. G. Valentine, Commissioner of Indian Affairs, 4 November 1910. Record Group 115, National Archives, Washington, D.C.
Opler, Morris E.
1983   The Apachean Culture Pattern and Its Origins. In *Handbook of North American Indians*, Vol. X, *Southwest*, ed. Alfonso Ortiz, 368–92. Washington, D.C.: Smithsonian Institution Press.
Peck, Fred R.
1956   An Archaeological Reconnaissance of the East Verde River in Central Arizona. Master's thesis, Department of Anthropology, University of Arizona, Tucson.
Perry, Richard J.
1991   *Western Apache Heritage: People of the Mountain Corridor*. Austin: University of Texas Press.
1972   Structural Resiliency and Danger of the Dead: The Western Apache. *Ethnology* 11:4:380–85.
Redman, Charles L., and John W. Hohmann, eds.
1986   *Small Site Variability in the Payson Region: The Flex Land Exchange*. Anthropological Field Studies, 11. Tempe: Office of Cultural Resource Management, Department of Anthropology, Arizona State University.
Roosevelt, Theodore
1902   Letter to Fredrick Newell, 15 September 1902. Record Group 115, National Archives, Washington, D.C.
Steele, Rufus
1918   On the Warpath for Fun. *Sunset* 40:52.
Stockel, Henrietta H.
1991   *Women of the Apache Nation*. Reno and Las Vegas: University of Nevada Press.
U.S. Congress, House of Representatives
1911   Hearings Before the Committee on Expenditures in the Interior De-

partment. House of Representatives 7 July 1911. Washington, D.C.: U.S. Government Printing Office.

U.S. Congress, Senate

1871   Senate Document Number 452, 57th Congress, 1st Session (1871:812).

U.S. Department of the Interior

1901   Annual Report of the Commissioner of the Indian Service. Washington, D.C.: U.S. Government Printing Office.

1902   Annual Report of the Commissioner of the Indian Service. Washington, D.C.: U.S. Government Printing Office.

1904   San Carlos Apache Reservation Annual Report to the Commissioner, Luther Kelly, Agent. Washington, D.C.: U.S. Government Printing Office.

1905   San Carlos Apache Reservation Annual Report to the Commissioner, Luther Kelly, Agent. Washington, D.C.: U.S. Government Printing Office.

Walde, D., and N. Willows, eds.

1991   *The Archaeology of Gender.* Proceedings of the 22nd Annual Chacmool Conference. Calgary: Archaeological Association of the University of Calgary.

4

The House of the Black Burghardts

An Investigation of Race, Gender, and Class at the W.E.B. DuBois Boyhood Homesite

Nancy Ladd Muller

> Cultural critics, especially those of us who are black, seeking to make a context for liberation, cannot ignore the issue of representation, as it determines who gets to speak to, with and for us about culture and be heard.
>
> (hooks 1990, 9)

William Edward Burghardt DuBois, an international figure, defined and reshaped the world's understanding of the "race concept" and its predicated action, racism (see Muller 1985, 1992). DuBois is considered a founder of the modern civil rights movement in the United States and the "father" of Pan-Africanist movements for colonial independence in Africa and the Caribbean. His voice as philosopher, educator, playwright, poet, historian, and social scientist only now is being recovered as potentially one of the most important in the twentieth century.

W. E. B. DuBois was born in Great Barrington, Massachusetts, in 1868. He was one of the fifth generation of African Americans to live and work in the Berkshires. His boyhood home, which he called the "house of the Black Burghardts," was one of his favorite places, and yet, as with many African Americans, his home and the lives of its inhabitants still remain largely invisible. DuBois was never able to implement his dream of restoring the house because of the economic and political realities of racism in the United States. He was hounded by the U.S. government throughout his career because of his relentless challenge to the racist structures of the United States and imperialism and colonialism in Africa and the Caribbean (DuBois 1975, vii-xii). In 1928, the "house of the Black Burghardts" was bought from DuBois's cousin Lena Wooster by friends and colleagues of DuBois, including Clarence Darrow and Jane Addams, as a gift for his sixtieth birthday; it was in poor condition and probably was uninhabitable. Of this occasion DuBois wrote in the *Crisis:*

> There it stood, old lonesome, empty. . . . It had lost color and fence and grass and up to the left and down to the right its sister homes were gone—dead and gone with no stick or stone to mark their burial. From that day to this I desperately wanted to own that house. . . . Then of a sudden somebody whose many names and places I do not know sent secret emissaries to me on a birthday . . . and said by telegram—"The House of the Black Burghardts is come home again—it is yours!" Whereat in great joy I celebrated another birthday and drew plans and from its long hiding place I brought out an old black pair of tongs. Once my grandfather and mayhap his used them in the great fireplace of the House. Long years I have carried them tenderly over all the earth and when the old fireplace rises again from the dead on Egremont Plain, its dead eyes shall see not only the ghosts of Tom and his son Jack and his grandson Othello and his great-grandson me but also the real presence of these iron tongs resting again in fire worship in the House of the Black Burghardts. (DuBois 1928, 133–34)

DuBois sold the house and land in 1954, probably because the repressiveness of the McCarthy years made his political and economic circumstances uncertain. In 1969, the site was named to the Registry of National Historic Places and is presently owned by the Commonwealth of Massachusetts, through the University of Massachusetts, Amherst (for more on this see Paynter 1990).

The DuBois Boyhood Homesite is now a poison-ivy patch on the side of the road, on the Egremont Plain just outside the town of Great Barrington. Nothing marks this place that had such significance to one of the most important voices of the twentieth century. No school children are bussed there for the day to reflect on the greatness of the individual who spent part of his boyhood there and wrote so extensively of the experience of U.S. African Americans. Only those who know of the site from contact with DuBois's writings or other sources make the trek to Great Barrington in order to pay homage.

This neglect of the DuBois site serves to reaffirm the prevailing myth that African Americans were not important to the history either of Massachusetts, which is considered a major "cultural hearth" (Paynter 1990) in the American experience, or of the United States. This in turn reifies a "history" that clearly demonstrates an insensitivity and a kind of cultural imperialism that places a premium on the recovery of the pasts of European Americans.

As the twentieth century comes to a close, there is a fundamental need to assess and evaluate the political, economic, and social circumstances of people of African descent, as well as other so-called minority groups, in the United States.

The conceptual production, reproduction, and distribution of the past, as "subject," is a culturally specific and ahistorical activity. In the United States, as well as in other Western nations, the pasts of non-European, nonwhite women and men are carefully controlled by white supremacist culture in an academic milieu largely funded by governmental institutions with a vested stake in the status quo. Academics should consider several questions. For whom does the recovery of these various pasts have meaning? In whose vernacular are the "stories" of the past distributed? Where are the "products" of the past located, if not in museums and laboratories or on bookshelves? The stories of the past are controlled by very few and are symbolically "owned" by privileged researchers who control the theories and methods created for and reproduced by the dominant Eurocentric culture. As these pasts remain largely the academic business of "white folks," often white men, in whose image are these pasts being recovered? Who goes back to these culturally created pasts as a reference point? In other words, who is experiencing whose past for whom?

This study of the "house of the Black Burghardts" provides an example of the meaning that house and land ownership had for African Americans living north of the slaveholding plantation South. Resources consulted include the documentary evidence of the family's presence in Great Barrington as well as information from historical archaeology conducted at the DuBois Boyhood Homesite. In addition, the Black Burghardts and their house are placed in the broader context of African American land ownership in Great Barrington. Finally, I focus in particular on the Black Burghardt women and their activity during a time of economic stress when the community's largely agrarian economy was replaced by an industrial economy in the mid- to late nineteenth century. They provide an example of agency and resistance by African American women as they created their own meaning out of house and land ownership and negotiated such ownership in a changing wage-labor environment.

The Black Burghardts of Great Barrington

The presence of African Americans in rural eighteenth- and nineteenth-century Massachusetts is not as unique as it may seem (see Greene 1968, 81, 337–43). There were a number of African Americans in Massachusetts towns, yet little information survives either in written records or in the annals of New England archaeological investigation. Some exceptions to the latter are Deetz's (1977) work on the Parting Ways Settlement in Plymouth; Baker's (1980) investigation of Black Lucy's Garden in Andover; Bower and Rushing's (1980) analysis of the African Meeting House in Boston; and Paynter et al.'s 1983–84 research at the W. E. B. DuBois Boyhood Homesite in Great Barrington (Paynter et al. n.d.).

The experience of African Americans in the North was not simply opposite to that of those in the South. A commonly held but incorrect assumption is that because of the complexity of the Northern economy, bonded labor was not in demand. However, although plantation capitalism did not root itself in the North, the use of bonded labor was not necessarily precluded (Litwack 1961, 5); Africans were in fact bondsmen and bondswomen in the North (see Greene 1968; Higginbotham 1978; Litwack 1961; Pierson 1975; Twombly and Moore 1982). And Litwack (1961) has proposed that racial bondage in the North was not abolished due to any abolitionist sentiments but was due instead to the "ire of white workers who wanted to charge more for their labor in a market which used slave labor" (5). Africans had a distinctive experience in the North, and specifically in the Northeast, because unlike their counterparts in the South, they were "engulfed in a pervasive whiter society," one that was much more forceful in inculcating European values (Pierson 1975, x).

In an interview about his origins, DuBois was asked this question: Please give any memories or achievements of your ancestors which have been the sources of family pride or have fired your ambition? He answered, "Our free birth and ownership of land" (DuBois n.d.).

The community of Great Barrington in the eighteenth and nineteenth centuries was unique in that it was a New England town mostly populated by Dutch, not English, settlers, and was more dependent on a New York rather than a Boston market. Geographically, it was isolated and depended on steamboats and the railroad for shipment and receipt of goods. The community's original inhabitants were Native Americans who were forced to give up their lands after King Philip's War.

DuBois's boyhood home had a great deal of personal meaning to him. It linked DuBois not only to his grandfather but to a vast network of kinfolk,

African and African American, many of whom lived or had lived in Massa-chusetts. His writings have led us to his maternal relatives, the Black Burg-hardts. Throughout his life he wrote extensively about his New England heritage and its influence on him. From these writings and his meticulous search for family background we learn that "the Black Burghardts were a group of African Negroes descended from Tom, who was born in West Africa about 1730 and was stolen by Dutch slave traders" (DuBois 1968, 62). "Tom" came to Great Barrington from Kinderhook, New York, with Coonrad Burghardt, the head of a white Dutch family, and originally was held in bondage by a family named Etton or Etson. Coonrad Burghardt was one of the original settlers of Great Barrington. According to DuBois, "Tom was reported a Negr [sic]. He enlisted to serve for three years; but how long or where he served the records do not show . . . this war service freed him and his family from slavery." For his service in the American Revolution under Captain John Spoor, Tom Burghardt was manumitted and given a small piece of land, approximately six acres, on the Egremont Plain just outside the town of Great Barrington.

Coonrad Burghardt and several other "entrepreneurs" obtained a land grant in Great Barrington sometime in 1733 or 1734. Until that time the land was in dispute among the English, Dutch, and Native Americans. This land included six hundred acres lying between Egremont Plain and North Egremont belonging to Captain John Spoor, which he had purchased from Native Americans about 1731 (see Brennan 1990 and Taylor 1928 for more on these transactions). Coonrad Burghardt owned two hundred acres lying in the extreme western part of Great Barrington, which adjoined the Spoor grant (Taylor 1928, 68).

There is a record of Tom Burghardt having a son, Jacob or Jack, born in 1760, and a daughter, Nancy (DuBois 1968), although the search thus far has not revealed any further documentation of this daughter. Of Tom's wife Violet, DuBois writes "she was a little Black Bantu woman, who never became reconciled to this strange land; she clasped her knees and rocked and crooned Do Bana Coba—gene me, gene me, Ben d'nuli, ben d'le—the song came down the years and I heard it at my grandfather's fireside" (62). In another source DuBois again writes of Violet's song and identifies it as African: "she brought with her a song, an African song, which became tra-ditional in the family even though no one understood the words" (DuBois 1975, 89).

Jacob or Jack Burghardt stayed in the employ of the Burghardt family but lived on the South Egremont Plain just outside the town limits of Great Barrington. DuBois (1968) writes, "Here in the late eighteenth- and early nineteenth-centuries the Black Burghardts lived. I remember three of these houses and a small pond. There were the homes of Harlow and Ira; and of my grandfather Othello, which he had inherited from his sister Lucinda" (63). DuBois's extensive writings about his family, their households and furnishings, and the larger community have served as a guide to interpretation of the site:

> It is the first house I remember. There my mother was born and all her nine brothers and sisters. There perhaps my grandfather was born. . . . At any rate, on this wide and lovely plain . . . lived for two hundred years the Black Burghardt clan. Up and to the east of a hill of rocks Uncle Ira; down and to the south was Uncle Harlow in a long, red house beside a pond—in a house of secret passages, sudden steps, low, narrow doors and unbelievable furniture. And here right in the center of the world was Uncle Tallow, as Grandfather Othello was called. . . . It was a delectable place—simple square and low, with the great room of the fireplace, the flagged kitchen, half a step below, and the lower woodshed beyond. Steep, strong stairs led up to Sleep, while without was a brook, a well and a mighty elm. (DuBois 1928, 360)

Historical Archaeology at the W. E. B. DuBois Homesite

Archaeological and documentary data from the DuBois Boyhood Homesite were collected by participants in a two-year field school at the DuBois site conducted in 1983 and 1984 by the Department of Anthropology, University of Massachusetts, Amherst, under the direction of Dr. Robert Paynter (see Paynter et al. n.d.).

This site at which DuBois spent part of his boyhood, and vacations later in life, contains about five acres of woodlot and gravelly field. The house and barn were torn down in the 1950s, and from the main road it is impossible to discern that the lot was once inhabited. In the early twentieth century a small parcel of land was sold, and presently the site is U-shaped with a house on that central parcel. The only other known activity on the site postdating the Burghardt/DuBois occupations was some landscaping done to the site by interested African Americans in the late 1960s.

As part of the field school, a preliminary deed chain was developed (Paynter and Gumaer 1983), and subsequently Muller (1986) looked at the transfer of ownership through the Black Burghardt women. Brennan (1990) added to this data by researching the origins of the site when the land belonged to Native Americans. The field schools also produced a genealogy and artifactual data.

Paynter et al.'s preliminary investigations have yielded what seem to be four major periods of land use from 1820 to the present. Artifacts representing virtually every aspect of daily life that were retrieved from two middens, several test pits, and a comprehensive surface collection have been analyzed (Paynter et al. n.d.). The myriad activities of generations of Black Burghardt men and women are reflected in fragments of dishes, glasses, bottles, and utensils; clothing; medicinal containers; recreational items; agricultural implements; and bicycles and automotive parts recovered from the site.

Few eighteenth- and nineteenth-century houses owned and occupied by African American families are known to have survived. Not many sources deal with the social history of African American settlements outside of the South (some exceptions are Geismar 1982 and Bridges and Salwen 1980). Even fewer have concentrated on land and house ownership by individual African American families. We have many examples of a "house" as a point of entry into the lives of important figures in our history, and obviously "the identity, lineage, and social status of a family determines whether a house is remembered or forgotten. The history of a house validates the social position of its occupants" (Yentsch 1988, 15). In most cases, however, the restrictions of the "color line" prevented African Americans from land and house ownership. Therefore, the documentary evidence of land ownership by African Americans such as DuBois's maternal relatives, the Black Burghardt women, is significant and may be the most important "artifact" recovered from the site.

African American Land Ownership in Great Barrington

The Black Burghardts did not originally choose to settle in Great Barrington. They were placed there by political and economic forces beyond their control, such as Tom Burghardt's movement with his "owner," Coonrad Burghardt. Since refusal to accompany Coonrad could have meant loss of life or becoming a fugitive, Tom decided to stay with Coonrad, and subsequently his family also remained. However, the Black Burghardts mediated these forces and participated in all the "legitimate" systems of the community of Great Barrington. They attended local integrated schools, worshiped at several local Protestant churches and also at the African church, had their land transactions recorded in the town register, and, in the case of Lucinda Burghardt, had their property probated. The Burghardts were buried in the cemetery of Great Barrington although in a separate area reserved only for African Americans. Some of their births, marriages, baptisms, and deaths are recorded in both town and church records. They moved freely about the community, seemingly without any restrictions. Letters were held for them at the local post office and announced in the local paper, the *Berkshire Courier.* In one instance, the name of Harlow Burghardt (DuBois's great uncle) was included in the "Gentlemen's List."

Yet there are definite signs of separation from the mainstream of Great Barrington. The only African Americans who owned a business were men, James Jacklyn and Caesar Freeman, who operated a distillery in the Seeconk area directly behind the Burghardt homesite. Taylor's (1928) *History of Great Barrington* mentions this distillery: "in that part of town, too James Jacklyn and Caesar Freeman (Negroes) located very early. Jacklyn settled about 1793 near the brook north of Bush Hill Road, where he long maintained a cider brandy distillery. He lived to the age of ninety-three and died in September of 1831" (359). The only other indication of a business owned by African Americans, also men, is in the *New York Globe*, an African American newspaper, 27 September 1894: "Mssrs. Cooley and Mason, our enterprising caterers to the public appetite, will reopen their restaurant at the Agricultural Fair which takes place here Sept. 24–26. Theirs is the only colored establishment on the grounds and we wish them the same success this year that has attended them in their former ventures."

No African American held any political office. In his writings DuBois mentions attending town meetings in Great Barrington but sitting in a segregated area. Of his family's economic status he states, "Their economic status was not high. These early members of the family supported themselves on little farms of a few acres then drifted to town as labourers and servants but did not go into the mills. Most of them rented homes, but some owned homes and pieces of land; a few had very pleasant and well furnished homes, but none had anything like wealth" (DuBois 1975, 91). Even though it seemed that the Black Burghardts were not completely shut out, they were excluded from certain economic opportunities. African American men and women were not employed in the mills, possibly due to racism. The labor of the "free" African American population was no longer in demand, as an economic shift from a largely agrarian economy to an industrial economy took place around 1880. Willing Irish and German immigrant populations were ready to work in the mills and in turn to become "consumer" laborers supporting the burgeoning influx of merchants into the town. Therefore, the Black Burghardts were not really "free" or able to participate in the mill economy. They were forced to move into other directions in order to survive. They did, however, manage to hold on to that small plot of land lying north on the Egremont Plain.

The Black Burghardt Women and Land Ownership

Occupational data recovered for Great Barrington reveal that over a period of thirty years, between 1850 and 1880, significant shifts occurred in the occupations of African American men and women (Paynter and Gumaer 1983). The numbers of men and women identified as "servant," "domestic," and "hotel employee" rose from less than 5 percent in 1850 to over 30 percent in 1870. This increase was accomplished by a noticeable decline in a previously stable African American professional sector, which included, for example, barbers, musicians, and clergy. African American men were not being hired in the mills in Great Barrington, and some had to leave the area, either permanently or seasonally, by working in the hotel, restaurant, and tourist business or as day laborers in New England, the Midwest, and as far away as Florida (DuBois 1968). This shift may be seen in ads in the local papers and also in DuBois's early writings for the *New York Globe*. DuBois wrote on 5 May 1883, "Mr. G. S. Jackson will leave the Miller House to go to Brunswick House in Troy, N.Y. We are sorry to lose so many colored people from our town but they have the best wishes of all"; on 22 November 1884, "Mr. Henry Jackson departs soon to Florida with Mr. Peck, where he will cater to the public appetite throughout the winter"; and on 10 January 1885, "Mr. J. T. Burghardt and G. S. Jackson will be found at the Kenmore Hotel Albany, N.Y. after that date."

The change in demand for servants in Great Barrington had its most profound effect on African American women. In 1850, 75 percent of these women were listed in census data as housewives and a small number (20 percent) employed as servants. The shift toward mills and factories in the Great Barrington economy pulled these women out of the home and into the paid labor force, so that by 1870, 60 percent of the African American women were listed as servants, with only 40 percent remaining as housewives (United States Census 1850, 1870).

It is in this period that "ownership" of land seems to have become an important issue for the Black Burghardt women. These women were forced to move in different directions because of the shifting economy, but between 1855 and 1928 they managed to transfer the land eleven times among themselves and their employers, the Kellogg sisters (Muller 1986). Ownership of this land by the Black Burghardt women may be seen both as an act of resistance to an outwardly imposed system and as a way of creating family solidarity. The house itself becomes a symbol of the Burghardt family. From DuBois's writings we see the meaning this house and land had to him. This meaning was also part of his familial heritage, and we can assume that the Black Burghardts, his maternal relatives, instilled in him the importance of securing his ancestral home, which he later did.

Although the deed chain of the Black Burghardt property transfers is still in the preliminary stages, it allows us to trace the movement of the Black Burghardt women. Ownership began to involve these women in 1831. In that transaction Harlow Burghardt was the grantor and Maria (Mariah) Burghardt the grantee. The next transaction, in 1836, involved Mariah as a grantor to James Freeman. The deed reads as follows: "I Mariah M. Burghardt of Great Barrington, Massachusetts single women in consideration of two hundred and fifty dollars paid by James Freeman of Great Barrington. . . . I do hereby acknowledge so hereby give grant . . . . unto the said James Freeman the following real estate in Great Barrington" (Great Barrington Town Hall 1836).

Mariah Burghardt married Samuel Van Ness in late 1836 and named her two daughters after the women to whom she was in service, Sarah and Mary Kellogg, the unmarried daughters of a local mill owner. Mariah's daughters were named Sarah Kellogg Van Ness and Mary Kellogg Van Ness. The latter was the great-great-grandmother of Denise Williams, a living relative of the Black Burghardts; she produced family documents to support the close relationship that existed between Mariah and the Kellogg sisters (D. Williams, pers. com. 1991). This relationship is clearly seen in the next transaction, in 1855, in which Sarah and Mary Kellogg were the grantees, buying the land back from James Freeman. On that same day the Kellogg sisters sold or granted the land to Lucinda M. Burghardt for the sum of one dollar, thus keeping the land in the family of the Black Burghardts.

In 1860, Lucinda Burghardt as grantor sold the land to her brothers Harlow, Henry, and Albert Burghardt. This sale seems to have been an economic necessity, since it was noted that Henry sent money from the Midwest to pay the real estate taxes that were owed.

It is not possible, in this essay, to present all the data from the deed chains of the Burghardt properties (see Muller 1986). But it is clear that the Black Burghardt women were not economically absent or politically powerless. This evidence contradicts approaches that present African American women in the past as having no significant effect in the private or public spheres, despite the fact that their impact is central to an appropriately rigorous interpretation of the historical and archaeological record. We can expand our understanding of these pasts by looking at African American women as rational decision makers, with the ability to participate in and adapt to social, economic, and political change.

The task of developing a theoretical framework within which to address the articulation of race, gender, and class in historical archaeology is a crucial one and, in the case of the recovery of African American pasts, a sometimes arduous task. But to analyze this articulation solely at the theoretical level yields very generalized observations that are undermined by a lack of reference to specific instances. The DuBois site becomes useful to address questions about the rural character of African American culture in the North. The lives of the Black Burghardt family and the unique problems of "free" rural African American women in a changing economy become a point of entry into the issues of how race, gender, and class intersect. Whether Great Barrington or the Black Burghardts are typical or unique is perhaps less important than the fact that this case exemplifies the superimposition of the urban/industrial pattern on the rural countryside and the subsequent shifts that occurred for African Americans as regional economic systems changed. Compared to information on Euro-American groups, documentation on African Americans in general and on African American women in particular is poor. However, as the foregoing discussion has shown, important information about at least some African American women can be gleaned from written records. This kind of knowledge cannot be recovered archaeologically. Only when archaeological information from sites such as DuBois's boyhood home is combined with evidence of women such as those of the Black Burghardts can we begin to see a fuller and clearer picture of the pasts of African Americans, both women and men.

Land ownership is significant not only as a point of entry into the larger issues of agency; it also becomes a way to record generational continuity in the African American family. This evidence serves to refute the myth of the inferiority of the African American family structure. Indeed, recent data point to a need for studying the process by which, in the changing socioeconomic and political context of the United States, family organization evolved from African patterns recreated in the New World by African women (Sudarkasa 1982).

Clearly, access to a strategic resource such as land will be affected by the color line. Yet we have data indicating that while African American men were out-migrating, selling their labor to more distant markets, the Black Burghardt women were creating their own unique position in this changing economic field. Therefore, any discussion of gender as an analytical category must pay attention to the roles, activities, and experiences of women and emphasize the ways in which gender intersects with race and class.

Any approach to the study of the pasts of African Americans must include attention to the cultural construction of race as identity and experience within what remains essentially a racist society. We must emphasize that race is not a universal, natural, or inevitable aspect of the human experience. It is, rather, a constructed category of domination, an assertion of "otherness" and inferiority that can be apprehended historically. We also need to incorporate approaches to issues of gender inequality that examine the disparity in the recovery of the pasts of European women and of women of color in the historical and archaeological record. It is not enough to restore some women to the "stage of history." These approaches should allow us to read between the lines of the cultural data we recover and to better interpret the pasts of minority peoples.

References

Baker, Vernon
1980   Archaeological Visibility of Afro-American Culture: An Example from Black Lucy's Garden, Andover, Massachusetts. In *Archaeological Perspectives on Ethnicity in America*, ed. R. L. Schuyler, 29–37. New York: Baywood Publications.

Bower, Beth, and Byron Rushing
1980   The African Meeting House: The Center for the Nineteenth Century Afro-American Community in Boston. In *Archaeological Perspectives on Ethnicity in America*, ed. R. L. Schuyler, 69–75. New York: Baywood Publications.

Brennan, Sheila
1990   Land Distribution and Use in Eighteenth Century Berkshire County, Massachusetts: A Preliminary Report. Manuscript in possession of the author.

Bridges, Sarah, and Bert Salwen
1980   Weeksville: The Archaeology of a Black Urban Community. In *Archaeological Perspective on Ethnicity in America*, ed. R. L. Schuyler, 38–47. New York: Baywood Publications.

Deetz, James
1977   *In Small Things Forgotten*. New York: Anchor Press.

DuBois, W. E. B.
n.d.   DuBois Archives. University of Massachusetts, Amherst.
1928   The House of the Black Burghardts. *Crisis* 35: 133–34.
1968   *The Autobiography of W. E. B. DuBois*. New York: International Publishers.
1975   *Dusk of Dawn*. New York: Krauss Thompson.

Geismar, Joan
1982   *The Archaeology of Social Disintegration in Skunk Hollow*. New York: Academic Press.

Great Barrington Town Hall
1836   Eighteen Thirty-Six Book of Deeds. Originals in Great Barrington Town
          Hall, Great Barrington, Mass.
Greene, Lorenzo
1968   *The Negro in Colonial New England 1620–1776.* New York: Columbia Uni-
          versity Press.
Higginbotham, Leon
1978   *In the Matter of Color.* New York: Oxford University Press.
hooks, bell
1990   *Yearning: Race, Gender, and Cultural Politics.* Boston: South End Press.
Litwack, Leon
1961   *North of Slavery.* Chicago: University of Chicago Press.
Muller, Nancy
1985   W. E. B. DuBois' American Pragmatism. *Journal of American Culture* 8:
          31–37.
1986   Preliminary Deed Chain for the DuBois Site. Manuscript on file, De-
          partment of Anthropology, University of Massachusetts, Amherst.
1992   DuBoisian Pragmatism and "The Problem of the Twentieth Century."
          Critique of Anthropology 12 (3): 319–37.
Paynter, Robert
1990   Afro-Americans in the Massachusetts Historical Landscape. In *The Poli-
          tics of the Past*, ed. P. Gathercole and D. Lowenthal, 49–62. London:
          Unwin Hyman.
Paynter, Robert, Susan Hautaniemi, and Nancy Muller
n.d.   The Landscapes of the W. E. B. DuBois Boyhood Homesite: An Agenda
          for an Archaeology of the Color Line. In *Unfinished Business: The Politics
          of Race and Identity*, ed. S. Gregory and R. Sanjek. New Brunswick, N.J.:
          Rutgers University Press (forthcoming).
Paynter, Robert, and Richard Gumaer
1983   Archaeology at the W. E. B. DuBois Boyhood Homesite, 1983. Field
          School. Unpublished paper on file with the Department of Anthropology,
          University of Massachusetts, Amherst.
Pierson, William
1975   *Afro-American Culture in Eighteenth-Century New England.* Bloomington:
          University of Indiana Press.
Sudarkasa, Niara
1982   African and Afro-American Family Structure. In *Anthropology for the
          Eighties*, ed. Johnetta Cole, 132–60. New York: Free Press.
Taylor, Charles
1928   *The History of Great Barrington 1676–1882.* Great Barrington, Mass.: Town
          History.
Twombly, Robert, and Robert Moore
1982   Black Puritan: The Negro in Seventeenth-Century Massachusetts. In

Race Relations in British North America 1607–1783, ed. Bruce Glasrud, 223–39. Chicago: Nelson Hall.

United States Bureau of the Census

1850   Manuscript Population Census of the United States, 1850. Washington, D.C.: U.S. Government Printing Office. Microfilm copy on file, National Archives and Records Administration, Washington, D.C.

1870   Manuscript Population Census of the United States, 1870. Washington, D.C.: U.S. Government Printing Office. Microfilm copy on file, National Archives and Records Administration, Washington, D.C.

Yentsch, Anne E.

1988   Legends, Houses, Families, and Myths: Relationships Between Material Culture and American Ideology. In *Documentary Archaeology in the New World*, ed. M. C. Beaudry, 5–19. Cambridge: Cambridge University Press.

III   All-Male and Predominantly Male Communities

5

"With Manly Courage"

Reading the Construction of Gender in a Nineteenth-Century Religious Community

Elizabeth Kryder-Reid

More than ten years ago Sherry Ortner and Harriet Whitehead argued persuasively in their introduction to *Sexual Meanings* that gender is a cultural construction and is inextricably intertwined with the formation of other aspects of subjectivity. In this way it is inseparable from status, age, ethnicity, race, and so forth. Because their position rejects biological determinism, Ortner and Whitehead (1981) assert that the analysis of gender must begin "by asking what male and female, sex and reproduction, *mean* in given social and cultural contexts. . . . Gender, sexuality, and reproduction are [to be] treated as *symbols*, invested with meaning by the society in question" (1).

But ten years also have seen some advances, and the concern of this paper is less with the static relationships among symbols or among social relationships than with the process by which gender is constructed and manipulated by social actors. As in other poststructuralist studies of social life (for example, Conkey 1982; Foucault 1979; Leone and Shackel 1987), the analysis of gender is not the discovery of a group identity or an artifact assemblage but rather is the discovery of the formation of that identity and the process by which those artifacts are made meaningful. Conkey and Gero (1991) state the point this way:

> As an issue of history gender is always "in production," emergent in the pro-
> cess of human existence. Thus, epistemologically, gender is not a bounded and
> static phenomenon, "out there" to be "found" and circumscribed; it is not a
> "thing" or an "it". . . . [G]ender . . . [is] a process that is constructed as a re-
> lationship or set of relationships, necessarily embedded within other cultural
> and historical social institutions and ideologies. (9)

The archaeological inquiry into this process of constructing gender is therefore a question of discerning both what sets of relationships are involved and how the material culture of the social group in question is implicated. In this case, the social group is a religious community of men in the second half of the nineteenth century; the relationships are those of the priests and lay brothers who professed to live according to vows of obedience, poverty, and celibacy; and the material culture is their common household assemblage and landscape. This chapter begins with a brief description of the site these men inhabited, presents a hypothesis of the construction of gender at this single-sex site, and examines the evidence in light of that hypothesis.

The Site

The site in question is the St. Mary's site (18AP45) in the Historic District of Annapolis, Maryland (fig. 5.1). Excavated by Archaeology in Annapolis for the past five summers, the site is best known as the home of Charles Carroll of Carrollton, signer of the Declaration of Independence. Since 1852, however, the property has been owned by the Redemptorists,[1] a congregation of ordained priests and lay brothers. Today, the Redemptorists use the site for their ministry to a parochial school and a parish of almost ten thousand communicants, but during the second half of the nineteenth century (from 1853 to 1862 and 1867 to 1907) the principal use of the site was as a Novitiate, a school for educating and training candidates for ordination. The site was also used as a base from which the priests led missions in rural areas.

The site today encompasses approximately 9 acres, including St. Mary's School buildings and facilities; a small convent used by the nuns who administer the school; the parish church; a large rectory where the priests' offices, private quarters, and dining hall are located; the former Carroll House now undergoing an extensive restoration and used until 1962 as an

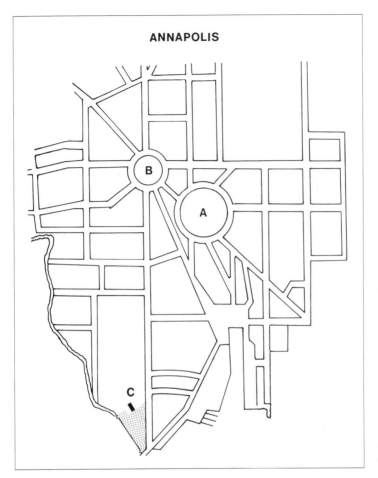

Figure 5.1. A plan view of contemporary Annapolis. The prominent focal points
of the town plan, State Circle and Church Circle, are marked (A) and (B)
respectively. The Redemptorist property (C), located on the point of land
where Spa Creek joins the Chesapeake Bay, is shown with the original Carroll
house and garden shaded.

extension of the rectory; and a nearly 2¼-acre garden containing the remains of Charles Carroll's 1770s terraced landscape garden.

The St. Mary's site offers an interesting challenge for the examination of
the construction of gender. During the second half of the nineteenth century it housed an all-male closed community—closed in the physical sense
of a cloister and in the ideological sense that it defined itself through a Rule

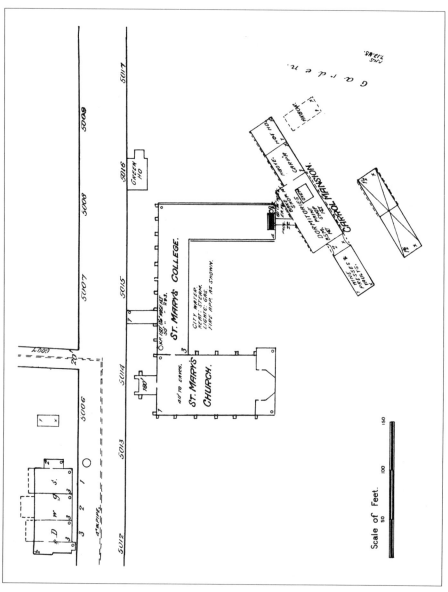

Figure 5.2. The Sanborn Fire Insurance Company's first map of the Redemptorist property in 1885 shows the addition of the church and rectory, the proliferation of outbuildings, and the renovation of the Carroll mansion

that prescribed daily conduct and dictated vows of obedience, poverty, celibacy, and perseverance.

The site is also rich in its archaeological and historical evidence. Because the transfer of property from the Carrolls to the Redemptorists dictated that the property always be used for the "purposes of religion," the spectacular waterfront location has been spared the development fate of much of Annapolis's Historic District. This remarkable archaeological preservation is complemented by equally remarkable archival material. Daily diary entries recorded in the congregation's official chronicles offer details of the liturgical life of the community: the transfers, illnesses, and activities of the residents, as well as alterations to the physical plant through building projects, fires, and renovations. In addition, the site is documented by a host of other records: maps, correspondence, insurance records, and, most notably, a photographic archive beginning in 1864 (fig. 5.2).

In sum, the archaeological and historical evidence make St. Mary's an intriguing test case of which to ask questions about the construction of gender in a single-sex site, and the ability or inability of archaeology to speak to the material correlates of gender.

Questions and Hypothesis

The most elemental question to be addressed is "What is the archaeology of gender in an all-male site?" However, even that question is complex. In one sense it asks, "Is a single-sex site necessarily a single-gender site?" I speak here not so much about the diversity of sexual behaviors possible among humans but about the associations of what it is to be male and female that are implicated in the creation and representation of self in any society. These associations may be ascribed to or resisted in varying degrees by any individual, but at their core is a cluster of values, connotations, and symbols made meaningful by the people who enact them as lived experience.

In another sense our basic question asks whether archaeology can distinguish gender differentiations from other cultural constructions. Here, too, the question is dependent on the premise that the production of gendered meanings and associations is part of the production of daily life and even to attempt to "separate" it from status, ethnicity, or age is to distort the conception of social life that fuels Conkey and Gero's statement above. To say that status differences mask gender-associated meanings is therefore to miss the point—gender is as inseparable from status as it is from ethnicity. The question is less whether or not we can distinguish gender, but whether we can understand its relation to other ideologically charged processes. In the case of the Redemptorists, the argument postulated here is that the lay brothers' association with female qualities was one means of maintaining their docile acceptance of menial tasks and their position on the lowest rung of the congregation's hierarchy.

In a third sense, the question provokes reflection on androcentric assumptions of male as normative. All too often we operate under the assumption that to find evidence of "gender roles" is to discover clues to the lives of women as they are differentiated from the lives of [hu]man beings, the latter of course unquestioningly associated with "maleness." But avoiding this bias in the study of past material remains is difficult unless one has access to corroborating sources, a problem fortunately easier for the St. Mary's site than for a prehistoric cave site. The prehistorian's dilemma of assuming universal gender roles is mitigated in this case by the wealth of literature on nineteenth-century United States gender relations. Instead of laying external standards of gender roles on the past, we can use that literature to discern contemporary categories and conceptions of gender ideals. While I acknowledge that these associations themselves are problematic and that what it means to be male or female is enacted uniquely by every individual, common stereotypes or ideologically charged ideals nevertheless remain. For late nineteenth-century America the period literature suggests several consistent themes of gender stereotypes. The construction of masculinity is only just beginning to be approached as a historical subject (as opposed to a contemporary social issue), and most recent work connects the nineteenth-century male identity to his place in a working world increasingly divorced from the domestic sphere.[2] Much more thoroughly studied have been the late nineteenth-century female stereotypes, which have been gathered variously under the titles "Cult of Domesticity" or "Cult of True Womanhood."

Using a survey of nineteenth-century American women's magazines, gift annuals, and religious literature, Barbara Welter argues that "the Cult of True Womanhood" identified the ideal woman by four cardinal virtues: piety, purity, submissiveness, and domesticity (the latter including nursing, housework, needlework, and gardening). It was by these attributes that "a woman judged herself and was judged by her husband, her neighbors and society" (Welter 1966, 152). While Welter's essay is somewhat dated, the categories are useful for understanding popular conceptions of gender ideals.

In a more recent study, Carroll Smith-Rosenberg notes the disparity between idealized feminine virtues and the roles most middle-class women played in the United States in the nineteenth century. She finds the disjunction to be a primary explanation for the prevalence of the "hysterical woman." Describing the "bourgeois ideal of proper womanhood," Smith-Rosenberg (1985) writes,

> Painful discontinuities existed between that ideal and the real world in which the bourgeois matron lived. The tensions [existed] . . . between the two central roles . . . that of the True Woman and that of the Ideal Mother. . . . The True Woman was emotional, dependent, and gentle—a born follower. The Ideal Mother, then and now, was expected to be strong, self-reliant, protective, an efficient caretaker in relation to children and home. She was to manage the family's day-to-day finances, prepare foods, make clothes, compound drugs, [and] serve as family nurse. (198–99)

These characterizations paint a picture of the True Woman as submissive, pious, and pure, while also a competent manager of domestic duties. Keeping in mind these ideals of feminine qualities and deportment, let me turn now to the specifics of the Redemptorist case.

As noted earlier, the Redemptorist ideology was codified by their Rules and Constitutions, the backbone of which was a set of vows: obedience, poverty, celibacy, and perseverance. But these ideals were fraught with tensions and contradictions. I propose that one of the ways those contradictions were mediated was through the differentiation of gender within the single-sex community. Specifically, despite an ideology which dictated equality, the social relations of hierarchy were reproduced in daily life, in part through the attribution of feminine qualities and roles to the most marginalized and least powerful members of the community, the lay brothers. I will first present the documentary evidence to support this hypothesis and then discuss some material manifestations of this construction of gender.

Historical Evidence

The Redemptorist vows, as presented in the Rule, dictated a life of profound equality:

> The members of the Congregation are bound by this vow [of poverty] to lead a perfectly common life, and to be uniform in all things. . . . As poor men they shall be content with frugal fare, without any respect of persons, no matter what may be the difference in their offices and claims. (*Constitutions* 1939, 26)

> Moreover, there should never be any contention as to precedence amongst the Subjects, for everyone's ambition should be to take the lowest place. (32)

Yet this egalitarian ideal was quickly translated into the hierarchy that defined daily life within the community. Within each house, the rector or superior was the ultimate authority, assisted by the minister. The ordained fathers stood next in precedence, ranked in seniority by date of their professions (257). The students preparing for ordination (novitiates or chorists) ranked next, followed lastly by the lay brothers whose vocation was "that they may aid . . . [the community] by service and bodily labours, they should most of all show themselves constant and careful in discharging the various domestic employments, always mindful that they have come to serve" (393). The commentary to the Rule elaborates on this seeming contradiction: "The Rule says, indeed, that all should be uniform in everything, but this should be understood of each in his own rank, that is, of the Fathers amongst themselves, and of the Brothers amongst themselves, but not of uniformity between the Fathers and the Brothers, because of the difference of state and duties" (394).

I propose that one of the ways this difference of "state and duties" was reinforced and naturalized was by the association of the lay brothers with roles and attributes that were by contemporary standards stereotypically feminine. In short, the "true" lay brother was a perfect example of piety, purity, submissiveness, and domesticity.

Like the other members of the community, the brother's ultimate goal was piety: to "earnestly strive to imitate the virtues and example of Jesus Christ our Redeemer" (21). Unlike the priests' primarily cerebral and spiritual instruction, the brothers' training was to unite a spiritual life with one of labor and service. The brothers were presented with the biblical models of Martha and Mary; "they should unite the repose of Mary, that is, the spiritual life, with the labours of Martha" (393). For example, the cook should "be a great lover of prayer and of union with God, and learn from the temporal fire to meditate on the eternal fire. Good cooks find time, even in the kitchen itself, to attend to God and to themselves" (409). Of the porter who received visitors, the rules dictate, "When he opens the door, he should beg of God to open the gate of Paradise to him; as he shuts it, that He may be pleased to close the gates of hell for him" (421).

Also like the other members of the community, the lay brothers were commanded to preserve their chastity above all else. For the "love of holy purity" the Redemptorists were instructed never to gaze upon a woman's face, touch the body of another person, or invite women to visit their country houses (168–69). Those teaching the Children's Catechism were told, "They shall never caress boys, for any motive how good, nor shall they take them to their rooms to instruct them, or to hear their confessions" (169). Within their own house, the priests and brothers were to guard their virtue strictly: "In undressing and in dressing they should be very cautious with themselves. At home, two shall never sleep in one bed. . . . During sleep they should always be covered, wearing drawers and shirt, and in the most modest posture. Similarly, whether in or out of their rooms, they should always wear the habit and cincture" (170).

The isolation of the Redemptorists and the impact of a celibate lifestyle on the construction of gender within the congregation are difficult to assess, but they must be noted nonetheless. The Redemptorists' vow of celibacy required them to abstain from all sexual activity, but the degree to which it repressed an individual's sexuality and the ways in which individuals responded to this denial must have varied greatly. More interesting than such speculation on sexuality, which is beyond the scope of this essay, is the implication of the vow of celibacy for construction of gender within the Congregation. Contact with women was extremely limited, although at least one of the priests carried on a lively correspondence with his sister. Furthermore, women were not only inaccessible but in the Redemptorist Rule and Chronicles were often presented as foreign, mysterious, and potentially dangerous. The training of the novitiates, therefore, occurred in a relatively cloistered setting where the denial of sexuality was accompanied by a more subtle denial of women as social beings as well.

In addition to the vow of celibacy, all members of the community were to be submissive and unquestioningly subject to the authority of the Redemptorist hierarchy. As the Rule chided, "The words 'I will' and 'I will not' have always been a crime in our Congregation, and he, who is not so disposed, can never live contentedly in our Institute" (185). The lay brothers, as the lowest-ranking members, were particularly admonished to "make it a special object of their care to show to all the chorists, and even more to those who are invested with the dignity of the priesthood, the honour, reverence, and service that they owe them" (394).

The final attribute of feminine virtue in nineteenth-century America, domesticity, covered a constellation of associations: the comforts a woman provided through cooking, nursing, sewing, cleaning, and other "wifely arts." This role of domestic manager and caregiver epitomizes the lay brothers' chief functions within the community. Their specific duties were the "infirmarian" or nurse, who "should regard the sick as the apple of his eye, and become all things to all, that he may console all, and see all consoled, tranquil, and cheerful in Jesus Christ" (403); the porter, who "should have much at heart modesty, kindness, and courteousness, and his behaviour to everyone should be such as will be commended by all, and give them good example" (421); the refectarian, whose "chief quality should be zeal for cleanliness and neatness" (409); and the cook, tailor, sacristan, caller, and Brother Procurator.

In each role, the lay brothers were called upon to manage the domestic functioning of the community life and to do so with the virtues associated with the "True Woman" of the day. Unlike the priests who were trained to

> "go ye into all the world and preach the Gospel" (Mark 16:15), the lay brothers' world was to be the community. The Rule dictated, "Loving solitude and recollection, they shall not go out of the House without necessity, nor without the Superior's leave. They shall avoid all familiarity with outsiders, and all curiosity about worldly affairs. . . . they may on no account read the newspapers, unless perhaps, on Sunday, one that does not deal with politics, and even this with the Superior's leave." (*Constitutions* 1939, 396)

The brothers' role was to serve the community, and their training was in a deportment naturally suited to the task.

One might argue that the entire community was marginalized socially in that it consciously dedicated itself to a religious vocation, removed itself from participation in sexual acts and inferences, and submitted to a rigid hierarchy of authority. But the degree to which members of the community were marginalized from the cultural associations of gender was not uniform. The Novitiate was a training ground for adolescents and young men. Its charge was instructing these novices to be obedient, chaste, and pious priests, equipped with the strength, knowledge, and discipline to be evangelical laborers to the world—in short, they were to be men without sexuality. One of the Redemptorist fathers, Henry Borgmann (1904), reflected on this process: "Many of the young men, nay, boys of 16 to 18, had left homes which every comfort rendered sweet . . . to consecrate themselves heart and soul to their Divine Master. . . . With manly courage they embraced the austerities of the religious life, remembering that, only by suffering and self-denial could they become true disciples" (24-25). The lay brothers, on the other hand, were to be trained as obedient, chaste, and pious domestic servants. They were to remain within the house and serve the community, not venture forth to spread the spiritual message of the missionaries.[3]

Archaeological Evidence

I turn lastly to the question of the material correlates of this process of gender construction within the Redemptorist community. Excavations over the past five summers have produced a rich assemblage of artifacts associated

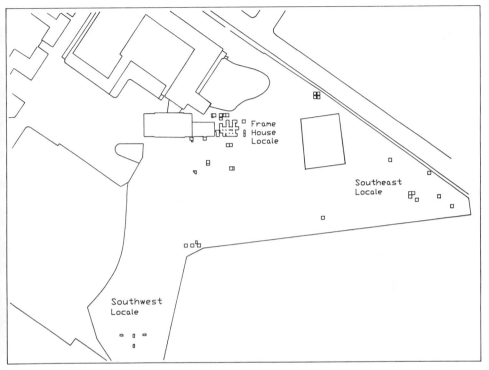

Figure 5.3. Autocad map of the St. Mary's site showing the location of units
excavated during the 1987–1990 seasons by Archaeology in Annapolis.

with the Redemptorist occupation of the site (fig. 5.3). The contexts for the
artifacts include massive fill deposits dating to the mid–twentieth century,
created by leveling a vineyard to become an athletic field in 1946 and by
moving graves from a mortuary chapel in 1948 to build a cemetery on the
terraces of the Carrolls' former garden. Archaeology also recovered sealed
contexts such as filled cisterns and the debris of a demolished greenhouse.
The artifacts themselves may be characterized as those expected from any
nineteenth-century institutional site: thousands of whiteware and iron-
stone sherds, hundreds of bottles found in the Redemptorist wine cellar,
and the myriad of flowerpot fragments from one of three greenhouses once
standing on the site. There were also numerous artifacts associated with
the site's religious identity: a crucifix, religious medals, holy water bowls,
a chalice and paten, and fragments of the Redemptorists' coarse woolen
habits.

The cataloguing and analysis of these artifacts is completed,[4] but their interpretation for gender associations is problematical, at least for the Redemptorists' nineteenth-century occupation. As noted earlier, the Redemptorist Rule explicitly prescribes, "The members of the Congregation are . . . to lead a perfectly common life, and to be uniform in all things. . . . As poor men they shall be content with frugal fare, without any respect of persons, no matter what may be the difference in their offices and claims" (*Constitutions* 1939, 26).

The Rule goes on to describe in exquisite detail which objects, such as scissors, thread, knives, needles, brushes, ink, and snuff, were to be kept in a common place for the use of anyone, and which objects were permitted in the rooms of individuals. Clothes were held in common as were all tablewares, bedding, furniture, and tools. Residents had to ask permission to use anything, including drinking water, and could not give or receive gifts. In short, bound by the vow of poverty, the Redemptorists were not permitted to own individual property of any kind. Although the dormitory rooms are still standing in the Carroll House, their contents have been emptied for years. Had such evidence been available for study it might have been possible to test the adherence to the Rule's dictum: "The rooms shall be small: their furniture, similarly shall be poor, but the same in all—namely, a small table with a drawer without a lock; three chairs; four paper pictures [to be black and white religious subjects only], a Crucifix of simple wood; two or three spiritual books" (26).

It might also have been possible to determine the spatial arrangement of the novitiates', lay brothers', and priests' sleeping quarters.

Instead, this antimaterialist ideology of poverty foils our most critical tool of analysis—the ability to associate archaeological context with the social context that produced it. Only in the historical record do we find evidence of status marked through material culture; in the debris of the greenhouse we excavated a collar button used to secure clerical collars. The Rule notes that fathers may wear white linen collars over their habits while brothers may not, but from the artifact alone, there is no way of discerning whether the collar button was worn by an obedient priest or a renegade lay brother. In another example, the Rule dictates that the priests wear birettas and the brothers only skull caps, but the distinction born out in photographs (fig. 5.4) is invisible in the excavated communal deposits. Because we have no way to connect a deposit with a lay brother, similar tests of the proposed gender division hypothesis, such as the distribution of artifacts associated with domestic duties, are not possible.

While artifacts from communal contexts such as the cistern make conclusions about differentiation within the Congregation difficult, some pos-

Figure 5.4. Photo of the Redemptorist community, 1928—29. The three men
without birettas or linen collars, on either end of the second row from the top,
are lay brothers (St. Mary's Parish Archives).

sibilities remain for testing the material correlates of the lay brother versus priest gender oppositions that might confirm the association of lay
brothers with domestic duties or indicate their interaction with the outside
world. If the lay brothers were relegated to domestic tasks and permitted
little access to the outside world, then one would expect that domestic
tasks were relatively self-sufficient and did not require extensive contact
with secular Annapolis. In at least one artifact class, faunal remains, this
trend appears verified. Analysis by Mark Warner (n.d.) reveals that faunal
remains from the nineteenth-century deposits show minimal processing,
while the analysis of a deposit of 597 cow bones buried by the 1911 greenhouse demolition revealed cut marks indicative of professional butchering.
As such food preparation was the lay brothers' task, the shift from processing their own meat to later participation in Annapolis' market economy
highlights the insular, domestic sphere of the brothers' daily regime in the

nineteenth century. In addition, ongoing analysis of the nineteenth- and early twentieth-century assemblage may reveal change through time in the relative cost and variety of artifacts, indicating a loosening of the strict adherence to the vow of poverty.

I turn, also, to another class of material culture: the landscape. Here too, the association of the physical—the organization of space—with the social —the people who used and inhabited that space—is made from evidence in the documentary sources. Maps compiled from archaeological, documentary, and photographic evidence indicate the extent to which the Redemptorists transformed the landscape. They turned what Carroll had groomed as an idyllic, open, terraced hillside into a crowded, productive farmyard. The lay brothers spent much of their day in this farmyard with its barns, grape arbors, greenhouses, and gardens. The material correlates of this labor—the white-washed brick walls, the thousands of flowerpot sherds, the remains of shell paths—are all evidence of the domestic and menial labor of the lay brothers. Furthermore, the duties were not only menial but often dangerous and sometimes "disagreeable." The Chronicles describe the brothers' frequent injuries during routine chores (falling from arbors, stepping on nails, and so forth) and their assignment to some less-than-pleasant tasks. One entry records, "At 2 PM the Solemn translation of our dead from under the Sacristy to new vault. There were 24 in all. They were placed in six boxes. . . . Bro. Leopold had a very hard and most disagreeable task to perform" (Redemptorist Chronicles n.d., 2 Nov. 1885 entry).

In contrast to the brothers' relative freedom of movement, the novices and priests were strictly controlled in their activities within and outside of the house. The novice's days were highly regimented, and it was listed as a "GRIEVOUS FAULT. . . . To go out into the garden, the kitchen, the Refectory, or the balcony, without the Superior's leave" (*Constitutions* 1939, 181). This differential access to activity areas may be interpreted as increased autonomy for the lay brothers, but it also reinforced their domesticity and servile role in the community. While the novices were being schooled in theological subjects or led through spiritual exercises designed to prepare them for their missions to the outside world, the brothers were being trained in the "religious labors" of gardening, nursing, cooking, cleaning, and mending, with the ideological mantle of being obedient, submissive, loyal, and loving caregivers.

The community was founded on the egalitarian notion that "there should never be any contention as to precedence amongst the Subjects, for everyone's ambition should be to take the lowest place" (32). Yet that same community succeeded in creating a highly stratified and harmonious social structure by training young men to be priests of "manly courage" or brothers "mindful that they have come to serve." One of the ways the potential inequity of duties apportioned to these young men was muted was that they were given to those with the disposition and "calling" for their vocations.

In her essay on female hysteria in the nineteenth century, Smith-Rosenberg (1985) writes that for women there was only "one prescribed social role, one that demanded continual self-abnegation and a desire to please others. . . . all required of women an altruistic denial of their own ambition and a displacement of their wishes and abilities onto the men in their lives" (213). I argue here that the same subservience of the lay brothers was achieved, in part, through a construction of gender in which these servants of the Congregation were instructed not only in their appropriate duties but were trained to be docile, pious, pure, and domestic—thus subjects ideally and naturally suited to the tasks.

This chapter contributes two points to the evolving discourse on the archaeology of gender. The first is that by playing hypotheses from documentary sources (such as the evidence for the "Cult of Domesticity") against the artifacts of a particular group or individual, the material correlates of gender distinctions may be tested. The challenge at the St. Mary's site, as at many others, is that the artifacts, which were communally owned and recovered from communal deposits, are difficult to connect to a single group or individual within the Congregation. The second implication of this study is that the differentiation of gender roles within a single-sex site is possible. Men's Studies are being taken up as a serious counterpart to Women's Studies, and work on the construction of masculinity is just coming into print. If the archaeology of gender is not to lag behind the history of gender, archaeologists must be aware that the duality of gender oppositions works both ways: that just as female is marked in reaction to male, so too male is formed in opposition to female. If we are on the right track of a "feminist archaeology," the trail of a "masculinist archaeology" cannot be far off. And perhaps in the inspection of what we hold to be the opposition of "female" and "male" we may begin to see dynamics and subtle nuances that suggest that the oppositions are not so different after all.

Acknowledgments

I would like to thank Elizabeth Scott for the invitation to participate in the SHA session where this paper was first presented, and Barbara Little for first pointing out the potential of viewing the Redemptorists from the perspective of gender. My thanks also go to the numerous people who assisted in this research along the way: Robert Worden opened the Parish Archives at St. Mary's and generously reproduced documents and photographs in the collection; Father Rush was a gracious host during my visits to the Redemptorist Archives in Brooklyn, N.Y.; Amy Grey was helpful in supplying bibliography leads. The excavations of the St. Mary's site were conducted 1987–91 by Archaeology in Annapolis, which is sponsored by the University of Maryland at College Park and Historic Annapolis Foundation. I am grateful to the colleagues and crews who made those seasons both so productive and so much fun.

Notes

1. Though commonly called "The Redemptorists," their full title is the Congregation of the Most Holy Redeemer (Congregationis Sanctissimi Redemptoris or C.Ss.R.).
2. Histories of sexuality have been part of the diversification of historical topics to include a variety of "private sphere" issues, and Michel Foucault's *The History of Sexuality* (1978) has been highly influential in this burgeoning literature. Often these histories fail, however, to place sexual behavior within a broader question of gender (e.g., Freedman 1982). E. Anthony Rotundo's *American Manhood* (1993) is one of the first historical surveys of the construction of masculinity in America. He argues a shift from the colonial man whose identity was derived from his position as head of household and active community participant to the nineteenth-century male worker's identity associated with competition and achievement in an expanding bureaucracy. Other treatments of the topic, such as Horlick (1975) and Ryan (1981), also have given primacy to men's changing social and economic situations but have been less critical of the effect of these material conditions on the ideological production of what it is to be male.
3. Unfortunately, no information is available on the demographics of the Redemptorist community. Anecdotally, the lay brothers seem to have been less well educated (some probably even mentally disadvantaged), and they were likely drawn from a lower economic and social class. But the difference of class origins among the Redemptorists only strengthens the marginalization of the lay brothers, and engendering them with female attributes is only one element in their subjugation within the Redemptorist hierarchy.

4. The artifact analysis was completed by Archaeology in Annapolis at labs at the University of Maryland at College Park and at the Historic Annapolis Foundation. A site report by the author for the 1987-1990 seasons is in progress.

References

Borgmann, Henry
1904   *History of the Redemptorists at Annapolis, Md., from 1853 to 1903.* Ilchester, Md.: College Press.
Conkey, Margaret W.
1982   Boundedness in Art and Society. In *Symbolic and Structural Archaeology*, ed. Ian Hodder, 129-54. Cambridge: Cambridge University Press.
Conkey, Margaret W., and Joan M. Gero
1991   Tensions, Pluralities, and Engendering Archaeology: An Introduction to Women and Prehistory. In *Engendering Archaeology: Women and Prehistory*, ed. Joan M. Gero and Margaret W. Conkey, 3-30. Oxford: Basil Blackwell.
The Constitutions and Rules of the Congregation of Priests Under the Title of the Most Holy Redeemer.
1939   Translated from the Latin and published with the authority of The Most Rev. Father Patrick Murray. London: St. Mary's, Clapham.
Foucault, Michel
1978   *The History of Sexuality.* Trans. Robert Hurley. New York: Pantheon Books.
1979   Discipline and Punish: The Birth of the Prison. New York: Random House.
Freedman, Estelle B.
1982   Sexuality in Nineteenth-Century America: Behavior, Ideology, and Politics. *Reviews in American History* 10 (4): 196-215.
Horlick, Allan Stanley
1975   *Country Boys and Merchant Princes: The Social Control of Young Men in New York.* Lewisburg, Pa.: Bucknell University Press.
Leone, Mark P., and Paul A. Shackel
1987   Forks, Clocks and Power. In *Mirror and Metaphor: Material and Social Constructions of Reality*, ed. Daniel W. Ingersoll, Jr., and Gordon Bronitsky, 46-61. Lanham, Md.: University Press of America.
Ortner, Sherry B., and Harriet Whitehead
1981   Accounting for Sexual Meanings. Introduction to *Sexual Meanings: The Cultural Construction of Gender and Sexuality*, ed. Sherry B. Ortner and Harriet Whitehead, 1-27. Cambridge: Cambridge University Press.
Redemptorist Chronicles
n.d.   Bound manuscripts on file. Redemptorist Archives, Provincial Headquarters, Brooklyn, New York.

Rotundo, E. Anthony
1993   *American Manhood: Transformations from the Revolution to the Modern Era.*
        New York: Basic Books.
Ryan, Mary P.
1981   *Cradle of the Middle Class: The Family in Oneida County, New York, 1790–
        1865.* Cambridge: Cambridge University Press.
Smith-Rosenberg, Carroll
1985   *Disorderly Conduct: Visions of Gender in Victorian America.* New York:
        Alfred A. Knopf.
Warner, Mark
n.d.   Faunal Remains from Feature 82. In "Preliminary Report of the St. Mary's
        Site (18AP45), 1987–1990 Seasons," ed. Elizabeth Kryder-Reid. Manu-
        script on file, Archaeology Lab, University of Maryland at College Park.
Welter, Barbara
1966   The Cult of True Womanhood: 1820–1860. *American Quarterly* 18 (2):
        151–74.

6

The Identification of Gender at Northern Military Sites of the Late Eighteenth Century

David R. Starbuck

Historical records indicate that American and British armies of the late eighteenth century in North America were accompanied by sizeable numbers of dependents—wives, camp followers, and children. Thus, it is not surprising that one of the most frequently asked questions by students and visitors to eighteenth-century military sites is "How can you tell whether any women or children were here? Which artifacts did *they* leave behind?" Regrettably, there is no ready answer, because the number of artifacts positively used by women is quite small, and only brief, anecdotal references to women and children appear in military journals and orderly books. Nevertheless, wives and various categories of "camp followers" accompanied British and American forces on most campaigns, and they were indispensable for such camp chores as nursing and laundering. While historical sources differ somewhat as to exact figures, we know that many more of these women traveled with the British army than with American militia or Continental forces (Blumenthal 1952, 60) (fig. 6.1).

The low visibility of women within what were predominantly male

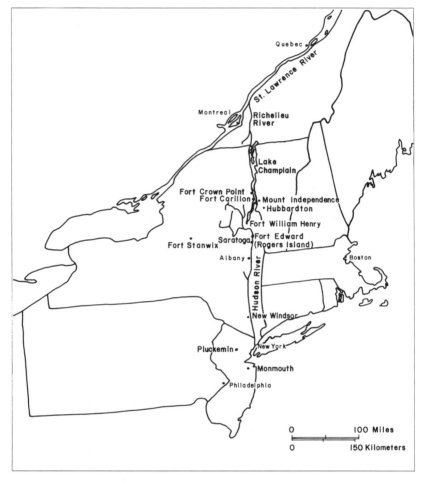

Figure 6.1. Location of eighteenth-century military sites mentioned in the text.

camps derives partially from the low status given to female activities. Additional bias results from the authorship of nearly all orderly books and diaries by white males, and even most of the historical archaeologists who work on military sites today are white males. Not surprisingly, most of the available literature on military sites pretends either that women did not exist or that because most were camp followers they need not be taken seriously. Additionally, historical archaeologists have only just begun to seek evidence for these dependents at military sites, and equating specific artifact types (or activity areas) with gender, age, or ethnicity is proving to be extremely difficult. Therefore, this study is a preliminary assessment of what is known and what needs to be done—it is not the final word on the role of women within military encampments. Unfortunately, while "seeing" women through the material culture that has survived in military settings may be difficult because men and women were consumers of the same technology, the fact that archaeologists rarely look for such evidence leads to the unacceptable impression that women were not even present.

Women with the Military

A review of the military literature of the eighteenth century suggests that the women who traveled with British and American armies in North America, during both the French and Indian War (1754–63) and the American Revolution (1775–83), have traditionally been placed into one or more of the following categories: (1) loyal wives, (2) larger-than-life heroines, (3) victims, (4) nurses, (5) camp maintenance workers, and (6) sources of disease. If a woman did not stand out within one of these areas, then historical sources typically ignored her altogether.

The first category, that of "loyal wives," is best exemplified by the Baroness von Riedesel and the Lady Harriet Ackland (both discussed in detail below). Wives such as these followed their husbands out of love and, perhaps, economic necessity. The wives of officers fared considerably better than the wives of ordinary soldiers; the status of a woman's husband directly determined her ranking within the military camp. The second category is rather more exclusive, for a few women achieved a status that, in retrospect, might be termed "larger-than-life." These are the women who sometimes fought alongside their husbands and lovers, and today we recognize them under the generic name "Molly Pitcher." During the American Revolution, Margaret Corbin and Mary Hays were two such women. When her husband was killed, Margaret Corbin took his place at a cannon during the defense of Fort Washington (Manhattan Island). For her part, Mary Hays operated a cannon together with her husband at the Battle of Monmouth in New Jersey (De Pauw 1975, 188–89). The almost mythical stature of these stories suggests that the numbers of women who actually fought in battle were relatively small.

Third, while all women attached to the military were in a sense "victims" of a system that gave them a great deal of work and few rewards, some of them achieved considerable fame through the atrocities inflicted upon them. The most famous murder of a woman during the American

Revolution was that of Jane McCrea, a young woman who was killed and scalped in Fort Edward, New York, in July 1777 by Native Americans who were part of General John Burgoyne's army (cited in many places, including Lossing 1855, 1: 96–100). Because she had been en route to see her fiancé, a Tory lieutenant attached to Burgoyne's army, the affair generated widespread publicity, and her death was often cited in anti-British, anti-Indian propaganda at the time. Her death became, in effect, a rallying cry for the American cause.

A fourth way in which women achieved prominence was as nurses. They worked in the hospitals and were quite effective in giving health care, much sought after *because* they were women. One example during the French and Indian War was when the British General Jeffrey Amherst, builder of the fortress at Crown Point, wrote on 9 June 1760 that "As many Women as may be Usefull to the Hospital are certainly very necessary for the Care of the Sick" (*Amherst Papers*, 1759–1763, 44). Occasionally, quantitative information exists for these caregivers; for example, during the American Revolution it was recorded in August 1777 that the flying hospital for the Northern Department of the Continental Army had a total of thirty-two nurses for 335 patients (Gillett 1981, 95). Unfortunately, there never were enough of these women, and much military correspondence of the period deals with the need to locate more nurses.

While neither sensational, nor sought after by the officers in their correspondence, a fifth category of women clearly existed, who sewed and repaired tents, uniforms, and other clothing and thus contributed significantly to the well-being and physical appearance of the army. These women who contributed to the maintenance of every military camp are almost unrecognizable in historical sources, yet they probably contributed the most to the morale of the military encampment.

Finally, women were sometimes mentioned in officers' reports for their rather unsavory reputations. A mixture of sweethearts, wives, mistresses, and prostitutes was thus subjected to periodic checks for venereal disease. Paul Kopperman (1982) notes that in 1755 the British officer Edward Braddock "ordered his soldiers' wives to be examined to make sure they were 'clean', and he added that the women who were not so, or who tried to avoid examination, were to be barred from his march" (17). Apparently, comparable inspections were not demanded of the men!

By modern standards, the women attached to eighteenth-century military camps led exceptionally difficult lives, often receiving little respect or even civility from males. In a little-known account by Captain Samuel Jenks, dated 24 July 1760, he noted that

Here is one of my men that was stationed at Ticondaroga, come up with a setler who has brought up a very fine mistress with him. On their passage they fell into disputes. At length he struck her, which inraged hir so that after several fits & efforts jumpt over board. This coold her courage, for her sweetheart held her under water untill she was amost expiring. They then took her in, stript off her cloaths & drest anew, & so the fray ended. I wish it were the fate of all these sort of ladys that follow the army. She apeard pretty likely & was very well drest. (*Proceedings of the Mass. Hist. Society* 1890, 364)

Mistresses often accompanied prominent officers, and it is well known that during the American Revolution Generals Burgoyne and Howe both had mistresses who were the wives of junior officers. In fact, both men spent so much time with their mistresses that they were widely perceived as being quite ineffectual officers. As Linda De Pauw (1975) notes, William Howe's mistress, Mrs. Loring, was known as "the sultana," and one jingle at that time expressed the popular attitude toward their relationship:

Sir William, he, snug as a flea,
Lay all this time a-snoring
Nor dream'd of harm as he lay warm
In Bed with Mrs. Loring.
(186–87)

Still, most of the women who accompanied the armies were tolerated well enough and granted partial rations (usually half-rations) by the commanding officer because they performed necessary functions, such as laundering. In fact, washing clothes for the men was viewed as a critical female activity and is noted in many officers' reports.

In one exceptional case, laundering led to disaster at the large British fort at Crown Point, constructed in 1759 on the New York shore of Lake Champlain. While references to women at that fort are rather meager, a soldier's wife, Jane Ross, became the best-known woman to have lived at that fort by virtue of starting a fire that resulted in the total destruction of the fortress. The "Court of Enquiry" created to determine how the fire had been set learned that Mrs. Ross and other women had customarily boiled soap within the soldiers' barracks, in order to wash the men's linen. On 21 April 1773 they were engaged in this activity when they caused a chimney fire that quickly spread and ended with the magazine (and most of the fortress) blowing up ("Proceedings of a Garrison Court" 1978). The Court of Enquiry noted that a number of wives and children resided at the fortress, and that the women in particular were running into the barracks to save their belongings at the time of the fire. Ironically, it required a major disaster for women to achieve recognition at Crown Point.

Contemporary Historical Accounts

Men's Accounts

The comments men made about army women were predictably diverse during the French and Indian War and the American Revolution. In 1757 Jabez Fitch was one of the soldiers who lived in the massive British and American encampment on Rogers Island in Fort Edward, New York. Fitch (1986) kept a daily diary of his experiences, and in it he made occasional references to women. For example, on 12 July 1757, "there Came Down with us one of ye Jersy Regt who was Going after His wife that Had Deserted from Him His Discors was Cheefly about Her on ye March" (11); and on 15 July, "this Day there was a Genl Revue of ye Women in ye Army to Examen Whether they Had the &c or Not" [The "&c" referred to venereal disease.] (12).

While men's diaries present the attitudes that ordinary enlisted men held toward women, Regimental Orderly Books are useful for revealing the official positions taken by officers. At the site of Mount Independence, on the Vermont shore of Lake Champlain, the importance of women for doing laundry work was noted on 10 December 1776, when the commanding American officer—Colonel Anthony Wayne of Pennsylvania—stated in his Regimental Orders, "Any Woman belonging to the Regt., who shall refuse to wash for the Men, shall be immediately drumm'd out of the Regt, as they are not found in Victuals [they are not being given rations] to distress and render the Men unfit for Duty, but to keep them clean and decent" (Munsell 1859, 116). And again on 23 December 1776, Wayne stated, "All such Women as will wash for the 4th P.B. [Pennsylvania Battalion] will be supplied with Wood and Water for that Purpose" (128).

Wayne also recognized the importance of women as nurses, noting on 13 July 1776 that: "One woman from each company of each of the Pennsylvania Battalions, now at this post to be draughted as soon as possible & sent to the General Hospital at Fort George, to nurse the sick; they will have the customary allowance of privision &c from Doctor Stringer, Director of the hospital there" (Wayne Orderly Book 1963, 95).

While both British and American officers appear to have been quite tolerant of the large numbers of women who accompanied both armies during the Revolution—especially because they performed useful services—

officers nevertheless liked to complain about the rations women consumed and about how they (and their children) slowed down the army while on the road. One of the harshest indictments came from George Washington himself, who issued the following order while he was maneuvering his army around Philadelphia in August 1777:

> In the present marching state of the army, every incumbrance proves greatly prejudicial to the service; the multitude of women in particular, especially those who are pregnant, or have children, are a clog upon every movement. . . . the Officers [are] earnestly called upon to permit no more than are absolutely necessary, and such as are actually useful, to follow the army. (cited in De Pauw 1975, 183–84)

Washington was loathe, however, to get rid of these women completely—many of whom were wives—because he believed it would cause some of his troops to desert (Fitzpatrick 1931–44, 9: 78–80, 199; also discussed in De Pauw 1975, 184).

Women's Accounts

During the eighteenth century, of the women usually only the wives of officers kept journals—or sent letters home—so only an upper class perspective has survived of what it was like to be a woman accompanying the army. One of the best such accounts is a diary kept by the Baroness von Riedesel, whose husband headed the Brunswick (German) soldiers under the British General John Burgoyne. The Baroness (and her children) traveled with Burgoyne's army from Canada to Saratoga in the summer of 1777, and her account is a colorful one, although it suggests how helpless she felt in the midst of the fighting. While waiting in a farmhouse a short distance from the Saratoga battlefield, she wrote,

> A terrible cannonade was commenced by the enemy against the house in which I sought to obtain shelter for myself and children, under the mistaken idea that all the generals were in it. Alas! it contained none but wounded and women. We were at last obliged to resort to the cellar for refuge, and in one corner of this I remained the whole day, my children sleeping on the earth with their heads in my lap; and in the same situation I passed a sleepless night. Eleven cannon-balls passed through the house, and we could distinctly hear them roll away. . . . My reflections on the danger to which my husband was exposed now agonized me exceedingly, and the thoughts of my children, and the necessity of struggling for their preservation, alone sustained me. (cited in Lossing 1855, 1: 89)

There were, however, some advantages to being a woman attached to the British army, for as the Baroness reported, "The want of water distressed us much; at length we found a soldier's wife who had courage enough to fetch us some from the river, an office nobody else would undertake, as the Americans shot at every person who approached it; but, out of respect for her sex, they never molested her" (1: 90).

Another prominent woman who traveled with the Burgoyne campaign was the Lady Harriet Ackland (Acland), who followed her husband, a major in the corps of grenadiers, from Canada to Saratoga. Unlike many of the officers' wives, she was anything but helpless: when her husband was sick in Canada, she attended him; when he was wounded in the battle of Hubbardton, Vermont, she dashed down from Montreal to join him; when he was shot through both legs in Saratoga on 8 October 1777 and captured by the Americans, she rowed to the American camp to nurse him back to health. Burgoyne, quite in awe of her, wrote "that a woman should be capable of such an undertaking as delivering herself to an enemy, probably in the night, and uncertain of what hands she might fall into, appeared an effort above human nature" (1: 67). Major Ackland might not have been long for this world if the courtesies of that period had not allowed officers' wives privileges and freedom of movement that male soldiers did not enjoy.

Discussion of Contemporary Sources

These contemporary sources strongly suggest that women were tolerated, but insufficiently appreciated, within military encampments of the eighteenth century. They consumed scarce rations and may have slowed down armies as they traveled, but this was more than counterbalanced by the fact that they performed activities the soldiers were reluctant to undertake themselves. Women unquestionably earned the partial rations they received and—except at times of actual combat—may well have worked harder than many of the soldiers. Rather than being a drain upon resources or hurting discipline, they contributed to a clean and well-kept camp.

The sources also suggest that the familiar appellation of "camp follower" is inadequate to describe the variety of roles in which women found themselves. Many appear to have been respected because of their loyalty to husbands or lovers, and others were much sought after for service as nurses and laundresses. True, some were despised as prostitutes and were driven from camp if found to be unmarried, but all were such a prominent feature of each military campaign that it is surprising that contemporary written sources did not deal with them in greater detail.

Modern Historical Scholarship

Twentieth-century interpretation of the women who traveled with the British and American armies is uneven in quality, and most authors have undertaken very little analysis of what is contained in eighteenth-century documents. Walter Blumenthal's study of *Women Camp Followers of the American Revolution* (1952) is unquestionably the most helpful source, but unfortunately it is all too brief. Blumenthal's book contains a mixture of anecdotal and quantitative information, but it does include useful tables listing the numbers of men, women, and children who composed selected British regiments in 1777 (93–95). Blumenthal's assessment of the numbers of women who accompanied the British army during the Revolution can be compared to estimates by other authors.

For example, Michael Cohn (1983) calculates that between 10 and 20 percent of the population of the camps consisted of women and children and notes that in ten New York regiments of the British Army in May 1777, 4,973 men, 787 women, and 566 children were being fed. In August 1781 the same ten regiments contained 5,183 men, 856 women, and 653 children. And a grand total of 3,621 wives and 4,156 children accompanied all forces under British command in 1781 (40–41). A higher estimate is proposed by John Seidel, who excavated a Continental Artillery Cantonment of 1778–79 in Pluckemin, New Jersey. Seidel (1987) has written that the ratio of females to males in Burgoyne's army may have been as high as one to four and has suggested that as many as 2,000 women may have accompanied Burgoyne on his trip south from Canada (23).

Many other historians in recent years have made passing reference to women accompanying these armies. For example, John Krueger, in a 1981 dissertation on the American Northern Army, wrote:

> Many soldiers exhibited a more than casual interest in camp followers. As might be expected, women of doubtful virtue followed the Northern Army, although by no means were all of the camp followers prostitutes. Camp followers included wives and children of the soldiers, sweethearts, prostitutes, and other hangers-on. Some of the camp followers cooked, washed laundry, and cared for the sick. (147)

In general, it appears that fewer women accompanied American forces than British forces, but this varied greatly among regiments. Krueger has noted that "The number of camp followers varied from regiment to regiment. In 1776, thirteen women and four children were officially attached to the four New York regiments. New Jersey laws allowed for soldiers in each company to have their wives in camp, while Pennsylvania regiments were permitted one woman for every eight soldiers" (147–48).

If a woman accompanying the army lost her husband, the practice was for her to remarry as quickly as possible so she would not be dismissed from the camp (Cohn 1983, 41). It was unquestionably a difficult existence for many women, and Linda De Pauw has quoted a Boston woman who left this description of the camp followers who accompanied the British army at Saratoga in 1777:

> I never had the least Idea that the Creation produced such a sordid set of crea-tures in human Figure—poor, dirty, emaciated men, great numbers of women, who seemed to be the beasts of burden, having a bushel basket on their back, by which they were bent double, the contents deemed to be Pots and Kettles, various sorts of Furniture, children peeping thro' gridirons and other uten-sils, some very young infants who were born on the road, the women bare feet, cloathed in dirty rags, such effluvia filld the air while they were passing, had they not been smoking all the time, I should have been apprehensive of being contaminated by them. (De Pauw 1975, 181)

Archaeological Perspectives

Linda De Pauw's work (1975) contains many useful insights, but other mod-ern scholars do not appear to be moving beyond the early stereotypes of the "camp follower." The role of women at eighteenth-century military camps continues to be neglected by most authors. But what did women actually wear or use on military sites that might distinguish them from men? What would they have dropped that can be recovered by archaeolo-gists? The list is amazingly short. Calver and Bolton (1950), who literally began Revolutionary War archaeology by digging in the New York City area in the first part of this century, found numerous children's toys—in the form of "whizzers," marbles, doll parts, and whistles—but they did not find artifacts that could clearly be associated with women (summarized in Cohn 1983). For them, and everyone who has followed them, what would fall into this category has been unclear.

A possible exception is the work conducted by Dick Ping Hsu (Han-son and Hsu 1975) at Fort Stanwix in Rome, New York, from 1970 to 1972. This archaeological study was one of the most thorough ever conducted at an eighteenth-century military site, and Hsu knew from historical records that women were living in the vicinity of the fort as early as 1758, when a group of camp followers established a small town nearby. (The British commander of the fort had their huts burned, and the women subsequently left with the British [162].) A small number of women were living in the fort in 1777, when British forces attacked the American garrison. In spite of the large scale of his excavation and the approximately 42,000 artifacts found that dated between 1758 and 1781, Hsu was left with extremely few items directly suggestive of women's activities: 6 small buckles (92), 2 tin-plated brass earrings (95), 3 brass thimbles, 3 steel needles, 5 hat pins, 635 straight pins (138), 3 sad irons (clothes irons) (146), and 3 brass or copper rings (151). Almost all of these—except, perhaps, the earrings—*could* have been used or worn by male soldiers, although Hsu believes that the sad irons were probably used by the women at the fort (by the "wives of soldiers") who washed the laundry of the garrison: "With 300 to 400 men stationed at the fort, there was plenty of laundry to keep the women busy" (146).

While the archaeological evidence for women at Fort Stanwix appears rather meager, it nevertheless may be the best we have for any eighteenth-century military site in the Northeast. No "women's artifacts" were found by Charles Fisher (1986) at the New Windsor Cantonment in New York, nor by John Seidel (1987) at Pluckemin, New Jersey, nor by David Starbuck at the Saratoga Battlefield (1988), at Mount Independence in Vermont (1991), or at Rogers Island in New York (1992). (A single thimble was found in 1991 at Rogers Island, a 1750s military camp, but sewing was practiced by both men and women.)

Of course, archaeologists have undeniably been uncovering material items that were used by women. However, in military settings, men and women were apparently often using and sharing virtually the same material culture, and so their identities are not easily distinguishable archaeologically. After all, there is nothing inherently "male" or "female" about the camp kettles, pottery, trenchers, wine bottles, cutlery, tobacco pipes, coinage, architectural remains, or food refuse commonly found in military camps. And even more similarities between male and female possessions would have been promoted by the difficulties in obtaining provisions at frontier sites, with sutlers (merchants attached to the army) stocking as much alcohol, sugar, and other food items as possible, but with any items used exclusively by women in the outside world (articles of clothing, sewing and cooking implements) simply not being a priority in the camp stores.

At the same time, we can be reasonably certain that those items that were standard military issue—or were necessary to the conduct of war—would have been used only by men in the camps. Those implements typically associated with men would include all types of armaments (gun parts, bayonets, swords, musket balls, gunflints, canister and grape shot), heavier brush-clearing tools, axes, marked regimental buttons, and cuff links.

While archaeologists have made little effort to locate artifacts that would have been used or worn principally or exclusively by women, such a list would include toy tea sets sometimes used by girls; "pins" used as fasteners by women (although occasionally their undergarments had buttons made from bone or materials such as peach pits); small shoe buckles sometimes worn by women (requiring a qualitative assessment of how small the buckles must be); earrings; hooks and eyes that, when present, would often be indicative of women's undergarments; sad irons, sewing needles, and thimbles (but male tailors also used these, making them unreliable for studies of gender); and small silver-plated or brass rings, occasionally worn by women but sometimes used as trade items for exchange with Native Americans. Women's undergarments used many snaps and drawstrings, but these have left scant evidence in the archaeological record.

In conclusion, women at eighteenth-century military sites in the northern colonies were underreported historically, and—because most activities cut across sex lines—traces of their material culture appear underrepresented archaeologically. Historical sources make it clear that women were critical to army maintenance by nursing, laundering, and sewing, that they effectively nurtured their families while far from home, and that sometimes they fought and served with distinction. Within the fields of history and historical archaeology we are now going from a period of ignoring these women to arguing that they were numerous and that they played significant support roles, but we still know very little about them.

It is now appropriate to define more precisely the items that women *alone* could have used and worn, and to search consciously for these during future archaeological research at military encampments. Chapters may need to be added to all field reports explicitly reporting on the roles of women, the very young, the elderly, and also the African Americans who fought alongside them. But minimally, as artifact patterning is examined at military sites, systematic consideration needs to be given to the gender of those who used the artifacts, the degree to which they had control over their own lives, and their economic and social status. Undeniably, more gender-specific information will be found within primary documents than will derive from material culture found at archaeological sites, but archaeologists need to make a more deliberate search for contexts within military camps where women are known to have lived, and testing strategies must be devised that will help us to find and identify them.

Acknowledgments

Special thanks are due to several scholars who assisted in the preparation of this article, notably Tim Titus, Interpretive Programs Assistant at Crown Point State Historic Site, who located several manuscripts pertaining to women at Crown Point; Paul Huey of the New York State Division for Historic Preservation; and Dick Ping Hsu of the National Park Service.

References

Amherst Papers
1759–63 Letters from the Commander in Chief to Officers at Crown Point, Dec. 1759–Oct. 1763. Public Archives of Canada, British Manuscripts, Public Record Office 240, War Office 34, Amherst Papers, Vol. 52.

Blumenthal, Walter Hart
1952 *Women Camp Followers of the American Revolution.* Philadelphia: George S. MacManus.

Calver, William Louis, and Reginald Pelham Bolton
1950 *History Written with Pick and Shovel.* New York: New-York Historical Society.

Cohn, Michael
1983 Evidence of Children at Revolutionary War Sites. *Northeast Historical Archaeology* 12: 40–42.

De Pauw, Linda Grant
1975 *Founding Mothers: Women in America in the Revolutionary Era.* Boston: Houghton Mifflin.

Fisher, Charles L.
1986 *Material Objects, Ideology, and Everyday Life: Archaeology of the Continental Soldier at the New Windsor Cantonment.* Waterford, N.Y.: New York State Parks, Recreation and Historic Preservation, Bureau of Historic Sites.

Fitch, Jabez, Jr.
1986 *The Diary of Jabez Fitch, Jr. in the French and Indian War 1757.* 3rd ed. Fort Edward, N.Y.: Rogers Island Historic Association.

Fitzpatrick, John C., ed.
1931–44 *The Writings of George Washington from the Original Manuscript Sources.* 39 vols. Washington, D.C.: U.S. Government Printing Office.

Gillett, Mary C.
1981 *The Army Medical Department 1775–1818.* Washington, D.C.: U.S. Government Printing Office.

Hanson, Lee, and Dick Ping Hsu
1975 *Casements and Cannonballs.* Publications in Archeology 14. Washington, D.C.: U.S. Department of the Interior, National Park Service.

Kopperman, Paul E.

1982   The British High Command and Soldiers' Wives in America, 1755–1783. *Journal of the Society for Army Historical Research* 60: 14–34.

Krueger, John W.

1981   Troop Life at the Champlain Valley Forts during the American Revolution. Ph.D. diss., Department of History, State University of New York at Albany.

Lossing, Benson J.

1855   *Pictorial Field Book of the Revolution.* New York: Harper Brothers.

Munsell, Joel

1859   *Orderly Book of the Northern Army at Ticonderoga and Mt. Independence from October 17, 1776 to January 8, 1777 with biographical and explanatory notes and an appendix.* Albany, N.Y.: published by the author.

Proceedings of a Garrison Court of Enquiry Regarding the Destruction of His Majesty's Fort of Crown Point on Lake Champlain

1978   Transcription of a microfilm copy in the Public Archives of Canada, Colonial Office 5, Reel B-2966. Library, Crown Point State Historic Site.

Proceedings of the Massachusetts Historical Society

1890   Second Series, Vol. 5, 1889–1890. Boston: Published by the Society.

Seidel, John L.

1987   The Archaeology of the American Revolution: A Reappraisal & Case Study at the Continental Artillery Cantonment of 1778–1779, Pluckemin, New Jersey. Ph.D. diss. in American Historical Archaeology, University of Pennsylvania.

Starbuck, David R.

1988   The American Headquarters for the Battle of Saratoga. *Northeast Historical Archaeology* 17: 16–39.

1991   *Mount Independence and the American Revolution, 1776–1777, Orwell, Vermont.* Montpelier: Vermont Division for Historic Preservation.

1992   *Rogers Island Archeological Site, Fort Edward, New York.* Fort Edward: Rogers Island Yacht Club.

The Wayne Orderly Book

1963   The Wayne Orderly Book. *The Bulletin of the Fort Ticonderoga Museum* 11 (2): 93–112.

7

Class, Gender Strategies, and Material Culture in the Mining West

Donald L. Hardesty

Gender is one of the principles that structure the social and cultural organization of human groups and that must be considered in interpreting the
documentary and archaeological records of the past (Conkey and Gero
1991). The urban mining frontier in the nineteenth-century American West
provides an interesting example of the role played by gender in the evolution of frontier communities under conditions of rapid social and cultural
change. Mining towns typically were "instantly" urban; unplanned; geographically remote and isolated; impermanent and marked by boom/bust
economic and demographic cycles; cosmopolitan; demographically unique,
with strongly unbalanced sex and age ratios and with high turnover rates;
ethnically diverse; and class structured (Barth 1975; Hine 1980; Paul 1963;
Smith 1967).

The impact of these unique societies upon gender relationships is not
well understood. Historians, for example, explain how the frontier experience affected women and men in the western United States with three
models (see, e.g., Petrik 1987, xiv–xv; Stefanco-Schill 1981): the Turnerian

or Heroic Model, the Reactionist or Oppression Model, and the Stasis Model. Following the Frederick Jackson Turner interpretation of the frontier experience, the Heroic Model portrays the frontier as congenial to the ambitions both of women, who became strongly independent, self-reliant, and masculine, and of men. In contrast, the Oppression Model interprets the experiences of men and women moving to the American West as quite different; men responded in a variety of ways but women rather consistently became "lonely, displaced persons, demeaned and worn out by the rigors of the frontier" (Petrik 1987, xv). Finally, the Stasis Model interprets the frontier experience as having no effect at all on women and men. Both continued to live in the same world and to play the same roles they played before emigrating. Julie Roy Jeffrey (1979), for example, found that women's lives changed little after moving to the frontier, commenting that "my original perspective was feminist; I hoped to find that pioneer women used the frontier as a means of liberating themselves from stereotypes and behaviors which I found constricting and sexist. I discovered that they did not" (xv–xvi). Whatever their differences, the three models are the same in stereotyping the responses of women and men to the frontier. In particular, the experiences of the few exceptional, downtrodden, or unchanged women who have been documented and the experiences of women in rural farming communities are taken as typical.

None of the models, however, adequately describes or interprets the great variety of ways in which men and women coped with the nineteenth-century U.S. frontier in general and with mining towns in particular (Petrik 1987). The archaeological remains of mining towns are an enormous repository of information about gender strategies. To date, however, the archaeological study of gender in the mining West has been limited mostly to brothels, all-male residences such as bunkhouses, and family residences. Excavations of brothels, for example, have taken place in the red-light district of the coal mining town of Blairmore in Alberta, Canada (Kennedy 1983), and at the Vanoli sporting complex in Ouray, Colorado (Baker 1972). In addition, Simmons (1989) reviewed documentary data on and developed a predictive model of the material correlates of brothels in Cripple Creek, Colorado; Virginia City, Nevada; Jacksonville, Oregon; Silver City, Idaho; and Helena, Montana. The three studies provide archaeological and documentary information about the material expression of brothels as a household strongly organized by the principle of gender. Other archaeological studies document all-male and family households in Nevada and elsewhere in the American West (e.g., Blee 1991; Hardesty 1988). All of these, however, focus upon the material expression or artifact "signatures" of households containing either all men or all women. None considers the more general problem of how to analyze and interpret the engendered archaeological record of mining towns with the aim of documenting the way in which the social and cultural organization of mining towns reflects gender. Toward this end, this chapter develops an interpretive framework within which an engendered mining archaeology can evolve. First is a more detailed documentary model of the class and ethnic structure of mining towns within which gender played a role, followed by a prospectus for an engendered archaeology of the nineteenth-century American West.

Class, Ethnicity, and Gender in Mining Towns

Mining towns in the western United States in the nineteenth century have been described as "class-conscious and masculine" first and foremost (Jameson 1977, 166; see also Hine 1980). How mining towns were organized by gender, therefore, has to be interpreted within the context of class divisions. The fundamental economic class structure of most of these towns included the poor, a lower class of unskilled and semiskilled workers, an artisan class of skilled workers, a middle class of white-collar professionals and merchants, and an elite class of mining capitalists and managers (Petrik 1987, xviii). How women interacted with this hierarchical scheme is not well understood; however, the class structure for women probably was similar enough for this to be a reasonable model that can be modified with additional information.

The extent to which mining towns had a well-developed class structure, however, varied enormously. Hogan (1990), for example, has classified nineteenth-century mining and other towns in Colorado as either "caucus" or "carnival" according to class and power structure. Large-scale corporate interests or elite groups working "behind the scenes" to manipulate economic and political power controlled caucus towns; power in the carnival town was controlled at the grassroots level by working-class miners and entrepreneurs. Peck (1993) also shows that the formation of a working class of wage miners on the Comstock was marked by the emergence of a new ideology of risk-taking that focused upon physical rather than financial risk, in contrast to the middle class.

In mining towns caucus-type and carnival-type organizations have to be understood within the context of technology and the workplace. The nineteenth-century mining frontier in the western United States was marked by two quite different patterns of mining technology: a nonindustrial pattern and a corporate industrial pattern (Hardesty 1988, 115–16).

The use of low-cost and low-energy mining technology with little capitalization characterized the nonindustrial pattern along with little variation in yield, wealth, and political power; a decentralized system of power control; and miner-owner entrepreneurs. Communities with Hogan's carnival-type power organizations and a poorly developed class structure emerged within this technological context. In contrast, the corporate industrial pattern included the use of high-cost and high-energy industrial mining technology with high capitalization; considerable variation in yield, wealth, and political power; centralized power control in elite groups; and wage laborers. This pattern encouraged the development of social organizations with well-developed classes and a caucus-type power structure. Class-based "coping strategies" focused on elite-group domination, and working-class resistance also emerged within this context. Both patterns strongly influenced how gender structured the social and cultural organization of mining towns.

Middle-Class Women

The largest group of women immigrating to the urban mining frontier were middle-class married women from the midwestern or eastern United States. Within this group, the stereotyped gender ideology and practice of nineteenth-century America included (1) the cults of true womanhood and domesticity, which made dedication to "home, morality, children, and femininity" and the personality of "submissiveness, self-sacrifice, and passivity" the ideal for women; and (2) the doctrine of separate spheres, which limited the social and economic activities of women to the home (Armitage and Jameson 1987; Jameson 1977, 186; Jeffrey 1979; Myles 1982; Petrik 1987, xvii; Schlissel et al. 1988). As the guardians of morality and children, the power base of these women resided in the churches and the schools. Another important institution was networking, which brought together friends, church groups, and civic organizations into an informal support group when needed. Working-class women of the time typically carried similar gender ideologies and practices but with significant differences. In general, the ideas about gender that women brought to the urban mining frontier varied along the lines of ethnicity, class, and regional culture.

Petrik's (1987) study of the gold and silver mining town of Helena, Montana, illustrates the experiences of middle-class women living on the U.S. mining frontier. Although she did not find dramatic "evidence that the influence of the frontier transformed women's lives and set them apart . . . from other nineteenth century American women," she did come to the conclusion that "the peculiar demography of the frontier created significant (and often contradictory) differences in their lives" (67). In early Helena, great age differences between married men and women, long absences by men on business trips, and high frequencies of divorce gave more independence to women than was typical of other U.S. middle-class women between 1865 and the 1880s. Partly as a result, the first women in Helena pursued a greater variety of economic activities both in and outside the home than was typical in the rest of the United States in that century. Furthermore, the shortage of women in mining towns such as Helena required more work in the home and made women increasingly critical of the ideologies of domesticity and sexual inequalities. At the same time, frontier mining towns broke up the informal "social network" of friends and relatives that acted as a support group to other nineteenth-century American women, making it more difficult for the women emigrants to break away from the private sphere of the home and the cult of domesticity. Finally, churches and schools, the institutional power base of American women of the time, were poorly developed if present at all on the urban mining frontier.

Working-Class Women

Although the experiences of middle-class women on the mining frontier are much better documented, working-class women typically arrived first. The 1860 federal population census for Virginia City, Nevada, for example, shows that the first group of women to arrive were the wives of teamsters. Two gender-based adaptive strategies (problem-solving rules or guidelines) developed by poor and working-class women to make a living and sometimes prosper illustrate the role of gender in the organization of frontier mining towns. The strategy of "prostitute-entrepreneurship" appears to have worked best in the early stages of community formation in "carnival-type" and nonindustrial frontier mining towns (Goldman 1981; Hogan 1990; Petrik 1987, 25–58). Masculine, "wide open," and not controlled by elite groups, carnival towns provided more opportunities for single young poor or working-class women to move out of the private sphere of the household and into the public marketplace. In a nineteenth-century society that greatly limited the social and economic opportunities of women outside the home, mining towns made prostitution an important way that single young underclass women could not only survive but also gain material wealth (Petrik 1987, 56). To be sure, prostitution exploited the sexuality of those women, but it did allow for a profit and control over the terms of the relationship. Carnival towns allowed prostitutes not only to practice their craft and to own their businesses but also often to move into the lofty ranks of "respectability" with no more effort than accumulating property and legally changing names and lifestyles. With the shift to a caucus-type power structure controlled by elite groups and a corporate industrial pattern, however, the municipal government increasingly circumscribed and licensed the brothels, forcing prostitutes to work as wage-laborers for pimps rather than as independent small-business entrepreneurs and owners.

Another type of "working-class" adaptive strategy developed by women in corporate industrial and caucus-type towns is illustrated by Cripple Creek, Colorado. Between 1894 and 1904, the Western Federation of Miners organized the Cripple Creek miners to oppose the interests of corporate capitalists; a militant and intense working-class identity emerged among both men and women that strongly affected gender strategies. Unions and wage work guaranteed good incomes to domestic households, attracted abundant working men, and left women with few paid jobs available outside the home. The labor union not only gained good wages for the miners but also supported the traditional nineteenth-century ideology of genteel "True Womanhood" and "True Manhood." Concepts of "home, morality, children, and femininity" and the private sphere organized the ideal middle-class domestic household (Jameson 1977, 186). As a result, the militant working-class women in Cripple Creek fought for and entered into a world that often was just the opposite of what middle-class women wanted. In contrast to the prostitute-entrepreneur strategy, the new labor-union strategy increasingly restricted the public sphere to working-class women. Rather than increasing their independence and self-reliance, labor unions made the working-class women of Cripple Creek even more dependent upon the wages of men. The strategies of working-class women in Cripple Creek more closely resembled and complemented the class/resistance strategies of the male-dominated labor unions than the women's rights/civic reform strategies of elite women during the same time period (Jameson 1977, 180). In many cases, in fact, the strategies of working-class and middle- or elite-class women and men conflicted directly. Women in the labor unions, for example, sometimes boycotted or picketed women owners of boardinghouses and restaurants for using non-union products or labor.

Ethnicity and Gender

In addition to class, gender also interacted with ethnicity in mining towns. Cosmopolitan mining towns absorbed a large variety of immigrants and emigrants carrying quite different cultural and social traditions, affecting the way in which gender structured the community. Perhaps the most dramatic example is the social and cultural context of overseas Chinese women. At first, most Chinese women arriving in the western United States came for arranged marriages or as wives of physicians and merchants who migrated with their families (Hirata 1979; Tsai 1986). A few, however, came on their own as prostitutes and worked as independent entrepreneurs (Hirata 1979, 225; Wegars 1993, 231). Only a handful of women came with the large Chinese immigration between 1850 and 1880. After the mid-1850s the Chinese tongs (voluntary associations) brought many more Chinese women into the American West either as domestic slaves or as prostitutes. During the 1860s and 1870s, overseas Chinese women living in mining towns and elsewhere in the West engaged in prostitution more than any other occupation (Hirata 1979; Wegars 1993, 233–39). The overseas Chinese community in California recognized both higher-class and lower-class prostitutes. Higher-class prostitutes, who serviced only Chinese men, worked under relatively good conditions; lower-class prostitutes engaged anyone who could pay their fees and worked under poor conditions. Overseas Chinese women in mining towns, however, also worked in other occupations. In addition to "keeping house," they worked as laundresses, actresses, lodging house operators, seamstresses, miners, servants, laborers, cooks, gardeners, fishers, and shoe binders.

Although wealthy merchants and professionals in the community had wives, family households could be established only with great difficulty by the Chinese working class in the mining towns. Wives literally had to be purchased from the Chinese tongs; the going price for wives on the Comstock in the 1870s, for example, was four to eight hundred dollars (Magnaghi 1981, 146). Once married, both kidnapping and abuse appear to have been a constant threat to wives. Living conditions varied considerably within the community. The wives of wealthy Chinese merchants, for example, often lived "leisured, secluded lives revolving around their husbands and children" and "until the birth of their first child, they were not often seen in public, and then only at Chinese New Year, weddings, and funerals, and sometimes at the (Chinese) theater" (Wegars 1993, 237).

The Archaeology of Gender in Mining Towns

How is gender reflected in the archaeological record of nineteenth-century frontier mining towns in the western United States? Comparative studies of towns such as Bodie, California; Shermantown, Nevada; Hayden Hill, California; Copperton, Wyoming; and Battle, Wyoming, suggest several

Figure 7.1. Map of major mining towns discussed in the text.

things about how gender is reflected in the archaeological record (fig. 7.1). As with the documentary record, class and ethnicity are the key variables. The evidence of gender principles, however, is arranged geographically and hierarchically in the archaeological remains of the household, the local settlement or town, and the mining district or regional settlement system.

Household Archaeology

The widespread nineteenth-century U.S. ideology of the separation of gender spheres into the home and the public domain suggests that the archaeological record of domestic households should contain much that is of importance to understanding how the principles of gender organized frontier mining towns. Certainly the activities reflected in archaeological remains of households can provide key information about how gender influenced labor and social relations at the grassroots level. Gibb and King's (1991) study of gender and houselot activity areas in the seventeenth-century Chesapeake Bay region, for example, illustrates the approach that should be taken in frontier mining towns. They found gender reflected archaeologically in the type and spatial arrangement of economic activities of men and women taking place in the household. Ruth Tringham's (1991) study of the "use life" of houses as a reflection of household cycles at the Neolithic Yugoslavian site of Opovo is another example. Architectural data on the "construction, duration, utilization, maintenance, abandonment, destruction, and replacement of buildings" were used to document transformations not only in household activities but also in household organization (107).

The most common patterns of organization of coresidential households in mining towns of the West reflect the principles of gender. These include family households, cooperative or mutual aid households, occupational households such as brothels, and all-male work-group households such as bunkhouses (Hardesty 1992). Features and artifact assemblages are sufficiently distinctive to identify the basic household patterns and suggest that variability and change in how gender organizes the domestic household can be studied through the archaeological record. Simmons (1989, 63–67), for example, develops a model of artifacts expected in the archaeological remains of high-, middle-, and low-status brothels in mining towns.

Blee (1991), however, goes further and analyzes several well-documented archaeological sites from the American West to more precisely define the artifact assemblages left by, among others, family households, all-male households, and brothels. Composite profiles of artifact assemblages from several excavated sites in Alaska, Colorado, Nevada, Oregon, Washington, and Utah were developed for each of the three patterns of household organization. The composite profile of artifact assemblages from the sites of fourteen family households, which ranged from working-class to wealthy, is dominated by artifacts used for the storage, preparation, and serving of food (e.g., canning jars, tablewares), which together make up nearly 40 percent of the total. Of these, decorated dishes make up about 8 percent of the assemblage. Male-specific (e.g., suspender clasps, tobacco pipes, pocket knives), female-specific (e.g, corset stays, garter snaps, perfume bottles), and child-specific (e.g., toys, diaper pins) artifacts each make up between 2 and 3 percent of the assemblage. Most interesting in many ways, however, is the relatively high percentage of liquor-related artifacts in the family household assemblage (over 18 percent), a considerably higher percentage than that of patent medicine and other pharmaceutical bottles (only 6 percent). One interpretation is that women members of the household consumed alcoholic beverages at home instead of in public places.

Personal artifacts (e.g., combs, coins, carpetbags, tooth powder), which make up nearly half of the total, dominate the composite profile of artifact assemblages from ten all-male household sites, mostly labor camps, from the western United States (Blee 1991). Male-specific artifacts are the next most abundant (16.1 percent), and artifacts associated with women and children are absent. Unlike family households, artifacts used for the storage, preparation, and serving of food are sparse — only one-ninth that of family household sites — and decorated tablewares make up less than 1 percent of the assemblage. Blee (1991) attributes this and the small size of the assemblage in general to the fact that all-male households tend to be transient rather than long-lasting (177). The artifact assemblages of all-male residences also have two other distinguishing characteristics: a low percentage of liquor-related artifacts and a relatively high percentage of armaments (9.9 percent). The low number of liquor-related artifacts suggests that men drank in saloons and other places outside the residence; drinking in public was acceptable behavior for men in mining camps but not for women.

Finally, the composite profile of artifact assemblages from two brothels is dominated by liquor-related artifacts and bottle stoppers/caps, both of which make up almost half of the total. Certainly the consumption of alcoholic beverages is one of the principal activities taking place in brothels, and in this way the artifact assemblages are quite similar to those of saloons. Female-specific artifacts are relatively common, greatly outnumbering male-specific artifacts and nearly three times as abundant in the assemblages of brothels as in family household assemblages. Undecorated dishes also are common, making up nearly 14 percent of the assemblage, and decorated tablewares make up less than 1 percent of the total; in this way the assemblages of brothels are similar to those of restaurants, hotels, and boardinghouses.

The material expression of overseas Chinese women in mining towns or elsewhere in the American West is poorly known, archaeologically or otherwise. Wegars (1993, 241–49) documents jewelry (such as gold earrings), hair ornaments and grooming devices (bone hair picks, hair combs, and fine-toothed lice combs), fan handles, cosmetics such as perfume bottles and toilet water (e.g., Florida Water), and Chinese medicine bottles. Archaeologists found a rosewood hairdressing stand with compartments for combs, brushes, and other things in the loft of a standing building in the Chinese settlement at Lovelock, Nevada. Excavations in Idaho recovered fragments of jade rings, which may have been used as bracelets by Chinese women and men or attached to the lids of sewing baskets. Other artifacts include inlaid boxes and trays and "Chinese marriage cups," shoes for bound feet (associated with upper-class women), and "a large-sleeved robe of silk or cotton, over a long garment, under which are loose trousers sometimes fastened around the ankle" (Williams 1941, 97, 99; cited in Wegars 1993, 248).

Whether the degree to which households were organized according to the traditional nineteenth-century American ideology of "home, morality, children, and femininity" can be studied archaeologically is a questionable but interesting proposition. Greater stress upon the cult of domesticity in the labor union towns of Cripple Creek, for example, may be reflected archaeologically in the exclusion of "public sphere" activities from the home. Church and school activities may be reflected in the middle-class households of women building their power base. Furthermore, the extent to which domestic households reflect this ideology is expected to vary by class and ethnicity.

Settlement Archaeology

If gender works on labor and social relations at the household level, it also plays a key role in structuring the social and cultural organization of the local community and beyond. Without question, the principles of gender structured the layout of frontier mining towns. Most had geographically separated poor, working-class, and middle/elite-class neighborhoods that incorporated women in various ways, and the spatial organization of the archaeological record of the towns is so structured. "Red-light" districts, for example, were a common feature of most towns and included many of the single young women (e.g., Goldman 1981; Petrik 1987). Thus, most of the brothels in Bodie, California, clustered downtown on Bonanza Street (Wedertz 1969, 28). The historian Paula Petrik (1987, 28) notes further that the Helena red-light district in Last Chance Gulch was organized along class lines. Elite-class brothels clustered in the upper section, working-class brothels further down the street, and poor Chinese brothels at the lower end of the street. Simmons (1989) documents similar patterns in Jacksonville, Oregon; Cripple Creek, Colorado; Silver City, Idaho; and Virginia City, Nevada.

Middle- and upper-class neighborhoods also were geographically segregated and typically included most of the married women. In the Gold Rush town of Nevada City, California, for example, the neighborhoods of Aristocracy Hill and Piety Hill had emerged by the end of the 1850s as residential islands containing not only most of the upper-class merchants and professionals but also most of the married women (Mann 1982, 65, 96).

Most of the middle/elite-class family households in Bodie, California, were in the Green Street neighborhood downtown, but a few were scattered in the "working-class" residential satellite settlements that grew up around outlying mines and mills (Wedertz 1969, 16). Archaeological studies of Shermantown, Nevada, suggest the presence of geographically separated "nucleated clusters" of house sites associated with what appear to be the archaeological remains of upper-class family households (Hardesty 1989).

In addition to the layout of mining settlements, gender also structured the architectural and archaeological remains of special-purpose community buildings. Special-purpose buildings include those used by fraternal organizations, churches, schools, union halls, and social clubs. The buildings typically are symbols of the class and power structure within the community (see, e.g., McGuire and Paynter 1991). Three patterns of special-purpose buildings emerge from the archaeological and architectural records of frontier mining towns: (1) towns in which special-purpose buildings did not occur; (2) towns with special-purpose buildings used mostly for men's activities; and (3) towns with special-purpose buildings used for both men's and women's activities. The first pattern is typical of mining towns that have been "truncated" abruptly by a complete bust in mining activity after a short boom period. White Pine City, Nevada, is a good example. Not only did men dominate the population of the town, but the town failed to survive long enough to establish a well-defined class structure marked by symbols of power. The second pattern is typical of working-class mining towns that survived long enough to establish a well-defined class structure but either had an unusually high percentage of men or were strongly dominated by labor unions. Copperton and Battle, Wyoming; Gold Hill, Nevada; and Cripple Creek, Colorado, are good examples. The third pattern is typical of mining towns that survived for a relatively long period of time, had a well-defined class structure, and had populations with a more balanced sex ratio.

Middle-class women in frontier mining towns created adaptive strategies that included reform movements centered around the organization and development of churches and schools. For this reason, the archaeological and architectural remains of schools, churches, and local clubs must be interpreted not only as locations of religious, educational, or recreational activities but also as reflections of gendered activities. Artifacts in the domestic household assemblages of frontier mining towns that are related to church and school activities, in fact, may be good markers of elite-group strategies intended to increase the traditional power base of women within the community.

Regional Archaeology

Finally, gender principles structure the archaeological record at the level of the mining district or the regional mining community. Because of large-scale and fluid social interaction networks, the effective geographical boundaries of mining communities are best defined at the scale of the region rather than of the local settlement (Hardesty 1988; Hine 1980). The mining district often is a close approximation of the community. For this reason, research strategies aimed at identifying the ways gender helped organize the mining community must take into account the larger region or mining district.

Two regional patterns reflecting gender are evident. In mining districts centered around a town with a variety of outlying settlements, gender strongly structured regional geography. Most of the women, for example, lived either in the town, with families at outlying ranches, or at toll stations managed by families. Men occupied the working-class satellite settlements clustering around the mines or mills scattered throughout the district. A few women lived at boardinghouses or with the families of managers at the satellite settlements. However, one notable exception to this pattern can be identified. In mining districts with company towns closely regulated by corporations, special-purpose satellite settlements outside company control often emerged around the entertainment industry. For example, what Elliott (1966, 210) calls a "parasite" settlement emerged as a center of prostitution and other recreational services at Riepetown outside the limits of the company towns of Ruth and Kimberly in the Robinson copper mining district of eastern Nevada. Working-class women living in Riepetown were spatially separated from the middle-class women living in the company towns; furthermore, only company towns had churches and schools.

In addition to spatial separation at the regional scale, geographic mobility characterized both men and women on the nineteenth-century urban mining frontier. Middle-class women in mining towns, for example, frequently complained about the long-term absence of men from the home (e.g., Petrik 1987). For their part, women often engaged in a pattern of geographic mobility that replicated traditional nineteenth-century American "informal female networks" as a support group for women. Purser's (1991) documentation of "visiting" by women in Grass Flats, California, and Paradise Valley, Nevada, illustrates this pattern.

Gender, class, and ethnicity worked together to structure the society and culture of nineteenth-century mining towns in the American West. The structuring took place at the levels of the household, the local settlement, and the regional community. Without question, the roles of women in mining towns were much more diverse than existing documentary models have implied. No place reflects the diversity better than the domestic household, where the impact of gender and power upon labor and social relations created the potential for enormous variability. Long-lived mining towns such as Helena and Virginia City expressed the most household variability, Shermantown and other short-lived towns the least.

The archaeological and documentary study of household cycles in frontier mining towns may be the key to understanding the role of gender in the community. At the same time, macrostudies of mining towns and regional analyses of mining districts and beyond also are clearly needed. Certainly the principles of gender not only structure the use of space and resources in towns and mining districts but also assign a gendered meaning to public and special-use buildings such as schools, churches, lodges, and union halls. As others have also stated, we need to maintain a proper balance of theory to inform and empirical data to guide the archaeology of gender on the mining frontier.

References

Armitage, Susan, and Elizabeth Jameson, eds.
1987   *The Women's West.* Norman: University of Oklahoma Press.
Baker, Stephen G.
1972   *A Prospectus of Continuing Research on the Goldbelt Theatre and Social History of the Vanoli Properties in Ouray, Colorado.* Montrose, Colo.: Centuries Research.
Barth, Gunther P.
1975   *Instant Cities.* New York: Oxford University Press.
Blee, Catherine Holder
1991   Sorting Functionally-Mixed Artifact Assemblages with Multiple Regression: A Comparative Study in Historical Archaeology. Ph.D. diss., University of Colorado, Boulder.
Conkey, Margaret, and Joan Gero, eds.
1991   *Engendering Archaeology: Women in Prehistory.* Cambridge: Basil Blackwell.
Elliott, Russell R.
1966   *Nevada's Twentieth Century Mining Boom.* Reno: University of Nevada Press.

Gibb, James G., and Julia A. King
1991   Gender, Activity Areas, and Homelots in the Seventeenth-Century Chesapeake Region. *Historical Archaeology* 25 (4): 109-31.

Goldman, Marion S.
1981   *Gold Diggers and Silver Miners: Prostitution and Social Life on the Comstock.* Ann Arbor: University of Michigan Press.

Hardesty, Donald L.
1988   *The Archaeology of Mining and Miners: A View from the Silver State.* Special Publication, 6. Ann Arbor, Mich.: Society for Historical Archaeology.
1989   Community and Settlement, Household and House Site on the Mining Frontier: Combining History and Archaeology. Paper presented at the annual meeting of the Western History Association, Tacoma, Washington.
1992   The Miner's Domestic Household: Perspectives from the American West. In *Sozialgeschichte des Bergbaus im 19. und 20. Jahrhundert*, ed. Klaus Tenfelde, 180-96. Munich: C. H. Beck.

Hine, Robert
1980   *Community on the American Frontier.* Norman: University of Oklahoma Press.

Hirata, Lucie Cheng
1979   Chinese Immigrant Women in Nineteenth-Century California. In *Women of America: A History*, ed. C.R. Berkin and M.B. Norton, 223-44. Boston: Houghton Mifflin.

Hogan, Richard
1990   *Class and Community in Frontier Colorado.* Lawrence: University Press of Kansas.

Jameson, Elizabeth
1977   Imperfect Unions: Class and Gender in Cripple Creek, 1894-1904. In *Class, Sex, and the Woman Worker*, ed. Milton Cantor and Bruce Laurie, 166-202. Westwood, Conn.: Greenwood Press.

Jeffrey, Julie Roy
1979   *Frontier Women: The Trans-Mississippi West, 1840-1880.* New York: Hill and Wang.

Kennedy, Margaret
1983   Final Report: Historical Resources Impact Assessment and Conservation Studies, Highway 3 Realignment Frank to Blairmore. Report prepared for Alberta Culture, Archaeological Survey of Alberta, Edmonton. Photocopy.

Magnaghi, Russell M.
1981   Virginia City's Chinese Community, 1860-1880. *Nevada Historical Society Quarterly* 24 (2): 130-57.

Mann, Ralph
1982   *After the Gold Rush*. Palo Alto, Calif.: Stanford University Press.
McGuire, Randall H., and Robert Paynter, eds.
1991   *The Archaeology of Inequality*. Cambridge: Basil Blackwell.
Myles, Sandra L.
1982   *Westering Women and the Frontier Experience, 1800–1915*. Albuquerque:
        University of New Mexico Press.
Paul, Rodman W.
1963   *Mining Frontiers of the Far West, 1848–1880*. New York: Holt, Rinehart
        and Winston.
Peck, Gunther
1993   Manly Gambles: The Politics of Risk on the Comstock Lode, 1860–1880.
        Journal of Social History 26 (4): 701–23.
Petrik, Paula
1987   *No Step Backward*. Helena: Montana Historical Society.
Purser, Margaret
1991   "Several Paradise Ladies are Visiting in Town": Gender Strategies in the
        Early Industrial West. *Historical Archaeology* 25 (4): 6–16.
Schlissel, Lillian, Vicki Ruiz, and Janice Monk, eds.
1988   *Western Women, Their Land, Their Lives*. Albuquerque: University of New
        Mexico Press.
Simmons, Alexy
1989   *Red Light Ladies, Settlement Patterns and Material Culture on the Mining
        Frontier*. Anthropology Northwest, 4. Corvallis: Department of Anthro-
        pology, Oregon State University.
Smith, Duane A.
1967   *Rocky Mountain Mining Camps*. Bloomington: Indiana University Press.
Stefanco-Schill, Carolyn
1981   Women on the American Frontier: An Historiographic Essay. Paper pre-
        sented at the annual meeting of the Social Science-History Association,
        Nashville, Tennessee.
Tringham, Ruth E.
1991   Households with Faces: The Challenge of Gender in Prehistoric Archi-
        tectural Remains. In *Engendering Archaeology*, ed. Joan Gero and Margaret
        Conkey, 93–131. Cambridge: Basil Blackwell.
Tsai, Shih-Shan Henry
1986   *The Chinese Experience in America*. Bloomington: Indiana University Press.
United States Bureau of the Census
1860   Eighth Census, 1860. Utah (Territory). Population Schedules, Washing-
        ton. Washington, D.C.: National Archives.
Wedertz, Frank S.
1969   *Bodie 1859–1900*. Bishop, Calif.: Chalfant Press.

Wegars, Priscilla

1993   Besides Polly Bemis: Historical and Artifactual Evidence for Chinese
        Women in the West, 1848–1930. In *Hidden Heritage, Historical Archaeology
        of the Overseas Chinese*, ed. Priscilla Wegars, 229–54. Amityville, N.Y.:
        Baywood Publishing.

Williams, C. A. S.

1941   *Outlines of Chinese Symbolism and Art Motives*. Third rev. ed. Shanghai:
        Kelly and Walsh. Reprint, New York: Dover, 1976.

IV Working Women in Urban Communities

8

Mrs. Starr's Profession

Donna J. Seifert

Mrs. Starr, an established Baltimore madam, arrived in Washington, D.C., in 1858. In 1862, she purchased property at No. 62 Ohio Avenue. One of her daughters, Mrs. Mary Jane Treakle (also known as Mollie Turner), moved from Norfolk, Virginia, to Washington to run the house (Hall, pers. com. 1989). The Provost Marshal's 1865 inventory of bawdy houses lists the establishment run by Mollie Turner as a class 1 house with three inmates (Provost Marshal 1865; Tidwell 1988, 337). Mrs. Starr's daughter Ellen Starr (also known as Ella Turner, Nellie Starr, and Fannie Harrison) was living at No. 62 Ohio Avenue[1] when she gave her statement to the police on 15 April 1865:

> My name is Nellie Starr. My native place is Baltimore, State of Maryland. I have been in Washington City D.C. since a week before Christmas. I am about nineteen or twenty years of age. I am not married. I have known John Wilkes Booth about three years; he was in the habit of visiting the house where I live kept by Miss Eliza Thomas, No. 62 Ohio Avenue in the City of Washington. The house is one of prostitution. I have never heard him speak unfavorable

of the President. I heard him speak of the President as being a good man just as other people did. I do not distinctly recollect how he was dressed, when I last saw him; I think he had on dark clothes. I think he wore a slough hat. I do not think it is the one shown me by the district attorney. I know nothing more about the case. I know not with whom he associated with, as I have not been on good terms with him for over a year. The last time I seen Mr. Booth was two weeks ago, at the said house. [signed] Nellie Starr, Ella Starr, Fannie Harrison (National Archives and Records Administration 1865)

The Starr family business was located in the Washington, D.C., neighborhood known as Hooker's Division. The appellation refers to the district frequented by the men of General Joseph Hooker's division, attractive to Union soldiers and officers during the Civil War because of its saloons and bawdy houses. Although prostitutes lived in the neighborhood from the 1860s until 1914, the neighborhood of the 1860s through 1880s was a working-class neighborhood that included prostitutes among the working women boarding there. During the 1890s, however, the neighborhood became a red-light district characterized by rows of brothels. Census records, contemporary accounts, and archaeological data document the change in the neighborhood and the changes in the business of prostitution.

At Home in Hooker's Division

The neighborhood historically known as Hooker's Division is within the modern Federal Triangle in Washington, D.C.—the triangle formed by Fifteenth Street, Pennsylvania Avenue, and Constitution Avenue (fig. 8.1). The neighborhood, then as now, is in the capital city's center, between the White House and the Capitol and north of the Smithsonian Mall. In the mid-nineteenth century, the neighborhood was occupied by households of working-class people, including native-born American blacks and whites as well as German, Irish, and Russian immigrants, among others. Although most households were headed by a male skilled or unskilled worker, several were headed by women. These female heads of household included Caroline Graniger (1367 Ohio Avenue), who kept a grocery, and Frances Johnson (1309 C Street), a forty-year-old, French-born woman who ran a boardinghouse occupied by a laborer, a housekeeper, a printing-office worker, a seven-year-old child, and two prostitutes. Mrs. Johnson, like Mrs. Starr, may have been running a family business: perhaps the twenty-year-old prostitute Fanny Johnson was Mrs. Johnson's daughter and the child, Mary Johnson, another daughter or granddaughter. A household at

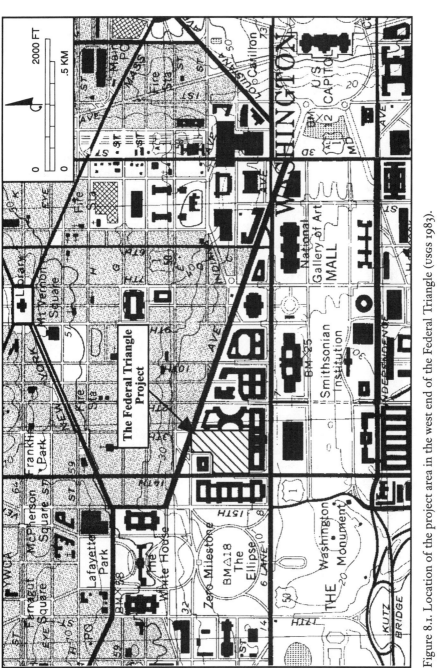

Figure 8.1. Location of the project area in the west end of the Federal Triangle (USGS 1983).

312 13½ Street was a brothel, occupied by four African American prostitutes, all born in Maryland or Virginia. Three were in their early twenties; the head of the household, Florence Hall, was thirty-five (United States Bureau of the Census [USBC] 1870).

Working-class households and brothels continued to share the neighborhood in the 1880s: prostitutes were living in brothels and boarding in working-class households with families and boarders working in other trades (USBC 1880). "Prostitute" is one of a limited number of occupations listed for working-class women in this Washington, D.C., neighborhood.

A review of occupations listed in the census records from 1870 and 1880 shows that the women of the neighborhood were engaged in traditionally female occupations: domestic servant, laundress, cook, housekeeper, seamstress, dressmaker, and nurse. In the mid-nineteenth century, the ideal woman's work was homemaking. However, even for many skilled workers, men's wages alone were inadequate to support a family, so daughters and wives often contributed to the family income. But wages for women's work were even lower and employment options were limited. There were few factory jobs in Washington, D.C.; most employment was in the service sector (Green 1962, 1: 356).

The women of Hooker's Division—whether they were wives, heads of household, daughters, or single women—were providing homemaking services for others or working in the clothing trades. Such women's work rarely paid a living wage, much less enough to support dependents. There were two notable exceptions in the neighborhood: Caroline Graniger, a widow, was a grocer, running an inherited family business. The other exception was the prostitutes. Prostitution was the only employment generally available to working-class women that offered a chance to escape poverty. The change in the organization of work from the productive household to wage labor in capitalist businesses (with the male provider and female homemaker) increased women's dependency on men (Stansell 1986, 45, 52, 218). The sudden loss of a male wage earner in a family—through death, disability, or desertion—immediately left a working-class family destitute. For a woman on her own with or without dependents, prostitution was one choice among limited, undesirable options (Stansell 1986, 177–79, 191).

Prostitution may have been a choice for some working-class young women on their own after leaving the natal household and before marriage (Stansell 1986, 185–86). Most prostitutes listed in census records are young women (in their teens and early twenties), and historical sources indicate that some of these young women went on to marry—rather than die horribly within a few years, as reformers argued (Stansell 1986, 188; Hobson 1990, 86–87; cf. Sanger 1939, 453). Young working-class women often worked in wage labor during early adulthood, and prostitution may have been an option selected, particularly by women living away from family.

By 1900, most of the households in Hooker's Division were brothels, headed by a female who ran the boardinghouse (the madam) and several women in their teens and early twenties for whom no occupation was listed. Some brothels included servants. Brothels were segregated by race, although some white brothels included black servants. The few family households were occupied by skilled and unskilled workers; most were native born (USBC 1900). The 1910 census shows a similar pattern of occupation (USBC 1910), although some immigrant families had moved in.

The brothels were closed in 1914, when Congress enacted legislation banning houses of prostitution in the District of Columbia (Commissioners of the District of Columbia 1914). Tax records and city directories indicate that some of the buildings housing brothels became vacant; some were reoccupied by working-class residents (Cheek et al. 1991, Appendix I).

Neighborhood, Household Type, and Material Culture

The household types that constitute a neighborhood are useful analytical units in studying the archaeology of urban life. Aggregate data from several deposits representing known household composition and function are more likely to represent the households characteristic of the neighborhood than data from any single documented household (see Cheek and Seifert 1994). In an urban setting where residents move frequently, as in Hooker's Division, correlating an archaeological deposit with a specific household is often difficult. However, where documents indicate that a lot was occupied by the same type of household over a period of time, the household type is the most useful unit of comparison. Different household types (defined by composition and function) can be compared within a period of time and over time. This approach proved successful in the analysis of the archaeological assemblage from Hooker's Division, where the character of the neighborhood and the types of household within it were known but specific residents could not always be correlated with specific deposits.

Examining household types in the context of the neighborhood is appropriate because of the importance of the neighborhood in working-class women's lives. By the middle of the nineteenth century, urban middle-class families carefully separated the public life of work, the milieu of men, from the private life at home, the domain of women and children (Stansell 1986, 41). The public and the private, work and home, were not so clearly divided for working-class women, who spent much of their time out of the home and in the neighborhood.[2] The daily tasks of getting food, fuel, and water consumed much of the working-class homemaker's time, and these necessities were acquired in the neighborhood. Few of the goods needed for the home were produced by the urban household, so women bought goods from street vendors and neighborhood shops. With little ready cash, working-class homemakers made frequent trips and small purchases. Bartering, pawning, and scavenging were also common aspects of the domestic economy of the working poor (Stansell 1986, 52). Before the advent of municipal utilities, the work of homemaking included hauling fuel and water (Stansell 1986, 46, 49). Although Washington, D.C., had a city water system by 1863, houses in poorer neighborhoods such as Hooker's Division were still not equipped with plumbing in the 1880s and 1890s, so women and children pumped water from cisterns or carried it home from wells in public squares (Green 1962, 2: 42, 45). Even houses with running water often had only one tap and one water closet.

In the crowded conditions of urban neighborhoods, the affairs of everyday life were rarely private, and neighbors involved themselves in each other's concerns, resulting in cooperation or confrontation, depending on the personalities and circumstances (Stansell 1986, 56). While some of the men living in the working-class neighborhood probably worked there also, most were employed in workplaces outside the neighborhood. Men, therefore, spent more of their time away from the neighborhood, associating with men involved in the same type of work. Working-class men might be involved in labor associations, but women in wage labor were less likely to belong to such associations, and the working-class homemakers' community was the neighborhood (Stansell 1986, 55).

Archaeological investigations in the neighborhood known as Hooker's Division recovered assemblages from two types of households, working-class households and brothels, for two periods, 1870 to 1890 and 1890 to 1920. The two types of households were defined on the basis of household composition as given in census records. Brothel assemblages were from households composed of a female head, resident prostitutes, and household servants. Working-class households included a family group; some also included boarders. While the census records also list households with family groups and boarders (including prostitutes), none of the archaeological deposits was from such a household.

Two time periods are represented by archaeological deposits that can be correlated with specific household types. The earlier period, 1870 to 1890, includes the post–Civil War economic and social dislocations and adjustments and the capital city's response to population growth during the war and the influx of freed slaves. The later period, 1890 to 1920, includes the depression of the 1890s, the recovery and building boom, and the closing of the brothels in 1914 (Green 1962). The year 1890 was selected as the dividing point for two reasons: archaeological deposits could be separated as earlier or later than 1890 on the basis of datable building episodes and artifacts, and, despite the lack of 1890 manuscript census records, other documents (such as Sanborn fire insurance maps from 1888 and 1903 and a newspaper article from the mid-1890s, "Within Sight of the White House" [1895]) indicate that by the early 1890s, the neighborhood had become a red-light district. While working-class women were involved in wage labor in both periods, the later period is marked by the national increase of middle-class women in commercial and industrial employment and the concomitant reformers' concern over the impact of such employment on these young women and on the next generation. Washington, D.C., was not an industrial city; nevertheless, the development of capitalist business changed the organization of work as the independent prostitute was replaced by the brothel inmate, who worked not for herself or the madam but for the owner of the business (U.S. Senate 1913, 28–29; Rosen 1982, 70–71; Seifert 1991, 88–89).

Prostitution's principal attraction was negotiable compensation, but archaeological evidence from Hooker's Division gives little indication that the material conditions of life in brothels were better than those of working-class households during the period from 1870 to 1890. By the turn of the century, however, there are indications that prostitutes enjoyed some of the comforts of life not available to their working-class neighbors.

The archaeological excavations conducted in historic Hooker's Division in 1989 sampled deposits from ten house lots. Census data were collected for a larger sample of lots, including all excavated lots and several neighboring lots near the corner of 13½ Street and Ohio Avenue (figs. 8.2 and 8.3). Four archaeological assemblages representing household types are analyzed and compared in this paper: early working-class, early prostitute, late working-class, and late prostitute households. The archaeological data for each household type from each period were aggregated from two or three deposits that had been dated and assigned to a household type on the basis of census data. Combining data from two or more archaeological samples was judged to produce more representative samples for comparison.[3]

To compare artifact assemblages among types of households, artifact pattern analysis developed by Stanley South (1977) was used (table 8.1).[4] Artifacts were grouped by function, and the relative percentages of the

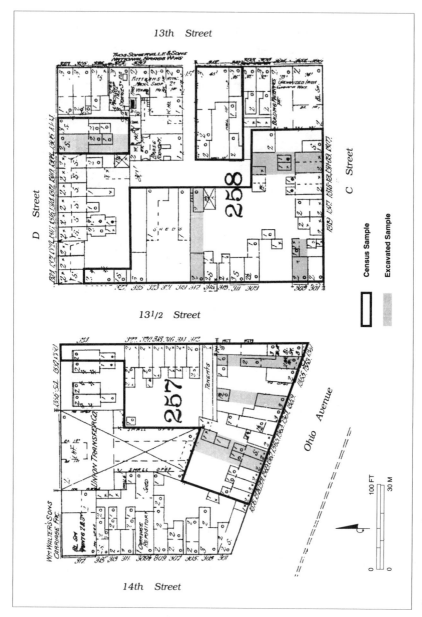

Figure 8.2. Detail of 1888 fire insurance map showing house lots included in excavated and census samples (Sanborn Map Company 1888).

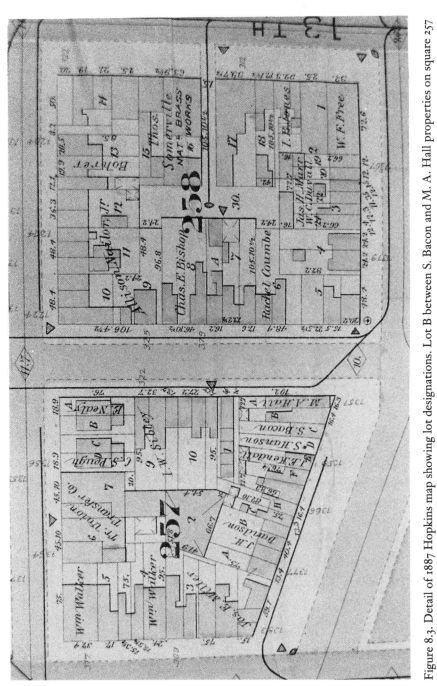

Figure 8.3. Detail of 1887 Hopkins map showing lot designations. Lot B between S. Bacon and M. A. Hall properties on square 257 was the lot owned by Mrs. Starr in the 1860s (Hopkins 1887).

158

functional groups were compared. In addition, the specific composition of
artifact groups was examined, and ceramic indices (using the methods developed by George Miller [1980, 1991] and Susan Henry [1987]) were calculated as a measure of socioeconomic status. The differences between early
working-class and early brothel assemblages reflect differences in house-

Table 8.1   Frequency of Selected Artifact Groups by Household Type
and Time Period

Artifact Group[1]	Working Class		Prostitute	
	n[2]	%	n	%
EARLY 1860–1890				
Assemblage total (all groups)	3,181	99.99	1,291	99.99
Architecture	737	23.17	557	43.14
Kitchen	2,228	70.04	641	49.65
Furniture	—	—	—	—
Arms	—	—	—	—
Clothing	10	0.31	11	0.85
Personal	22	0.69	7	0.54
Tobacco	24	0.75	39	3.02
Activities	160	5.03	36	2.79
LATE 1890–1920				
Assemblage Total (all groups)	7,699	100.00	10,727	100.00
Architecture	1,896	24.63	3,403	31.72
Kitchen	5,391	70.02	5,441	50.72
Furniture	8	0.10	26	0.24
Arms	—	—	2	.02
Clothing	34	0.44	240	2.24
Personal	35	0.45	125	1.17
Tobacco	32	0.42	136	1.27
Activities	303	3.94	1,354	12.62

[1]South 1977
[2]number of fragments

hold composition and function; the differences between the late working-
class and late brothel assemblages also suggest differences in material comforts. The distinctive assemblage of the late brothels reflects an increase
in the acquisition of consumer goods, related to changes in the business of
prostitution.[5]

Hooker's Division, 1870–90

Kitchen and architecture artifacts make up about 90 percent of both assemblages (table 8.1). Obvious construction and destruction deposits were
excluded from the data base used for this study. Therefore, the higher percentage of the architecture group in the brothel is a reflection not of building activities but of different consumption patterns.

The kitchen group accounts for a higher percentage of the working-
class assemblage compared to the brothel, which may reflect the importance of providing sustenance for a family household. While plate and bowl
ceramic indices from the assemblages overlap, cup-and-saucer indices for
the working-class assemblage are consistently higher (table 8.2). The higher
cup-and-saucer indices for the working-class assemblage may reflect families' display of status through use of more expensive tewares. However,
both brothel and working-class indices are relatively low, a reflection of
the limited means of working-class people (Cheek et al. 1991, 47).

Minor differences exist in the relative proportions and composition of
the personal and clothing groups. (The only sewing tool is in the working-
class assemblage, and the only bead is in the prostitute assemblage.) Differences in the personal, tobacco, and activities groups' percentages are
worth examining, however. Relatively small differences in percentages and
composition in these groups may reflect important differences in household consumption patterns.

Table 8.2 Ceramic Indices by Period and Household Type

Period/Household	Cup and Saucer[1]	Plates	Bowls	Mean Index
Early Working Class	2.15	1.54	1.89	1.80
Early Prostitute	1.89	1.72	2.31	1.87
Late Working Class	1.37	1.52	1.26	1.44
Late Prostitute	1.91	1.40	1.44	1.51

[1]Indices for the early-period households are based on Miller (1991); indices for the
late-period households are from Henry (1987).

Although the percentages of the personal group are close, the composition of the group is different. The brothel assemblage includes mirror fragments, slate pencils, and hair combs. The working-class assemblage includes these types of artifacts as well as jewelry. There is a higher percentage of mirror fragments in the prostitute assemblage but a lower percentage of hair combs. The differences are small, suggesting that the prostitutes' personal effects were not much different from those of working-class women.

The activities group includes toys, tools, hardware, flowerpots, and lamp glass. Over 80 percent of the artifacts in the activities group for both working-class and brothel assemblages is lighting glass. However, there are other interesting differences in the composition of the activities group by household type. The working-class assemblage also includes toys (marbles and a toy dish), hardware, and tools (hammers), probably reflecting children and laborers in residence. The brothel assemblage includes a marble, hardware fragments, and flowerpot sherds.

The tobacco group is represented primarily by pipe stems and bowls. The higher frequency of pipes in the brothel assemblage is probably related to the frequency of visiting men, although the resident prostitutes may have smoked as well (see Cook 1989, 224).

Evidence of neighborhood foodways is reflected in the faunal and floral remains recovered during excavation. Pork is well represented, but there are only three elements of beef in the early working-class assemblage. Rabbit, duck, fish, and opossum are also represented. The early prostitute assemblage has a lower frequency of pork bones and four elements of beef. Chicken, pigeon, and fish are also represented. Neither assemblage includes many expensive cuts, such as steaks or roasts (Cheek et al. 1991, 53–54). Overall, the two assemblages are similar and are consistent with assemblages recovered from other working-class sites in the East (Holt, pers. com. 1991).

Household composition and related consumer patterns are probably responsible for the differences in the assemblages: family groups and boarders of both sexes and a range of ages acquired more food storage, preparation, and serving vessels, more tools, and more toys. Single women living and working together apparently did not enjoy a lavish lifestyle, but lived much as their neighbors did.

Hooker's Division, 1890–1920

While the material culture of working-class households changed only slightly, changes in the material life of prostitutes at the turn of the century were pronounced. These changes were probably related to increased purchasing power in the brothel households as the business of prostitution became more lucrative. The archaeological assemblage of the late brothel household is distinctly different from the late working-class household.

The relative percentages of architecture and kitchen groups from the early period are essentially the same in the later period (table 8.1). Mean ceramic indices for both late working-class and brothel assemblages are lower than the indices from the earlier period, and the cup-and-saucer index for the working-class assemblage is lower than the brothel index (table 8.2). The low mean indices, however, suggest little difference in socioeconomic status: both indices are within the range found for other working-class households in the East (Cheek et al. 1991, 46–48, table 11).

The clothing group percentage for the late working-class assemblage is slightly higher than in the earlier period. The late brothel assemblage evidences a greater increase, however. In both early-period assemblages, 90 percent of the clothing group is buttons. In the later period, a wider variety of artifacts is represented, including other fasteners, beads, shoe parts, and sewing tools (represented in both the working-class and brothel assemblages). The most important difference between the two late assemblages is in the types of buttons: the working-class assemblage is made up of simple white porcelain buttons of the kind used on undergarments and plain clothing. The brothel assemblage, however, also includes fancy black-glass buttons, used on dressy outer clothing. Such buttons are probably evidence of prostitutes' "putting on style," the distinctive and flamboyant dress style affected by working-class young women at the turn of the century (Peiss 1986, 66). Based on the archaeological data, prostitutes apparently had the income to dress in the style to which working-class young women aspired (Seifert 1991, 99, 104).

Through time the personal group percentage increases for the brothel assemblages and decreases slightly for the working-class assemblages. In the later period, the working-class assemblage has more pencils and coins, while the brothel assemblage includes more mirror fragments, jewelry parts, and hair combs, suggesting greater expenditures by the prostitutes on personal adornment. Pharmaceutical and cosmetic bottles are not included in the personal group in the version of artifact pattern analysis used in this study. However, there are some interesting differences in the kinds of such artifacts in each assemblage. The working-class assemblage includes a Fletcher's Castoria bottle and a perfume bottle stopper. The brothel assemblage includes Putnam's White Satin Bouquet, Chesebrough Mfg. Co. Vaseline, Mrs. Winslow's Soothing Syrup, Bromo Seltzer, and

Valentine's Meat Juice, which has been identified as a cure for "social diseases" (Herskovitz 1978, 16).

The tobacco group percentage declines for both working-class and brothel assemblages in the later period, although the brothel percentage is still higher. The decline in both assemblages may be related to an increase in cigarette smoking (replacing pipe smoking) by the early twentieth century (Peiss 1986, 99; Cook 1989, 224).

A dramatic change is seen in the activities group: the percentage of the group declines in the late working-class as compared to the early working-class assemblage but increases from about 3 percent to 13 percent from the early to late brothel assemblage. The composition of the late assemblages is similar to the composition of the activities group in the earlier period: both include toys (though there are more in the working-class assemblage), and there are more tools and more hardware in the working-class assemblage and more flowerpots in the brothel assemblage. While 80 percent of the late working-class activities group is made up of lighting glass, over 90 percent of the late brothel activities group is lighting glass. The high frequency of lighting glass may be related to the brothel as workplace where most of the workday was after dark (Seifert 1991, 101).

Another distinctive aspect of the late brothel assemblage is the high frequency of expensive meat cuts represented in the butchered bones recovered. No beef elements were recovered from the late working-class assemblage, but pork continues to be well represented. Duck and fish are included as in the earlier period, and pigeon is added to the late working-class assemblage. Beef, pork, sheep, rabbit, chicken, duck, turkey, and fish are represented in the late brothel assemblage. While the early brothel, early working-class, and late-working class assemblages exhibit frequencies of steaks and roasts within the expected range for households with limited means, the late brothel had startlingly high frequencies of these expensive cuts (Holt, pers. com. 1991). The majority of these bones were from steaks, which are considered individual portions. The high frequency of steak bones suggests eating well and eating alone. The bones may represent individual meals served to clients (see Rosen 1982, 94–95) or meals eaten by resident prostitutes (Cheek et al. 1991, 55).

The evidence for good food, along with the archaeological evidence for personal adornment, suggests that late-period prostitutes enjoyed greater material comforts than their working-class neighbors. A major inducement to enter the profession (cited by social workers and prostitutes alike) was the high wages and amenities of middle-class life available to prostitutes (Rosen 1982, 145–47; Seifert 1991, 87). While higher wages were also a factor during the period from 1870 to 1890, practicing prostitution, at least in Hooker's Division, does not appear to have translated into material conditions that were dramatically different from those of their working-class neighbors. Differences in the social climate and business of prostitution may account for the differences observed in the archaeological record of the later period.

Daily Life for the Working Women of Hooker's Division, 1870–1920

Complementary data from historical sources and archaeological excavations provide the basis for a better understanding of life in Hooker's Division during the late nineteenth century and early twentieth century. Census records and historic maps indicate that the 1870-90 neighborhood, which included industrial facilities, commercial establishments, and residences occupied by working-class households and brothels, changed in the early 1890s to a red-light district. Archaeological evidence demonstrates that both working-class households and brothels were households of limited means during the earlier period. Because of low wages for unskilled and semiskilled workers, such as those living in Hooker's Division, families were always struggling to make ends meet. Women in working-class households contributed to the household income by taking in piecework, laundry, and boarders. Adolescents worked in unskilled jobs, contributing most (for boys) or all (for girls) of their income to the household.

Household furnishings were limited, and families moved frequently— often when the rent was due (Stansell 1986, 55, 247n). Homemakers were taxed with the physical hardships of cooking, washing, and cleaning for their families and boarders. Daily tasks included hauling water for cooking and laundry and fuel for stoves and lamps. Nearly all clothing was sewn by hand. Working-class households usually included boarders as well as family members. Although boarders provided extra household income, they also meant extra work for the homemaker. Modest consumer purchases were a function of low income. The working-class households of Hooker's Division reflect the limited means of the residents: little was spent on ceramics (mean ceramic indices are low), and few expensive meat cuts were purchased (few steak and roast bones).

Women living in early-period brothels in the neighborhood lived very much like their neighbors in terms of material possessions. In fact, without documentary evidence, the brothels could not have been identified on the basis of archeological evidence: the content of the assemblage is different, but the socioeconomic status the assemblage reflects is essentially working-class. Although madams such as Mrs. Starr may have enjoyed the profits of the business, the prostitutes in Hooker's Division in the 1870s and 1880s were apparently women of limited means like their neighbors in working-class households.

The neighborhood changed to a red-light district during the 1890s, and the business of prostitution changed as well. The madam-owned brothels were replaced by capitalist business with nonresident owners, madam-managers, and employee-prostitutes. The material culture of the brothel changed as well. Based on the archaeological evidence, brothel residents enjoyed some material comforts that their working-class neighbors did not. Expensive meat cuts and buttons from fancy clothes suggest that prostitutes ate better and dressed better than their neighbors. The few working-class households remaining in the neighborhood at the turn of the century were households of limited means, and the residents may not have been able to afford to live in a more desirable neighborhood. On the basis of the archaeological evidence alone, the brothels were clearly unusual households: the meat cuts represented suggest expenditures more like middle-class households, but the ceramic indices are comparable to working-class households. With the aid of documentary sources, a sharper picture emerges of life in the best-known red-light district of Washington, D.C.

Nineteenth-century prostitution was largely an institution of working-class young women selling sexual services to middle- and upper-class men. Women resorted to prostitution particularly in response to loss of a male wage earner to avoid destitution without seeking charity. Prostitution might be occasional (when need was urgent) or practiced for a period during young adulthood by women living away from family (either by choice or necessity) before marrying. Most prostitutes practiced for a few years, rarely past their mid-twenties. Contemporary reformers argued that this short time was a period of precipitous decline from loss of virtue to utter ruin and death. However, other documents indicate that some women left prostitution and married. Working-class people accepted a flexible definition of virtue, unlike the middle-class policymakers and reformers (see Rosen 1982, 70; Stansell 1986, 179–80; Hobson 1990, 106).

The census data from 1870 and 1880 for Hooker's Division indicate that prostitutes lived in the neighborhood among practitioners of other professions, sometimes in the same houses. The segregation and protection of the brothel was less important than later, when pressure from reformers and police harassment accelerated. While these prostitutes may have been able to earn more than the seamstresses, laundresses, and servants in the neighborhood, there are several factors to consider in understanding the similarity of material culture. Several members of the family were contributing to the income of a working-class household; some of the other women in the neighborhood may also have been practicing occasional prostitution to supplement earnings from sewing or laundry; and all residents of this neighborhood were probably included in the growing class of the working poor whose material possessions were few (see Stansell 1986, 46–50).

By the turn of the century, prostitution had changed in organization, like most other trades, from the independent practitioner or small shop (like the family brothel) to a capitalist business (Rosen 1982, 70–71; Hobson 1990, 103). Increasing pressure from the antiprostitution movement may have made the shelter of the brothel more attractive. The brothels in Hooker's Division were managed by women but were probably owned by businessmen who realized much of the profit (U.S. Senate 1913, 28–29; Seifert 1991, 89; cf. Shaw 1951,.3). Mrs. Starr's family business was replaced by the organization of corporate owners that characterized the profession of George Bernard Shaw's Mrs. Warren.[6] The change in the organization of the profession may have cost practitioners some independence, but it offered greater material comfort for those living in brothels. The archaeological evidence suggests that the prostitutes in Hooker's Division enjoyed a higher standard of living by the turn of the century (and the houses may have served a wealthier clientele).

The results of the archaeological investigations in Hooker's Division demonstrate the utility of the household type as analytical unit and the neighborhood as context. In urban settings where it is not possible to correlate individuals or families with specific archaeological deposits, the household type is an appropriate unit of comparison. The working-class households and brothel households reflect the differences in material culture between households of different composition and function. Understanding the neighborhood is critical to understanding the daily life and social community of working-class women. The privacy and separate sphere of the home cultivated by middle-class women of comfortable means was not the experience of working-class women, who spent as much of their day in the street as in the home, struggling to make ends meet. Such differences in the patterns of everyday life are important to understanding the archaeological record: the use history of consumer goods recovered from middle-class deposits is likely to be simpler than the use history of the same kinds of goods in deposits in working-class neighborhoods. The simple model of purchase, use, and discard is appropriate for the middle-class consumer item. However, the use history of consumer items associated with a working-class household may also include exchange through barter, pawn, and secondhand purchase and use by more than one household before discard and deposition in an archaeological context. Analyzing data by household type (based on aggregate data) within the context of neighborhood provides more reliable results in situations where the acquisition of consumer goods is a complex process.

The historical and archaeological investigations of Hooker's Division have contributed to understanding the material conditions of those whose lives are documented in the census records, city directories, and police records and in the debris cleared from their tables and swept from their floors and thrown on the ash heap. The remains recovered through archaeological excavations reflect economic decisions that were made in the face of limited options by all of the women of Hooker's Division—seamstresses, laundresses, and servants, as well as the ruined girls and fallen women and the practitioners of Mrs. Starr's profession.

Acknowledgments

I am grateful to James O. Hall, who generously shared his information on Civil War Hooker's Division and the careers of Mrs. Starr and her daughters Ellen and Mary Jane. Mr. Hall sent me copies of documents and provided information on Mrs. Starr's purchase of the property at 62 Ohio Avenue; my research in the tax records confirmed her ownership of the property from 1862 to 1868.

Cheryl Holt shared her knowledge of meat consumption patterns in Hooker's Division in contrast to patterns she has observed in other Eastern urban contexts. Elizabeth Scott offered many useful comments on the early draft of this chapter; I am grateful to her also for her willingness to organize and introduce this collection.

The archaeological data on which this chapter is based are from the investigations at the Federal Triangle, which were undertaken in accordance with the National Historic Preservation Act of 1966. The project was sponsored by the Pennsylvania Avenue Development Corporation and conducted by John Milner Associates, Inc., in cooperation with TAMS Consultants, Inc., and in consultation with the District of Columbia Historic Preservation Office and the Advisory Council on Historic Preservation. The graphics used in this paper were prepared by Joe McCarthy and Sarah Ruch; Dana Heck assisted in the data retrieval; and support for the preparation of the manuscript was provided by John Milner Associates, Inc.

Notes

1. Historical sources provide conflicting information concerning the location of No. 62 Ohio Avenue and the location and address of the house occupied by the younger Ellen Starr. However, most of the information supports the interpretation that No. 62 Ohio Avenue was the second lot from the corner of Ohio Avenue and 13½ Street in Northwest Washington, D.C.

Various records document Mrs. Starr's ownership of lot B, subdivision of lot 1, square 257, in Washington, D.C., during the 1860s. Lot 1 of square 257 was subdivided in 1858 by Eugene Schwingerhamer, and lot B was the second lot from the corner of Ohio Avenue and 13½ Street West (Faehtz and Pratt 1874). Ellen Starr bought lot B on 18 August 1862 (Hall, pers. com. 1989). She began paying tax on the improved property in 1862. From 1864 through 1866, taxes were paid by Thomas D. Donn, in trust for Mary Jane Tauch, who may be Mrs. Starr's daughter Mary Jane Treakle. In 1867 and 1868, Ellen Starr is again listed in the tax books as the owner, but she sold the property in 1868. Between 1864 and 1867, Mrs. Starr was also paying taxes on several other properties in the city (District of Columbia Tax Books 1862–69).

The evidence suggests that the address in the provost marshal's list for the house run by Mollie Turner (62 C Street) is incorrect. The entry for Mollie Turner is probably the house at 62 Ohio Avenue, on square 257, facing Ohio Avenue, not C Street. The address may have been mistakenly recorded as C Street because of the way Ohio Avenue, a diagonal street, crosses C Street (which runs east-west) at 13½ street (which runs north-south). The 1864 city directory lists Mrs. Mary Turner at 62 Ohio Avenue (Boyd 1864). A contemporary newspaper account places the house of Mollie Turner, where Ellen Starr (identified as Ella Turner, Booth's mistress) lived, at the corner of 13th Street and Ohio Avenue (*Evening Star* 17 April 1865, 2). The 1865 city directory includes a street directory that indicates that 62 Ohio Avenue is at the corner of Ohio Avenue and 13½ Street (Boyd 1865); however, in the 1860s, the corner lot (lot A) may have been vacant, so No. 62 was the house closest to the corner.

The house numbering system in Washington, D.C., changed after the Civil War. The new address of the house at 62 Ohio Avenue was 1353 Ohio Avenue, N.W.

2. The home as workplace is discussed in another study based on data from Hooker's Division (Seifert 1991). Many working-class women contributed to the household income by taking in piecework and providing services for boarders.

3. Archaeological deposits were dated by using stratigraphic position, type of deposit (such as fill, construction or destruction debris, or midden), and datable artifacts in conjunction with documentary records such as building permits, Baist (1903) and Hopkins (1887) real estate maps, Sanborn (1888, 1903) fire insurance maps, city directories, and general assessments, which document building construction and modifications. Census records and city directories were used to correlate specific, dated deposits with household occupants. The deposits from the lot at

62 Ohio Avenue/1353 Ohio Avenue, which was owned by Mrs. Starr in the 1860s and occupied by Ellen Starr in 1865, were included in the early prostitute assemblage. However, based on datable artifacts, these deposits are probably related to the brothel household listed in the 1880 census (USBC 1880). No deposits that could be clearly associated with the 1865 occupation of the lot were identified.

4. Pattern analysis is designed to identify patterns in the percentages of the artifact groups that reflect patterns in cultural and historical processes (South 1988, 27). The artifact pattern analysis used in this study is based on Garrow's (1982) version, used in his analysis of the archaeological investigations at the Washington, D.C., Civic Center. This version was selected because it has been used in the analysis of several Washington, D.C., sites, including Howard Road (Louis Berger & Associates 1985, 1986) and N Street/Quander Place (Cheek et al. 1983). The following functional groups are used in this analysis: architecture, kitchen, furniture, clothing, personal, tobacco, and activities. Artifacts of several materials and types are included in each group. For example, the kitchen group includes ceramic and glass tableware, glass bottles, and metal utensils. The clothing group includes clothing parts as well as sewing tools. The personal group includes coins, keys, mirrors, and jewelry. The activities group includes tools associated with traditionally male activities, such as hammers and hardware, as well as lamp glass, toys, and marbles. Note that in this version of pattern analysis lighting glass is included with the activities group and pharmaceutical bottles are included with the kitchen group. Artifact pattern analysis is most useful for broad comparisons. Careful analysis of specific artifacts is necessary to evaluate the differences between assemblages. For example, artifacts representing men's work are primarily placed in the activities group, while those reflecting women's work are placed in the kitchen, clothing, personal, and activities groups.

5. Consumer goods refer to the material items purchased for use by the occupants of the household. In the context of late nineteenth-century Washington, D.C., most of the goods consumed in the household were market purchases; an increasing amount of such goods were mass-produced. Ceramic tablewares and meat cuts are generally thought to be the most sensitive of the common consumer purchases reflected in the archaeological record (Cheek et al. 1991, 5). Selection of housing is a consumer decision, but architectural artifacts are not useful in addressing consumer behavior, although selection of a neighborhood is important in understanding the socioeconomic status of a household (Cheek and Seifert 1994, 3). Since household purchases vary according to several factors, including market access, availability, household income, social status, and ethnicity, analysis of archaeological remains of consumer goods indicates consumer behavior. Evidence from the archaeological investigations in Hooker's Division shed light on differences in consumer behavior among the four household types considered in this paper.

6. Mrs. Warren is partner and managing director of several high-class brothels on the Continent in Shaw's 1894 play about the business of prostitution. During the course of the play, Mrs. Warren's daughter learns of the source of her

mother's wealth from her business partner. In response to her daughter's disapproval, Mrs. Warren argues that hers is the only business in which she could accumulate capital; therefore, she chose prostitution—rather than earn nine shillings a day in a mill and die of lead poisoning, as her sister did (Shaw 1951, 66–67, 82–83). In his preface, Shaw describes his objectives in writing the play:

> Mrs. Warren's profession was written in 1894 to draw attention to the truth that prostitution is caused, not by female depravity and male licentiousness, but simply by underpaying, undervaluing, and overworking women so shamefully that the poorest of them are forced to resort to prostitution to keep body and soul together. Indeed, all attractive unpropertied women lose money by being infallibly virtuous or contracting marriages that are not more or less venal. If on the large social scale we get what we call vice instead of what we call virtue it is simply because we are paying more for it. No normal woman would be a professional prostitute if she could better herself by being respectable, nor marry for money if she could afford to marry for love.
>
> Also I desire to expose the fact that prostitution is not only carried on without organization by individual enterprise in the lodgings of solitary women, each her own mistress as well as every customer's mistress, but organized and exploited as a big international commerce for the profit of capitalists like any other commerce, and very lucrative to great city estates, including Church estates, through the rents of the houses in which it is practiced. (3)

References

Baist, G. W.

1903   *Baist's Real Estate Atlas of Surveys of Washington, District of Columbia*. Philadelphia: G. W. Baist. Map on file, Geography and Map Division, Library of Congress, Washington, D.C.

Boyd, Andrew

1864   *Boyd's Directory of Washington and Georgetown*. Washington, D.C.: Boyd's Directory Company. Washingtoniana Room, Martin Luther King, Jr., Branch, District of Columbia Public Library, Washington, D.C.

1865   *Boyd's Directory of Washington and Georgetown*. Washington, D.C.: Boyd's Directory Company. Washingtoniana Room, Martin Luther King, Jr., Branch, District of Columbia Public Library, Washington, D.C.

Cheek, Charles D., Amy Friedlander, Cheryl A. Holt, Charles H. LeeDecker, and Teresa E. Ossim

1983   Archaeological Investigations at the National Photographic Interpretation Center Addition, Washington, D.C., Navy Yard Annex. Prepared for Soils Systems, Inc., Alexandria, Virginia. Photocopy.

Cheek, Charles D., and Donna J. Seifert

1994   Neighborhoods and Household Types in Nineteenth-Century Washington, D.C.: Fannie Hill and Mary McNamara in Hooker's Division. In *The*

Historical Archaeology of the Chesapeake, ed. Paul A. Shackel and Barbara J. Little, 267–81. Washington, D.C.: Smithsonian Institution Press.

Cheek, Charles D., Donna J. Seifert, Patrick W. O'Bannon, Cheryl A. Holt, B. R. Roulette, Jr., Joseph Balicki, Glenn Ceponis, and Dana B. Heck

1991   Phase II and Phase III Archeological Investigations at the Site of the Proposed International Cultural and Trade Center/Federal Office Building Complex, Federal Triangle, Washington, D.C. Prepared by John Milner Associates, Inc., West Chester, Pennsylvania. Photocopy.

Commissioners of the District of Columbia

1914   *Acts of Congress Affecting the District of Columbia*. Washington, D.C.: Commissioners of the District of Columbia.

Cook, Lauren J.

1989   Descriptive Analysis of Tobacco-Related Material from Boott Mill Boardinghouses. In *The Boarding House System as a Way of Life*, ed. Mary C. Beaudry and Stephen A. Mrozowski, 187–208. Interdisciplinary Investigations of the Boott Mills, Lowell, Massachusetts, 3. Cultural Resources Management Studies, 21. Boston, Mass.: Division of Cultural Resources, North Atlantic Regional Office, National Park Service, U.S. Department of the Interior.

District of Columbia Tax Books

1862–69 District of Columbia Tax Books. On file, National Archives and Records Administration, Washington, D.C.

Evening Star [Washington]

1865   *Evening Star*, 17 April 1865, page 2, col. 2.

Faehtz, E. F. M., and F. W. Pratt

1874   *Real Estate Directory of the City of Washington, D.C.* Washington, D.C.: E. F. M. Faehtz and F. W. Pratt. Map on file, Geography and Map Division, Library of Congress, Washington, D.C.

Garrow, Patrick H., ed.

1982   Archeological Investigations at the Washington, D.C., Civic Center. Prepared by Soil Systems, Inc., Marrietta, Georgia. Photocopy.

Green, Constance McLaughlin

1962   *Washington: A History of the Capital, 1800–1950*. 2 vols. Princeton, N.J.: Princeton University Press.

Hall, James O.

1989   Letter to Donna J. Seifert, 27 December 1989.

Henry, Susan L.

1987   Factors Influencing Consumer Behavior in Turn-of-the-Century Phoenix, Arizona. In *Consumer Choice in Historical Archaeology*, ed. Suzanne M. Spencer-Wood, 359–82. New York: Plenum Press.

Herskovitz, Robert M.

1978   *Fort Bowie Material Culture*. Anthropological Papers of the University of Arizona, 31. Tucson: University of Arizona Press.

Hobson, Barbara Meil
1990   *Uneasy Virtue: The Politics of Prostitution and the American Reform Tradition.*
        Reprint, with new preface. Chicago: University of Chicago Press.
Holt, Cheryl
1991   Telephone conversation with Donna J. Seifert, January 1991.
Hopkins, G. M.
1887   *A Complete Set of Surveys and Plats of Properties in the City of Washington,*
        District of Columbia. Philadelphia: G. M. Hopkins. Map on file, Martin
        Luther King Memorial Library, Washington, D.C.
Louis Berger and Associates, Inc.
1985   Archaeological, Architectural, and Historical Investigations at the How-
        ard Road Historic District, Washington, D.C. Vol. 2, Technical Ap-
        pendices. Prepared by the Cultural Resources Group, Louis Berger and
        Associates, Inc., East Orange, New Jersey. Photocopy.
1986   Archaeological, Architectural, and Historical Investigations at the How-
        ard Road Historic District, Washington, D.C. Vol. 1, Final Report. Pre-
        pared by the Cultural Resources Group, Louis Berger and Associates,
        Inc., East Orange, New Jersey. Photocopy.
Miller, George L.
1980   Classification and Economic Scaling in Historical Archaeology. *Historical*
        Archaeology 14: 1–40.
1991   A Revised Set of CC Index Values for Classification and Economic Scaling
        of English Ceramics from 1787 to 1880. *Historical Archaeology* 25 (1): 1–25.
National Archives and Records Administration
1865   Deposition of Nellie Starr, United States vs. J. Wilkes Booth, Preliminary
        Examination. Investigation and Trial Papers Relating to the Assassination
        of President Lincoln, M-599, reel 6, frame 0258. National Archives and
        Records Administration, Washington, D.C.
Peiss, Kathy
1986   *Cheap Amusements: Working Women and Leisure in Turn-of-the-Century*
        New York. Philadelphia: Temple University Press.
Provost Marshal
1865   List of Bawdy Houses in Washington, D.C. Provost Marshal's Depart-
        ment of Washington, 22nd Army Corps, 1864–1865. Vol. 289, RG 393.
        National Archives and Records Administration, Washington, D.C.
Rosen, Ruth
1982   *The Lost Sisterhood: Prostitution in America, 1900–1918.* Baltimore, Md.:
        Johns Hopkins University Press.
Sanborn Map Company
1888   *Fire Insurance Map of Washington, D.C.* New York: Sanborn Map Com-
        pany. Map on file, Geography and Map Division, Library of Congress,
        Washington, D.C.
1903   *Fire Insurance Map of Washington, D.C.* New York: Sanborn Map Com-

pany. Map on file, Geography and Map Division, Library of Congress, Washington, D.C.

Sanger, William W., M.D.

1939   *The History of Prostitution, Its Extent, Causes, and Effects Throughout the World*. Reprint of 1858 edition. New York: Eugenics Publishing Company.

Seifert, Donna J.

1991   Within Sight of the White House: The Archaeology of Working Women. *Historical Archaeology* 25 (4): 82–108.

Shaw, George Bernard

1951   Mrs. Warren's Profession. In *Seven Plays by Bernard Shaw*, 1–122. Originally published 1898. New York: Dodd, Mead & Company.

South, Stanley

1988   Whither Pattern. *Historical Archaeology* 22 (1) 25–28.

1977   *Method and Theory in Historical Archeology*. New York: Academic Press.

Stansell, Christine

1986   *City of Women: Sex and Class in New York, 1789–1860*. New York: Alfred A. Knopf.

Tidwell, William A.

1988   *Come Retribution: The Confederate Secret Service and the Assassination of Lincoln*. With James O. Hall and David Winfred Gaddy. Jackson: University Press of Mississippi.

United States Bureau of the Census (USBC)

1870   Manuscript Population Census of the United States, 1870. Washington, D.C.: U.S. Government Printing Office. Microfilm copy on file, National Archives and Records Administration, Washington, D.C.

1880   Manuscript Population Census of the United States, 1880. Washington, D.C.: U.S. Government Printing Office. Microfilm copy on file, National Archives and Records Administration, Washington, D.C.

1900   Manuscript Population Census of the United States, 1900. Washington, D.C.: U.S. Government Printing Office. Microfilm copy on file, National Archives and Records Administration, Washington, D.C.

1910   Manuscript Population Census of the United States, 1910. Washington, D.C.: U.S. Government Printing Office. Microfilm copy on file, National Archives and Records Administration, Washington, D.C.

United States Geological Survey (USGS)

1983   *Washington, District of Columbia-Maryland-Virginia, Quadrangle Map*. 7.5 minute series. Reston, Va.: U.S. Geological Survey.

U.S. Senate

1913   *Abatement of Houses of Ill Fame: Hearings Before a Subcommittee of the Committee of the District of Columbia, United States Senate 62nd Congress, Third Session on S. 5861*. Washington, D.C.: U. S. Government Printing Office.

Weiner, Lynn Y.

1985   *From Working Girl to Working Mother: The Female Labor Force in the United States, 1820–1980*. Chapel Hill: University of North Carolina Press.

Within Sight of the White House

[1895]   *Within Sight of the White House*. Unidentified newspaper clipping on file, Geography and Map Division, Library of Congress, Washington, D.C.

9

Diversity and Nineteenth-Century Domestic Reform

Relationships Among Classes and Ethnic Groups

Suzanne M. Spencer-Wood

This chapter grew out of a search to develop a feminist theoretical approach in historical archaeology. The search began with a critique of the projection of Western gender stereotypes onto other cultures in Eggan's (1950) classic historical ethnography of western pueblos. A critical reading revealed evidence of the actual complexity in Pueblo gender roles and relationships, contrary to Eggan's conclusions (Spencer-Wood 1971). Subsequently, some of the early feminist anthropology oversimplified women's roles by projecting the Victorian dichotomy between domestic women and public men as a cross-cultural universal (Rosaldo 1980; cf. Rosaldo and Lamphere 1974). Over the years a wide variety of sources in feminist theory (e.g., de Lauretis 1986; Mascia-Lees et al. 1989), science, (e.g., Reed 1978; Harding 1986) anthropology (e.g., Reiter 1975; Moore 1988), archaeology (e.g., Conkey and Spector 1984; Gero and Conkey 1991; Tanner and Zihlman 1976; Wylie 1991), and history (e.g., Hartman and Banner 1974; Kelly 1984; Scott 1988) contributed to development of a feminist approach in historical archaeology (Spencer-Wood 1991a, 1991d, 1992a, 1992d).

A case study in which women created major culture change using material culture would help correct the normative androcentric portrayal of men as the important shapers of history and material culture. However, at the time, most histories, archaeologies, and cultural models either were ungendered or assumed gender stereotypes. Victorian women usually were portrayed as house-bound, except for factory workers. Starting in the mid-1960s, feminist historians critiqued and corrected male-focused, often ungendered, histories with previously overlooked evidence of women's important domestic and public roles (e.g., Carroll 1976; Scott 1971). Feminists revealed the significant role of housewives and others who did not fit Victorian gender stereotypes (including feminists), a wide variety of working women, and women's organizations (including reformers) (e.g., Gordon 1976; Kraditor 1965; Rossi 1973; Strasser 1982; Wertheimer 1977). However, feminist histories seldom mentioned material culture. I sought a research topic for which archaeological data would not simply illustrate history but could contribute information not usually available in historic documents.

Research into domestic reform movements provides an example of the utility of a feminist theoretical approach in historical archaeology. By bringing to light previously overlooked information about the complexity of historic gender systems, this research critiques and corrects (1) ungendered constructions of the past, (2) stereotypical constructions of gender (e.g., Deetz 1977; South 1977), and (3) constructions of historic women as passive victims of male-controlled cultural processes (McGaw 1989; Spencer-Wood 1987, 1989, 1991c). Feminists, rather than simply adding gender to male-focused histories, have critiqued them for considering women's organizations private or domestic and historically insignificant (Scott 1990, 1991). For traditional historians, domestic reform was of such little note that it was usually overlooked entirely. Feminist histories demonstrated the importance of women's organizations in advancing women's education, suffrage, upward mobility, the development of community, and sisterhood (e.g., Berg 1978; Cott 1977; Hewitt 1990).

First and foremost, a feminist approach to domestic reform fundamentally changes our understanding of the past by considering the historical significance of reform women's activities in both domestic and public spheres. Second, in contrast to essentialist constructions of universal womanhood, feminist historians revealed that the reformers diverged from the Victorian ideal of passive, subordinate domesticity. Most were middle- and upper-class women who had time for reform because they had domestic servants. In fact, while this research is concerned with the re-forming of the domestic sphere, domestic reform was originally the name for the movement to professionalize domestic service into standardized wage labor with specified hours, conditions of work, and time off (Women's Educational and Industrial Union [WEIU] n.d.a, 1898, 1903). The large number of women's public organizations involved in a variety of reform programs obviates any argument that these reformers were just a few exceptions to the purported norm of house-bound Victorian women. Instead, feminists have shown that reformers were powerful social agents who used a variety of ideologies, strategies, and material culture to transform the U.S. gender system from the nineteenth century into the twentieth century (e.g., Hayden 1981; Spencer-Wood 1991c). Finally, such an approach builds on feminist histories to address the dialogue among people of different classes, ethnic groups, religions, and ideologies participating in domestic reform. Rather than viewing women in binary opposition to men, it is concerned with the ways that women reformers cooperated and negotiated with diverse men and women to physically contest male dominance in public landscapes. Without feminist theory and research questions, the evidence of large-scale changes in U.S. culture created by reform women never would have been found, nor would their significance have been understood.

The present study focuses on relationships among diverse women and their families participating in reform programs. Recently, feminist historians have begun to research African American women's organizations (e.g., Hine 1990; Shaw 1991; Scott 1991) and Latin American women's societies (Hewitt 1990), including some class relationships within these organizations. Some research also has been conducted on class relationships within middle-class Anglo women's organizations (e.g., Deutsch 1990; Hayden 1981; Scott 1991). In this chapter, a feminist approach is extended beyond gender to other social divisions, such as classes, religious groups, and ethnic groups. The main question is how individuals in oppressed social groups —including women, working classes, and minorities—acted as powerful social agents to shape their own lives and, through relationships, the lives of individuals in dominant social groups (Spencer-Wood 1992c). This approach rejects the dominant ideology thesis that the working class and minorities were passive recipients of middle- and upper-class reformers' programs and ideologies (e.g., Ginzberg 1990). It builds instead on historians' examples of ways in which the working class contested reformers' actions (e.g., Hayden 1981, 126) and ways in which ethnic groups, such as Italian women, resisted reformers' suggestions (Cohen 1980). Further, I am concerned with the ways in which women, and their families, of different

classes, religions, and ethnic groups used both voices and actions to nego-
tiate for reform programs that they felt would most improve their lives
(Spencer-Wood 1991b, 1992b).

This research also demonstrates that neither Victorian women, ethnic
groups, religious groups, nor social classes were monolithic. Instead, these
social categories crosscut each other. Therefore, each group is a flexible
polythetic (Clarke 1978, 36–7) set of diverse individuals whose wide variety
of experiences and behaviors partially overlap (Kosko 1993). That is, while
each individual's experiences are unique in the details, some significant
fundamental similarities are shared with some but not necessarily all other
members of the group. For instance, oppression and devaluation each takes
many different forms. Similarly, a variety of actions were taken to alleviate
oppressive conditions. This chapter gives a few examples of actions taken
by oppressed groups to empower themselves, and of the responses of the
dominant reformers, most of whom sought to assist the oppressed.

Domestic Reform Movements

The term *domestic reform* refers here to a variety of activities by a large
number of interrelated but diverse nineteenth-century social movements
that shared the goals of improving the status and conditions of women's
lives by expanding women's roles, economic independence, and power in
both the public and private spheres. This expansion was accomplished by
professionalizing women's domestic roles in the home and in the public
sphere. Instead of directly confronting male dominance in the public sphere
through the suffragists' equality argument, domestic reformers changed
the meaning of the dominant cultural ideology. They transformed women's
domesticity from a perceived subordinate role into a gendered source of innately superior abilities that powerfully justified increasing women's roles
and power in both spheres. Most reformers argued that women should control their expanded domestic sphere as separate but equal to men's public
sphere (Spencer-Wood 1991c).

The reformers blurred and shifted the boundary between domestic and
public by combining the separate spheres in two ways. First, they argued
that women's domestic labor could become equal in status to men's professions by applying public sphere scientific methods and technology to
housework. Innovative and ordinary household furniture and equipment
was arranged for the most efficient performance of tasks. Second, the reformers successfully argued for female dominance in a number of public
professions by claiming that they were really part of women's domestic

sphere, thus making it acceptable for women to work in public. The domestic sphere was expanded to include many areas of the public sphere, which were thus feminized. Starting in the early nineteenth century, women's supposedly innately superior domestic abilities were used successfully to transform a number of men's professions into women's professions, including primary-school teacher, sales clerk, typist, and overseer of girls and women in charitable homes, industrial schools, reformatories, and prisons. Further, domestic tasks were transformed into new public female professions, such as nurse, nutritionist, infant educator, playground supervisor, and social worker. While some women's occupations were overseen by men, reformers created and controlled women's professions at their public cooperative housekeeping enterprises. The transformation of housework from a craft into industrial professions was symbolized by special tools, equipment, methods, and training in special classes and schools. In these ways, reformers increased the number and variety of women's professions and institutions on public landscapes. Most fundamentally, domestic reformers believed that every aspect of social life had "domestic meaning" (Leach 1980, 209; Spencer-Wood 1991c). This belief redefined the "domestic sphere" as virtually unlimited, justifying the immense variety of women's domestic reform activities in both spheres. Due to space limitations, this chapter focuses on public reform institutions, although the adoption of domestic innovations did vary among classes and ethnic groups.

The reformers transformed the Cult of True Womanhood (Welter 1966) or Domesticity (Kraditor 1965), which glorified women's private roles, into ideologies and strategies of public domesticity, including cooperative housekeeping and municipal housekeeping. In cooperative housekeeping, domestic tasks that were individually performed in each household were socialized and recreated as organized group labor in public housekeeping enterprises and professions; this practice domesticated urban landscapes with female-dominated and -controlled public places. Public cooperative housekeeping enterprises included neighborhood cooperative kitchens or laundries, dining clubs, cooked-food delivery services, day nurseries, kindergartens, settlement houses, and working women's homes. Although Hayden (1981) called cooperative housekeeping movements "material feminism," I prefer to call these and a number of other reform movements *domestic reform* because many members did not view themselves as feminists and were initially antisuffrage. However, most of these women became prosuffrage around the turn of the century, at least partly as a result of their reform experiences.

In municipal housekeeping, women's values and roles as housekeepers, mothers, and guardians of morality were metaphorically extended from individual homes into the larger household of the community. Women applied their values to morally reform men's sinful public sphere, as they saw it, by campaigning to clean up the environment, including public water, sewers, food, air, streets, alleys, and tenement yards. Women's role in maintaining family health was extended to roles in promoting public health, including founding the field of public health nursing at settlements and creating some housekeeping cooperatives such as public baths, laundries, and kitchens (Beard 1915; Spencer-Wood 1992b). Reformers, as the moral mothers of society, also worked to protect women and children from economic and social exploitation by capitalists. Anne Scott (1991, 157) has noted that "standard histories of the age of reform" have not included municipal housekeeping. Yet these women's movements were important in transforming the U.S. gender system by increasing the number and variety of culturally accepted female public roles across the country. Domestic reformers were instrumental in gaining women's suffrage, by arguing that as public citizens women would bring their superior moral influence to government (Spencer-Wood 1991c).

Women's economic independence through work in the public sphere was supported by a number of alternative ideologies. The Cult of Real Womanhood advocated careful marriage, physical fitness, and training in the event a woman had to work (Cogan 1989). The antidomestic Cult of Single Blessedness argued that women should support themselves and not marry (Chambers-Schiller 1984). The Cult of Domesticity was also rejected by many working women and middle-class religious women who viewed the idleness of wealthy women as sinful and glorified work as the moral option (Preston 1987; Spencer-Wood 1989).

A wide variety of women's organizations have been classified as domestic reform groups because nineteenth-century women viewed these as organizations interrelated in ideology and practice (e.g., Beard 1915). Further, many domestic reform organizations cooperated with each other, and women often belonged to a number of different organizations and wrote journal articles, resulting in many shared ideas and strategies of reform (Spencer-Wood 1991c).

Historical Archaeology of Domestic Reform

This research on domestic reform was undertaken because it is particularly appropriate for a feminist approach to archaeological research. While some historians have analyzed how women and their housework were affected by men's architectural and technological innovations (e.g., Wright 1980; Cowan 1983; Stilgoe 1988), few took a feminist approach to analyze how women used material culture to create major cultural changes. A few feminist historians have discussed how women reformers ideally structured material culture and behavior in homes and cooperative housekeeping institutions (Cohen 1980; Hayden 1981; Strasser 1982). In a feminist materialist approach, material culture is actively shaped by women as well as men, and it in turn actively shapes cultural behaviors. This chapter is concerned with women's domestic reform movements as cultural contexts that gave new meanings to material culture in order to change gender ideology, roles, and relationships. Many reforms were symbolized by and implemented with innovative architectural designs and spatial arrangements of material culture, to be used by women and children. The cultural construction of gender was changed physically by reformers who created new female-dominated professions in female-controlled institutions on the public landscape (Spencer-Wood 1991b).

This chapter contributes to our understanding of domestic reform through the conjunctive analysis of historical documents, architecture, preserved material culture, and archaeological reports. Historical documents and photographs assist with the methodological problem of distinguishing which gender, class, religion, ethnic group, or age group usually used particular types of sites or artifacts. Critical historical research was undertaken to avoid overgeneralized assumptions of the kind traditionally made by prehistorians, such as universally identifying stone tools as male-related and pottery as female-related (critiqued by Conkey and Spector 1984). The feminist approach in this chapter involves not simply engendering historic material culture with idealistic stereotypes but rather applying a contextually interpretive approach that recognizes multiple uses and meanings of material culture (Beaudry et al. 1991; Hodder 1986; Spencer-Wood 1991b). Archaeological data may reveal the material culture actually used at a reform site, which is seldom recorded in documents about domestic reform institutions.

Historical documents about domestic reform mostly prescribe special innovative material culture, such as vacuum cleaners, dishwashers, scientific measuring equipment, or Froebelian kindergarten toys (fig. 9.3), and interior spatial designs to create the most efficient performance of tasks in private and public kitchens, dining rooms, and laundries (e.g., Beecher and Stowe [1869] 1985; Dodd 1914; Peabody and Mann 1877). Archaeology can contribute new information about the extent to which special ideal material culture was actually used at reform sites. Thus, archaeological data could indicate whether reformers at a particular site actually practiced ideally prescribed behaviors or modified them. A few feminist historians have discussed some particular situations in which actual material implementation of reforms differed from ideals, due to class differences among women participating in domestic reform (e.g., Cohen 1980; Hayden 1981; Strasser 1982). These cases provided a starting point for further research on diversity in domestic reform. Because the middle- and upper-class women who operated most reform institutions usually wrote the historic documents, these had to be critically read and analyzed for the viewpoints of the mostly working-class participants in reform programs. Evidence emerged of dialogue and negotiation between middle-class domestic reformers and working-class women and their families, especially concerning domestic reform uses of female-controlled public spaces and material culture. This chapter explores how the material implementation of domestic reforms was shaped by women's relationships across class, ethnic, and religious boundaries (Spencer-Wood 1991b).

The use of historic documents is essential to this research. It often would be difficult or impossible to identify domestic reform sites from their physical remains alone. Domestic reform buildings can be indistinguishable either from ordinary domestic buildings in some cases or, in other cases, from other large-scale institutions. Working women's cooperatives that were housed in domestic-type structures and used ordinary material culture may be difficult to distinguish archaeologically from an ordinary domestic site. Even archaeological identification of domestic reform sites that used ideal material culture can be difficult, because such special equipment was often curated. Few archaeological remains can be expected at urban institutions that either had no yards or at sites that were used by middle- and upper-class reformers concerned with sanitation and the neat appearance of their sites. Thus, little discard is expected at the homes of reformers or their friends, who first implemented domestic innovations, unless they were located in rural areas and had on-site dumps. As domestic appliances became more widely adopted in the twentieth century, more discard may be expected in house yards in rural areas or poor neighborhoods that did not have municipal trash collection. Institutions that had yards where children played with ideal domestic reform material culture, including kindergartens, day nurseries, and industrial schools for girls, have relatively high archaeological potential (Spencer-Wood 1991c).

Survey of Domestic Reform Sites in Boston, ca. 1860–1925

Boston and New York were primary cities in which many domestic reform movements developed. Since 1981, my systematic survey of reform institutions on Boston's landscape has located and assessed the condition of over 120 sites (Spencer-Wood 1984, 1987, 1991b, 1993). This survey focuses more on domestic reform sites than do available historic sources, which highlight selected women's historic sites (e.g., Dubrow 1991; Harrell and Smith 1975). A few historic guidebooks and tours contribute valuable information about a few individual sites in the survey (e.g., Kaufman et al. 1991; McIntyre 1975). Histories of women reformers analyzed ideal designs for towns and buildings but provided only one address for this survey (e.g., Hayden 1981; Ryan 1990). Although archaeologists have excavated utopian communes (e.g., Starbuck 1984), almshouses (e.g., Baugher 1991; Cook 1991; Huey 1991; Peña 1991), and a prostitute reform home (De Cunzo 1991, 1989), domestic reform sites controlled by women have yet to be excavated.

My research to date has been concerned principally with identifying the sites of domestic reform institutions in the Boston area, assessing their historic importance in the urban built environment and landscape, and assessing their present condition (Spencer-Wood 1987). First, domestic reform institutions were identified from histories, historic guidebooks, and records of historic organizations (e.g., King 1885; Woods and Kennedy 1911; Woods 1898; WEIU 1917, 2). Nineteenth-century city histories and guidebooks included few non-Anglo, non-Christian organizations or institutions, some of which I found in modern guidebooks to Jewish and African American sites (e.g., Grossman 1981). Addresses of institutions were most often identified from historic Boston street directories. The geographical location of sites and their movement over the urban landscape were mapped by finding these addresses on historic maps. The shape of buildings outlined on the maps was compared with existing structures to assess their degree of alteration by subsequent construction. Architectural style also was used to assess the age of existing structures. Unfortunately, many domestic reform sites were found to have been destroyed by subsequent construction. Due to space limitations for this chapter, mapped sites (see figs. 9.1, 9.2) have been grouped by their primary function without details, such as name, date, or condition (for details see Spencer-Wood 1987, 1991b, 1993). Sites are numbered, with letters to indicate the geographical movements of organizations over time.

The survey found abundant physical evidence of the ways that domestic reformers combined the public and domestic spheres, in contrast to the

184

SPENCER-WOOD

Victorian separate-spheres ideology. They generated an increasing variety of sites in row houses and larger-scale institutional structures that either domesticated urban public landscapes with female-dominated places (e.g., fig. 9.1: 7, 8, 25, 27, 28, 30, 32, 33, 36) or were women's public institutions for cooperative housekeeping in residential areas (e.g., fig. 9.1: 8–18, 29, 31, 34, 35, 37, 41–53, 55–59, 61–65). Architecturally, most domestic reform sites are distinguished by large communal rooms used for cooperative living, socialized housekeeping, and sometimes for educational classes, recreation, or production of domestic goods and services by unrelated individuals (Spencer-Wood 1987, 1993).

This survey reveals how domestic reformers changed the gender geography of Boston by founding new public housekeeping institutions that increased the physical presence of women in culturally acceptable "domestic" roles and professions in the public landscape. Over time the increasing number and variety of female-dominated and -controlled institutions changed the meaning of public landscapes from male-dominated toward one of greater gender equality. A number of areas in Boston's landscape came to be dominated by clusters of domestic reform institutions and/or the expansion of some institutions into many buildings (e.g., fig. 9.1: 37; 43, 49, 62–64, 29, 17, 7b; 16, 38a,d, 41, 56; 8, 11, 30b, 44a, 59a,c, 45).

Fig. 9.1 and 9.2. Boston proper (9.1, opposite) and greater Boston (9.2, p. 186) domestic reform sites.

Cooperative hotels: 1, 2, 3, 4, 5, 6
Cooperative homes for working women: 7, 8, 9, 10, 11, 12, 13, 58, 59, 62, 64, 65, 69
Charitable reform homes for working-class women: 14, 15, 16, 17, 18, 45
Women's charitable associations: 19, 20, 21
Schools and classes for women's higher education: 22, 23, 28, 33, 35, 36
Women's schools for domestic professions: 24, 25, 27, 34, 46, 60
Domestic reform associations: 26, 33, 54
Public kitchens: 29, 30, 31, 32

Industrial schools and settlements: 37, 53
Kindergartens: 51
Day nurseries: 38, 39, 41, 49
Day nurseries that became settlements: 40, 66, 67
Settlements: 42, 43, 52, 55, 57, 63, 68
Settlements and cooperative homes for working women: 44, 50, 56, 61
Working women's clubs: 47, 48
For site names, dates, and condition, see Spencer-Wood 1987 (for sites 1–50); for updated survey with additional details, see Spencer-Wood 1991a and 1993.

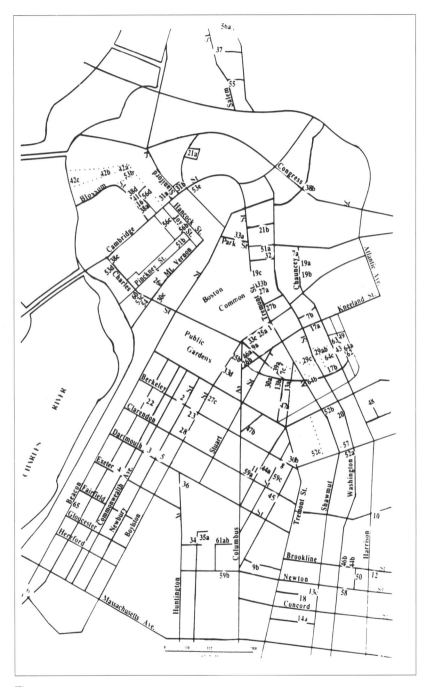

Fig. 9.1.

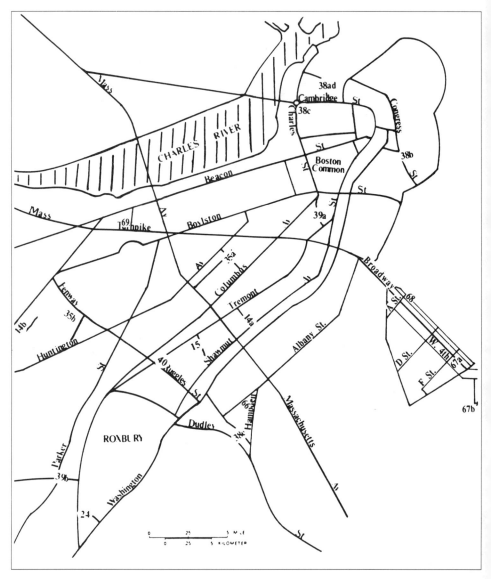

Fig. 9.2.

Over time the reformers increasingly contested male dominance and shaped the public built environment in more permanent ways, as many women's institutions grew from small rented quarters to ownership and sometimes construction of larger structures and grounds. Many organizations remodeled existing structures. A few designed and constructed their own buildings with the large communal rooms specifically needed for domestic reform activities (e.g., fig. 9.1: 7c, 8, 10, 11, 18, 42c, 52c, 58). Some of the now-destroyed domestic reform structures had towered over the surrounding built environment (e.g., fig. 9.1: 7c, 8, 42c, 52c), and others are still prominent buildings in their neighborhoods (fig. 9.1: 10, 11, 18, 58).

Class and Ethnic Relationships on Boston's Landscape

The rest of this chapter discusses material evidence of class and ethnic relationships between reformers and their client working-class communities. This research addresses the social control thesis, in which many historians have contended that the real purpose of nineteenth-century reform was the construction of class distinctions and social control of the burgeoning, mostly immigrant lower class by the middle and upper classes, who felt that their dominance and the existing social order were threatened (e.g., Blumin 1989; Gettleman 1963a, 1963b; Karger 1987; Lissak 1989). Americanization has been considered a major mechanism used to impose middle class values on the passive working class.

The survey provided geographic evidence of class and ethnic relationships. Domestic reform organizations, classes, and schools run by and for women in the upper classes (fig. 9.1: 22, 23, 28) were located in the fashionable Back Bay where many of these women lived, often in hotels with cooperative housekeeping by servants, which freed middle- and upper-class women for public activities such as domestic reform (fig. 9.1: 1–6; Spencer-Wood 1991c, 1987). Many employment bureaus, classes, and schools of cooking, housekeeping, salesmanship, and millinery, run by middle-class reformers to train working women, were located near the interface of the Back Bay and the downtown business district, easily accessible to both the reformers and working women (fig. 9.1: 25, 27, 33, 34, 35, 36). Working women's cooperative homes, often founded by religious orders, were mostly located in the South End to be near work (fig. 9.1; fig. 9.2: 9, 10, 11, 12, 13, 14). Religious separatism led each sect to establish its own homes for working women, which often had elitist restrictive rules for residents because they were founded *for*, not *by*, working women (Stein 1898, 406–7). Some types of domestic reform institutions included both centralized and neighborhood geographic distributions. For instance, the main New England Public Kitchen was centrally located to distribute school lunches throughout Boston (fig. 9.1: 30), but branches were located in the neighborhoods of the immigrant groups they served (fig. 9.1: 29, 31). Middle-class reformers operated kindergartens, day nurseries, housekeeping cooperatives, playgrounds, clubs, and a wide variety of industrial and domestic classes in poor ethnically mixed neighborhoods, often in settlements (fig. 9.1: 38, 39, 41). The distributed nature of sites providing similar services to different neighborhoods indicates that reformers were reaching out to make it easy for the lower classes to use their services rather than making people come to a centralized location, as in the modern welfare system.

While most domestic reform institutions founded by middle- or upper-class Anglo women remained in a neighborhood as its ethnic composition changed (fig. 9.1: 37, 42, 43), institutions founded by non-Anglo women usually moved across the landscape with their ethnic group (e.g., fig. 9.1: 53, 61). However, some institutions established by elite reformers changed both function and location through time. For instance, the Willard Settlement started in 1894 as a working women's club in the North End and became a working women's cooperative home in 1897. The following year it expanded into a settlement on Beacon Hill and moved into the West End in 1908 (Woods and Kennedy 1911, 132; fig. 9.1: 56).

While most women's reform organizations were integrated (Denison House Reports [DH Reports] 1914, 13; Elizabeth Peabody House [EPH] 1909, 15; North Bennet Street Industrial School Records [NBSIS] 1881, 10; Stanton 1985, 9), many Anglo institutions were racially segregated, including early kindergartens, kitchen gardens, and South End House, Boston's earliest settlement, founded by and for men (Hayden 1981, 126; South End House 1910, 1-2, 4, 26-27). Social work developed in settlements, where mostly middle-class, college-educated women and/or men lived cooperatively and offered educational and social programs to surrounding poor immigrant neighborhoods.

By using a feminist perspective I found evidence that minority women were not passive victims of the racism of some Anglo and/or Christian domestic reform institutions. Instead, minority women empowered themselves by organizing separate parallel institutions, which demonstrates that domestic reform institutions offered services that were valuable to, and desired by, minority women. In Boston one example of parallelism was the French YWCA established in 1902 in a residential-type row house near the larger Anglo YWCA (Eaves 1917, 108; fig. 9.1: 59). African American women, excluded from many white institutions by racism, founded their own parallel institutions, including YWCAs in the South and the Women's Era Club of Boston, which did not exclude Anglos. In these organizations African American women expressed group solidarity and mutual aid. Further, they held leadership positions that they could not have held in racist Anglo organizations (Calkins 1960, 46; Scott 1991, 109, 219n39). African American women also founded cooperative homes to meet the particular needs of their sisters migrating from the rural South to Northern cities. The Harriet Tubman House in Boston was founded for this purpose in 1904 by six middle-class African American women (Garcia n.d.; fig. 9.1: 61). The house became a settlement after 1910 (Garcia n.d.). In this case, class relationships paralleled those of Anglo-American reformers, in which cooperative homes for working women were usually founded by middle-class women. However, some African American cooperative homes were founded by, as well as for, working women, such as the Phillis Wheatley homes across the United States, started in Cleveland by Edna Jane Hunter in 1911 (Hine 1990, 78–81).

Jewish women, excluded from many Catholic and Protestant institutions, founded their own clubs, industrial schools, and settlement houses. Jewish organizations were founded not simply in reaction to exclusion but also as an expression of the strong self-identity among Jews as a group (fig. 9.1: 48, 53). Yet class and ethnic divisions existed within Jewish organizations, just as in Anglo organizations. In Boston, the Hebrew Ladies' Sewing Circle, founded in 1869, was copied after the high-status, Yankee, Boston Sewing Circle, which excluded Jews. Both sewing circles employed poor women to sew garments that were then given to other poor people. This organization declined to be revived in 1879 by Lina (Mrs. Jacob H.) Hecht as the Hebrew Ladies' Sewing Society. In 1889, several young women were encouraged by Mrs. Hecht to found the Hebrew Industrial School for girls on Chambers Street (fig. 9.1: 53; Schindler 1889). This institution had ethnic and class divisions similar to those at the Protestant-run North Bennet Street Industrial School (NBSIS), which once served a largely Jewish community. The established middle-class German Jewish reformers sought to "Americanize" and lift up poorer East European Jews into the middle class by teaching them proper personal hygiene and healthy, sanitary living habits. However, the reformers offered manual training classes, such as sewing, that would only fit the poorer Jews for low-paid manual labor, such as domestic service. The East European Jewish immigrants did not passively accept this but instead demanded intellectual education.

Parents often refused to send their girls to classes that they felt were training for domestic service, such as kitchen gardens (Hayden 1981, 126;

Lincoln House Records [LHR] 1905, 44). However, many parents would send their girls to similar classes in cooking, sewing, and housekeeping as preparation for wifely homemaking roles. It may be that upwardly mobile working-class families were emulating the middle-class cult of domesticity. As a result, girls were often trained in domestic handicrafts using ordinary household equipment, although some settlements in Boston did offer courses in laundry machines, typing, and machine-sewing (NBSIS 1881, 11; 1909; LHR 1906, 27–28), which prepared women and men for industrial occupations. In the yards of industrial schools for girls and of settlements, archaeologists might find small lost artifacts possibly indicating, for instance, the popularity of hand-sewing classes by numbers of needles and thimbles. Excavation of bobbins and other small parts of sewing machines might indicate the extent to which they were used.

After the Hebrew Industrial School became the Hecht House settlement in 1921, Mrs. M. H. Solomon successfully fought to open it to Italians and other white non-Jews. She attributed the success of this effort partly to the fact that Mrs. E. W. White opened the Elizabeth Peabody House (EPH) to Jews, stating in the 1908 report, "This year, at last, we have recognized no difference in creed or race" (EPH 1909, 15). Thus, segregation by both Anglos and Jews decreased together. However, according to Mrs. Solomon, when Hecht House moved to Dorchester with the Jewish community in 1936, it was only partly opened to African Americans, and subsequently closed as this group increasingly dominated the community and the Jews fragmented into the suburbs (Solomon 1977, 2: (7), 336–38, 346, 381–83, 390; (8), 425–26).

Archaeologists might be able to distinguish whether reform institutions were segregated or integrated, which often was not recorded in documents. Religious segregation would be suggested by the distinctive artifacts of only one religion, while artifacts from more than one religion would indicate some integration. Archaeologists also might contribute undocumented information about variation in nonreligious artifacts due to religious, ethnic, or class segregation. For instance, excavation of weights, measures, or parts of bunsen burners would indicate courses in scientific cooking that were mostly for the white middle and upper classes. In contrast, ordinary household utensils were used in courses that trained poor whites and African Americans for homemaking and/or domestic service (Spencer-Wood 1991c).

Over time many kinds of domestic reform institutions shifted away from segregation by class and ethnicity and became more integrated. For instance, the movement for American kindergartens, started in 1860 in

Boston by Elizabeth Peabody, was initially for elite white children and used special Froebelian toys that were invented to develop children's mental, spiritual, and manual abilities (fig. 9.3; Weber 1969, 1–11, 22). Elizabeth Peabody's first kindergarten was initially located in downtown Boston, but it later moved to the middle- to upper-class neighborhood of Beacon Hill, where many of her friends lived in a radical intellectual community (fig. 9.1: 51). Kindergartens in many cities developed from private classes for children whose parents could afford it to popular, charitable, ethnically integrated classes that the reformers then persuaded public schools to adopt, starting in 1873 (Snyder 1972, 61; Weber 1969, 41). In Boston, starting in 1877, Pauline Agassiz Shaw founded thirty-one racially integrated charitable kindergartens that used both ideal Froebelian equipment and a variety of other toys. Five of the kindergartens became settlements (Woods and Kennedy 1911; Women's Educational Association [WEA] 1924). At these popular kindergartens poor children were given preference and middleclass children placed on a waiting list (Blodgett 1971, 279; Ross 1976, 12, 20).

Buildings with yards where children played and would lose artifacts, such as kindergartens, have relatively high archaeological potential, especially if located in poor neighborhoods without municipal garbage collection. Archaeologists might contribute undocumented information about the extent to which kindergartens used Froebel's special equipment and methods versus more ordinary toys and kinds of play (fig. 9.3; Ross 1976, 20). While most photographs are ideally posed with Froebel's blocks on tables in front of orderly children (Massachusetts 1893, plate LXX), a unique realistic lithograph indicates that a variety of toys and play activities were used at racially integrated North Bennet Street School kindergarten, which served a poor immigrant neighborhood (fig. 9.4; Blodgett 1971, 279; Stanton 1985, cover). Similarly, in the kindergarten founded in 1891 at her Hull House settlement in Chicago's immigrant section, Jane Addams used both ideal and ordinary equipment and toys and displayed Italian madonnas and cherubs on the walls (Addams 1960, 127–28; Hayden 1981, 97, 126, 165; Weber 1969, 43). These records suggest that some reformers varied from ideal Froebelian methods and equipment, whether for economic reasons or to appeal to the ethnic or religious orientation of the neighborhood.

Negotiations

Several documented examples illustrate verbal and nonverbal dialogue and negotiation between reformers and working-class and/or minority women and their families over the uses of domestic reform spaces and material cul-

Figure 9.3. Advertisements for Froebel kindergarten gifts with durable parts that archaeologists might recover. These include metal rings (top left), wire model parts (below left), pricking needles (top right), weaving needles (below right), shells, and seeds (bottom). Children's clay products could also be found by archaeologists, but Froebelian blocks usually would not be preserved. The relative numbers of Froebelian and other toys would indicate the degree of adherence to Froebel lessons (Peabody and Mann 1884, 14, 16–18, 21, 26, 36–37; Palmer 1916, 130–131, 136–137, 146–147).

Figure 9.4. Unusually realistic lithograph of late 19th-century kindergarten at
    North Bennet Street Industrial School, showing miniature furniture and a
    variety of ordinary toys and drawings, language instruction, and Froebelian
    square, rectangular, and triangular blocks. From *Frank Leslie's Illustrated
    Newspaper* 4 June 1881: 239—40. Courtesy North Bennet Street School.

ture. These cases show that poor women and their families were not passive
recipients of reform. While many programs, such as day nurseries, kindergartens, gardening, and clubs, were popular, changes were requested in
some programs (NBSIS 1888-96, 1906). In addition, new programs sometimes were requested, as when neighborhood boys persuaded reformers to
set up carpentry classes at North Bennet Street School (NBSIS 1881, 16-
19; fig. 9.1: 37). However, some people contested reformers' actions and
sometimes used reform programs to empower themselves in ways not intended by reformers. Reformers often modified their behavior and services

because most sought to improve the lives of poor women. Poor people had power because their participation was needed for reform programs to be successful.

Thus, for instance, reformers changed their ideology, activities, material culture, and landscapes at the Magdalen Society Asylum in Philadelphia, a reformatory cooperatively run by men and women for women that they considered to have "strayed from the paths of virtue." The reformers changed their behavior both in response to actions of residents and as part of the societal shift from religious ideologies emphasizing repentance and punishment for "sinners" to a more positive view of "fallen" women as victims who could be reformed through a physically and morally uplifting environment. In the first half of the century, attempts at reform were thwarted by women who mostly used the home for temporary shelter in hard times, especially winter. Excavations in the yard of the home produced a mix of unmatched donated and purchased tableware. The "family," "inmates," or "Magdalens" (reformers' terms for residents) probably used the large numbers of plain glass tumblers, creamware, and edged pearlware that materially expressed the moral values of modesty, frugality, simplicity, and conservatism that the Society sought to instill in "fallen" women. The few items of unmatched, more expensive decorated stemware and teaware probably were used by the matron and to serve wine or tea to wealthy patrons and benefactors in the well-appointed parlors and garden of the Magdalen Asylum. The reformers were constantly constructing fences around the yard, which were replaced with a massive brick wall in 1843 after a storm damaged the wooden fences. Similar to a cloister, the enclosed yard separated and protected the Magdalens from worldly temptations and disorderly undesirable elements. At the same time, walls and restrictive rules kept inmates secluded in the Asylum, leading to an increasing number of escapes after a one-year stay was required in the 1870s (De Cunzo 1991).

In the last quarter of the nineteenth century the reformers modified their behavior and beliefs in some positive ways, in accordance with ideological changes in society. After 1880, a new matron had a playground and swing constructed in the yard, a gymnasium added, and nonreligious entertainments, classes, and outings increased. All of these changes indicate a shift toward a belief that "fallen" women were socially disadvantaged and could be reformed by creating a healthy social and physical environment (De Cunzo 1989, 27–33; 1991). In 1907, the matron noted in replacing the old, mostly plain and edged white ceramics (of types excavated by De Cunzo [1991]), that "new decorated dishes have been purchased . . . all go to make a new departure from the old, old ways of a century ago" (De

Cunzo 1989, 31). These changes suggest that the ideologies of the Cult of Real Womanhood (Cogan 1989) and Domestic Reform were combined to promote health, self-respect, and self-improvement as well as training for domestic work. The more empowering reform program, and increasing recruitment of sexually wayward girls who had recently come to the city from the country, resulted in far fewer escapes, deaths, and dismissals for improper conduct in the last decades of the nineteenth century (De Cunzo 1991, 19). While many residents resisted being reformed, others had a benign view of the experience as an alternative to prison (Rosen and Davidson 1977, 193–96). Positive ideologies supported the reformers in developing an approach that more successfully negotiated an acceptable common ground between the interests of the reformers and those of the Magdalens. Such reformatories can be viewed as working women's cooperative homes, in accordance with the recent feminist critique of historical archaeologists who took the male view of prostitutes as entertainment (Spencer-Wood 1991d).

Working women's cooperative homes were the most numerous type of domestic reform site in this survey and across the United States (Hayden 1981). Middle-class reformers operated most "charitable" working women's homes, including YWCAS. Although these homes were often patronizing, moralistic, and restrictive, the increasing number of women voluntarily using them over the nineteenth century indicates that working-class women still found cooperative homes to be better on balance than commercial boardinghouses. Working women benefitted from "charitable" homes' lower costs for room and board, and from facilities such as laundries, libraries, gymnasiums, classes, and social clubs (Meyerowitz 1988, 80–83; Stein 1898). Architecturally, cooperative homes offering services or classes, and those with workrooms where residents could produce sewed goods or laundry for market, had more large communal rooms than homes where the residents only cooperated in housekeeping (Spencer-Wood 1991c). Around the turn of the century, elite women maternalistically running Chicago YWCAS responded to working-class residents' complaints by loosening some rules, setting up resident governance bodies, and permitting more socialization with men in the parlors. The residents also requested more privacy, resulting in the construction of more single rooms in the early twentieth century (Meyerowitz 1988, 86–89). Thus, working-class residents of YWCAS empowered themselves by giving feedback that led elite women to modify their behavior in running the YWCAS.

Working women's cooperative homes have high archaeological potential because they usually had yards in which some artifacts were lost or discarded, often because they were located in poor neighborhoods without municipal garbage collection. The philosophy of women's homes and their attitude toward residents may be inferred from the kinds of ceramics and glass excavated, as indicated in the shift from a wide variety of donated ceramics to the transfer-printed set bought by the Magdalen Home in Philadelphia. Inexpensive plain white ceramics would communicate a different meaning than the institutional monogrammed ceramics used at the YWCA (fig. 9.1: 7, 8) or middle-class transfer-printed sets at women's hotels (e.g., fig. 9.1: 58). Archaeologists might find remains of unusually large foundations of specifically constructed buildings such as settlements and cooperative homes for working women (e.g., fig. 9.1: 10, 11, 42c), including the Boston YWCA (fig. 9.1: 7c, 8), which had dividing walls for a large basement dining room, a kitchen with footings for a large stove, and a laundry with footings for large-scale equipment (Boston Young Women's Christian Association Records [BYWCA] 1875, 15; 1885, 16–17; EPH 1915; Eva Whiting White Papers [EWW] n.d.a, n.d.b, c.1934, 2).

Poor women and their families successfully negotiated with reformers over the kinds of food to be produced and sold to them at low prices by public kitchens, which were founded in the 1890s in Boston by Ellen Swallow Richards, MIT's first female professor. Subsequently public kitchens were established at Hull House in Chicago, in New York City, and near Providence, Rhode Island (Hunt 1912, 220). The bland Yankee menu offered by reformers was rejected by poor non-Anglo women and their families, who demanded that the kitchens offer flavorful ethnic dishes if they were to be patronized for more than hot water and broth (Hayden 1981, 124–26, 287, 320n54; Strasser 1982, 208–9). One working-class woman protested, "I don't want to eat what's good for me; I'd ruther eat what I'd ruther" (Addams 1960, 102). A man from Southern Europe pointed to a baked Indian pudding and declared "You needn't try to make a Yankee out of me by making me eat that" (Hunt 1912, 220). The middle-class reformers who ran public kitchens responded by modifying their kitchen menus and selling food for school lunches, to hospitals, and to factory workers (Hayden 1981). They had to overcome their elitist ethnocentrism and learn from women in other ethnic groups in order to provide services of real utility to them. Minority women successfully negotiated with the dominant reformers to obtain specific uses of reform spaces.

Although reformers were very concerned with sanitation, public kitchens in poor neighborhoods—often in settlements—might have yards where some remains of food or special equipment might be deposited. Assemblages could include parts of Aladdin ovens, special insulated heat-retaining containers to transport food, bunsen burners, scales, weights, and scientific measures and glassware. Unless broken, such equipment would usually be curated. Few such archaeological remains can be expected at the downtown sites with municipal garbage collection (e.g., fig. 9.1: 30, 32; Spencer-Wood 1991c). More remains might be deposited at public kitchens in poor neighborhoods without garbage collection (e.g., fig. 9.1: 29, 31).

Historians frequently have interpreted the real purpose of women's and men's voluntary organizations to be the construction of class distinctions, the social control of the working classes, and the Americanization of immigrants (e.g., Hewitt 1984; Rothman 1978; Ryan 1981; Stansell 1986). While these may have been goals of some reformers, this research supports Scott's (1991) conclusions that these explanations are too simplistic. First, I found reformers met their goals of creating useful "respectable" female public professions, and in the process materially shifted the public landscape from male dominance toward greater gender equality prior to women's suffrage. Further, I found, as Scott did, that many women's organizations worked to dissolve existing social boundaries between women (fig. 9.1: 33, 37, 43; Scott 1991, 4). The most commonly expressed goal of reform organizations was to share middle-class privileges, in order to uplift the lower classes (Blair 1980, 73; Young Women's Christian Association of Cambridge Records [YWCAC] 1902, 5; EWW 1947, 7; BYWCA 1883, 20-22; Denison House Records n.d., 1-2; NBSIS 1881, 23; 1889, 22; Scott 1991, 105; WEIU n.d.b). Many women's organizations promoted social order (*not* social control) and Americanization not to keep people "in their place" but to assist the lower classes in reaching their own goals of economic independence and upward mobility into the middle class (Crocker 1992, 61; Scott 1991, 4; Solomon 1977, 2: 7-366). Thus, many institutions, especially settlements, taught not only English, civics, and patriotic songs but also promoted immigrant pride in their own cultures, songs, and skills, including facilitating the manufacture and sale of hand-crafted goods (e.g., DH Reports 1916, 28-30; LHR 1899, 1902; Stanton 1985, 31-32).

This research supports Crocker's (1992) conclusion that her initial leftist perspective of "social welfare as social control" (4) was not useful in analyzing settlements because it stressed manipulation and coercion by the dominant class, thereby overlooking the ability of the lower classes to resist and turn "controlling institutions to their own ends" (19). The dominant ideology thesis of social control is fundamentally flawed in the case of domestic reform organizations because participation in their programs was usually voluntary (except for reformatories that were alternatives to prison). Working-class and minority people could and did exert power over reform services by founding their own institutions and by voicing objections or not participating in reformers' programs that they did not think were useful. Therefore, middle- or upper-class reformers could not impose their values and preferences on the lower classes. The elitism and racism of the age did hamper many services offered by reformers, as in the Yankee menu offered non-Anglo poor women and their families at public kitchens. However, reform programs created dialogue among diverse women, increasing understanding across ethnic and class boundaries. This research found many examples (more than could be included here) demonstrating that working classes and minorities were not passive recipients of reform but that they acted and communicated to empower themselves through reform organizations. Many participants contested programs, such as training for domestic service, that addressed middle-class concerns such as the "servant problem" but not the upwardly-mobile aspirations of many working-class people. Further, working-class women requested, demanded, and gained greater social independence in institutions controlled by middle-class women, such as YWCAS. Because most reformers really intended to assist and protect working women rather than control them, they modified their behavior and the services offered working families at their request (e.g., NBSIS 1881, 16–19; Spencer-Wood 1991b). This chapter has demonstrated how archaeological data can contribute to our understanding of the ways that material implementation of reform programs varied from prescribed ideals due to class, ethnicity, and negotiations among the diversity of women and families empowering themselves through domestic reform.

Acknowledgments

First and foremost, this chapter has benefited from comments by Elizabeth Scott. LuAnn De Cunzo generously provided the data on the Magdalen Society Asylum in Philadelphia. In addition, I am also grateful for assistance from the staff of the Schlesinger Library at Radcliffe College and two undergraduates in the Radcliffe partners program. This research also drew on sources at Wellesley College library, Wheelock College library and archives, Simmons College archives, MIT archives, North Bennet Street Industrial School, and Widener Library at Harvard.

References

Addams, Jane
1960   *Twenty Years at Hull-House.* New York: New American Library. Reprint of 1910 edition, Phillips.

Baugher, Sherene
1991   An Archaeological and Historical Perspective on New York City's First Municipal Almshouse (1736-1797). Paper presented in the symposium "Visible Charity: The Archaeology of the Almshouse" at the 1991 Conference on Historical and Underwater Archaeology, Richmond, January 10.

Beard, Mary R.
1915   *Woman's Work in Municipalities.* New York: D. Appleton & Co.

Beaudry, Mary C., Lauren J. Cook, and Stephen A. Mrozowski
1991   Artifacts and Active Voices: Material Culture as Social Discourse. In *The Archaeology of Inequality*, ed. R. H. McGuire and R. Paynter, 150-91. Oxford: Basil Blackwell.

Beecher, Catharine E., and Harriet Beecher Stowe
1985   *The American Woman's Home, or Principles of Domestic Science.* New York: J.B. Ford & Co.; reprint of 1869 edition with introduction by Joseph Van Why, Hartford, Conn.: Stowe-Day Foundation.

Berg, Barbara J
1978   *The Remembered Gate: Origins of American Feminism. The Woman and the City 1800–1860.* Oxford: Oxford University Press.

Blair, Karen J.
1980   *The Clubwoman as Feminist: True Womanhood Redefined, 1868–1914.* New York: Holmes and Meier.

Blodgett, Geoffrey
1971   Pauline Agassiz Shaw. In *Notable American Women 1607–1950: A Biographical Dictionary*, ed. Edward T. James, Janet W. James, and Paul S. Boyer, 278-80. Cambridge: Belknap Press of Harvard University Press.

Blumin, Stuart
1989   *The Emergence of the Middle Class: Social Experience in the American City, 1760–1900.* Cambridge: Cambridge University Press.

Boston Young Women's Christian Association Records (BYWCA). Schlesinger Library, Radcliffe College, Cambridge, Mass.
1875   *Ninth Annual Report of the Young Women's Christian Association, Boston.* Boston: J. M. Hewes, Printer.
1883   *Seventeenth Annual Report of the Young Women's Christian Association, Boston.* Boston: Frank Wood, Printer.
1885   *Nineteenth Annual Report of the Young Women's Christian Association, Boston.* Boston: Frank Wood, Printer.

Calkins, Gladys Gilkey. Schlesinger Library, Radcliffe College, Cambridge, Mass.
1960   The Negro in the Young Women's Christian Association: A Study of the

Development of YWCA Interracial Policies and Practices in Their Historic Setting. M.A. thesis, Department of Religion, Columbian College of George Washington University.

Carroll, Berenice A., ed.
1976   *Liberating Women's History.* Urbana: University of Illinois Press.

Chambers-Schiller, Lee Virginia
1984   *Liberty a Better Husband. Single Women in America: The Generations of 1780–1840.* New Haven, Conn.: Yale University Press.

Clarke, David L.
1978   *Analytical Archaeology.* Columbia University Press, New York.

Cogan, Frances B.
1989   *All-American Girl: The Ideal of Real Womanhood in Mid-Nineteenth-Century America.* Athens: University of Georgia Press.

Cohen, Lizabeth
1980   Embellishing a Life of Labor: An Interpretation of the Material Culture of American Working-Class Homes, 1885-1915. *Journal of American Culture* 3 (4): 752-75.

Conkey, Margaret W., and Janet D. Spector
1984   Archaeology and the Study of Gender. *Advances in Archaeological Method and Theory* 7: 1-38.

Cook, Lauren J.
1991   The Uxbridge Poor Farm in the Documentary Record. In *Archaeological Investigations at the Uxbridge Almshouse Burial Ground in Uxbridge, Massachusetts,* ed. R. J. Elia and A. B. Wesolowsky, 40-81. British Archaeological Reports International Series 564. Oxford: Tempus Reparatum.

Cott, Nancy F.
1977   *The Bonds of Womanhood: "Woman's Sphere" in New England, 1780–1835.* New Haven, Conn.: Yale University Press.

Cowan, Ruth S.
1983   *More Work for Mother: The Ironies of Household Technology from the Open Hearth to the Microwave.* New York: Basic Books.

Crocker, Ruth H.
1992   *Social Work and Social Order: The Settlement Movement in Two Industrial Cities, 1889–1930.* Urbana: University of Illinois Press.

De Cunzo, Lu Ann
1991   The Material Culture of a Prostitute's Reform: The Magdalen Society of Philadelphia, 1800-1916. Paper presented at the annual meeting of the Society for Historical Archaeology, Richmond, January 10.
1989   Final Phase II Report: Cultural Resources Survey of the Magdalen Society Site at the Site of the Futures Center, The Franklin Institute Science Museum, Philadelphia, Pa. Philadelphia: The Clio Group, E.R. No. 88-0592-101-C.

Deetz, James
1977   *In Small Things Forgotten*. Garden City, N.Y.: Anchor Press/Doubleday.
de Lauretis, Teresa
1986   Feminist Studies/Critical Studies: Issues, Terms, and Contexts. In *Feminist Studies/Critical Studies*, ed. Teresa de Lauretis, 1–19. Bloomington: Indiana University Press.
Denison House Records. Schlesinger Library, Radcliffe College, Cambridge, Mass.
n.d.   Denison House. The Boston College Settlement. Box 6, Folder 39.
Denison House Reports (DH Reports)
1914   *Denison House: The College Settlement in Boston. Annual Report for the Year Ending October 1, 1914*.
1916   *Denison House: The College Settlement in Boston. Annual Report for the Year Ending October 1, 1916*.
Deutsch, Sarah
1990   Learning to Talk More Like a Man: Boston Women's Cross-Class Organizations, 1870–1950. Paper presented at the annual conference of the Organization of American Historians.
Dodd, Margaret E.
1914   *Chemistry of the Household*. Chicago: American School of Home Economics.
Dubrow, Gail Lee
1991   Preserving Her Heritage: American Landmarks of Women's History. Ph.D. dissertation, Department of Urban Planning, University of California, Los Angeles.
Eaves, Lucile
1917   *The Food of Working Women in Boston: An Investigation by the Department of Research of the Women's Educational and Industrial Union, Boston, in cooperation with the State Department of Health*. Boston: Wright and Potter.
Eggan, Frederick R.
1950   *Social Organization of the Western Pueblos*. Chicago: University of Chicago Press.
Elizabeth Peabody House (EPH). Boston.
1909   *Thirteenth Annual Report of the Elizabeth Peabody House: Report for the Year 1908*. Boston: Thomas Todd Co.
1915   *Nineteenth Annual Report of the Elizabeth Peabody House: Report for the Year 1914*. Boston: Thomas Todd Co.
Eva Whiting White Papers (EWW). Schlesinger Library, Radcliffe College, Cambridge, Mass.
n.d.a   Elizabeth Peabody House General Description by Schlesinger Library.
n.d.b   Elizabeth Peabody House. Settlement Council Neighborhood Service Center. Service Report.
c.1934   The Elizabeth Peabody House, 357 Charles St. 1945 Chronology of Elizabeth Peabody House (to 1945).

1947   Sixty years of Settlements: 1887–1947. United Settlements of Greater Boston. Box 2, Folder 22.

Frank Leslie's Illustrated Newspaper.

1881   North End Industrial Home. 4 June 1881: 239–40.

Garcia, Frieda

n.d.   Harriet Tubman and the Harriet Tubman House of United South End Settlements in Boston, Massachusetts. Pamphlet, n.p.

Gero, Joan M., and Margaret W. Conkey, eds.

1991   *Engendering Archaeology: Women and Prehistory.* Oxford: Basil Blackwell.

Gettleman, Marvin E.

1963a   Charity and Social Classes in the United States, 1874–1900, I. *American Journal of Economics and Sociology* 22 (April): 313–29.

1963b   Charity and Social Classes in the United States, 1874–1900, II. *American Journal of Economics and Sociology* 22 (July): 417–26.

Ginzberg, Lori D.

1990   *Women and the Work of Benevolence: Morality, Politics and Class in Nineteenth Century United States.* New Haven, Conn.: Yale University Press.

Gordon, Linda

1976   *Woman's Body, Woman's Right: A Social History of Birth Control in America.* New York: Grossman.

Grossman, Brigite S.

1981   *Experiencing Jewish Boston.* Jewish Community Center of Greater Boston.

Harding, Sandra

1986   *The Science Question in Feminism.* Ithaca, N.Y.: Cornell University Press.

Harrell, Pauline C., and Margaret S. Smith

1975   *Victorian Boston Today: Ten Walking Tours.* Boston: New England Chapter, Victorian Society of America.

Hartman, Mary S., and Lois W. Banner

1974   *Clio's Consciousness Raised: New Perspectives on the History of Women.* New York: Harper and Row.

Hayden, Dolores

1981   *The Grand Domestic Revolution: A History of Feminist Designs for American Homes, Neighborhoods, and Cities.* Cambridge: MIT Press.

Hewitt, Nancy A.

1984   *Women's Activism and Social Change: Rochester, New York, 1856–1872.* Ithaca, N.Y.: Cornell University Press.

1990   Charity or Mutual Aid? Two Perspectives on Latin Women's Philanthropy in Tampa, Florida. In *Lady Bountiful Revisited: Women Philanthropy and Power,* ed. Kathleen D. McCarthy, 55–69. New Brunswick, N.J.: Rutgers University Press.

Hine, Darlene C.

1990   "We Specialize in the Wholly Impossible": The Philanthropic Work of Black Women. In *Lady Bountiful Revisited: Women, Philanthropy and*

Power, ed. Kathleen D. McCarthy, 70–93. New Brunswick, N.J.: Rutgers University Press.

Hodder, Ian

1986   *Reading the Past: Current Approaches to Interpretation of Archaeology*. Cambridge: Cambridge University Press.

Huey, Paul R.

1991   The Almshouse in Dutch and English Colonial North America and Its Precedent in the Old World: Historical and Archaeological Evidence. Paper presented in the symposium "Visible Charity: The Archaeology of the Almshouse" at the 1991 Conference on Historical and Underwater Archaeology, Richmond, January 10.

Hunt, Caroline L.

1912   *The Life of Ellen H. Richards, 1842–1911*. Boston: Whitcomb and Barrows.

Karger, Howard

1987   *The Sentinels of Order: A Study of Social Control and the Minneapolis Settlement House Movements, 1915–1950*. Lanham, Md.: University Press of America.

Kaufman, Polly Welts, Patricia C. Morris, and Joyce Stevens

1991   *Boston Women's Heritage Trail*. Booklet, n.p.

Kelly, Joan

1984   *Women, History, and Theory: The Essays of Joan Kelly*. Chicago: University of Chicago Press.

King, Moses

1885   *King's Handbook of Boston, 1885*. Cambridge, Mass.: Moses King.

Kosko, Bart

1993   *Fuzzy Thinking: The New Science of Fuzzy Logic*. New York: Hyperion.

Kraditor, Aileen S.

1965   *The Ideas of the Woman Suffrage Movement 1890–1920*. New York: Columbia University Press.

Leach, William

1980   *True Love and Perfect Union: The Feminist Reform of Sex and Society*. New York: Basic Books.

Lincoln House Records (LHR). Widener Library, Harvard University.

1899   Lincoln House Bulletin 1899. N.p.

1902   Lincoln House Report for 1902. N.p.

1905   *The Annual Report of Lincoln House for the Year 1905*. Boston: Merrymount.

1906   *The Annual Report of Lincoln House for the Year 1906*. Boston: Merrymount.

Lissak, Rivka

1989   *Pluralism and Progressives: Hull House and the New Immigrants, 1890–1919*. Chicago: University of Chicago Press.

Mascia-Lees, Frances E., Patricia Sharpe, and Colleen Ballerino Cohen

1989   The Postmodernist Turn in Anthropology: Cautions from a Feminist Perspective. *Signs* 15 (1): 7–33.

Massachusetts
1893   *Report of the Commission Appointed to Investigate the Existing Systems of Manual Training and Manual Education.* Boston: Wright and Potter.
McGaw, Judith A.
1989   No Passive Victims, No Separate Spheres: A Feminist Perspective on Technology's History. In *In Context: History and the History of Technology. Essays in Honor of Melvin Kranzberg,* ed. S. H. Cutcliffe and R. C. Post, 172–91. Bethlehem, Pa.: Lehigh University Press.
McIntyre, A. McVoy
1975   *Beacon Hill: A Walking Tour.* Boston: Little, Brown.
Meyerowitz, Joanne J.
1988   *Women Adrift: Independent Wage Earners in Chicago, 1880–1930.* Chicago: University of Chicago Press.
Moore, Henrietta L.
1988   *Feminism and Anthropology.* Minneapolis: University of Minnesota Press.
North Bennet Street Industrial School (Boston, Mass.) Records (NBSIS). Schlesinger Library, Radcliffe College, Cambridge, Mass.
1881   *Report of the North-End Industrial Home: 39 North Bennet Street, January 1880 to April 1881.* Boston: Frank Wood, Printer.
1889   *The Work of the North Bennet Street Industrial School from 1888 to 1889.* Boston: Industrial School Press.
1888–96 Reports of North Bennet Street Industrial School. Handwritten.
1906   *The Work of the North Bennet Street Industrial School: Its First Quarter-Century, 1881–1906. Annual Report for the Year 1904–05.* N.p.
1909   *North Bennet Street Industrial School. Annual Report. 1906–1909. 39 North Bennet St. Boston, Massachusetts.* Worcester, Mass.: Davis Press.
Palmer, Luella A.
1916   *Play Life in the First Eight Years.* Boston: Ginn & Co.
Peabody, Elizabeth P., and Mary Mann
1884   *Guide to the Kindergarten and Intermediate Class; and Moral Culture of Infancy.* 1877. New York: E. Steiger.
Peña, Elizabeth S.
1991   The Albany Almshouse: Eighteenth-Century Wampum Production in Colonial New York. Paper presented in the symposium "Visible Charity: The Archaeology of the Almshouse" at the 1991 Conference on Historical and Underwater Archaeology, Richmond, January 10.
Preston, J. Anne
1987   Millgirl Narratives: Representations of Class and Gender in Nineteenth Century Lowell. *Life Stories/Recits de vie* 3: 21–30.
Reed, Evelyn
1978   *Sexism and Science.* New York: Pathfinder Press.
Reiter, Rayna R.
1975   *Toward an Anthropology of Women.* New York: Monthly Review Press.

Rosaldo, Michelle Z.
1980   The Use and Abuse of Anthropology: Reflections on Feminism and Cross-Cultural Understanding. *Signs* 5 (3): 389–417.
Rosaldo, Michelle Z., and Louise Lamphere
1974   *Woman, Culture and Society.* Stanford: Stanford University Press.
Rosen, Ruth, and Sue Davidson
1977   *The Maimie Papers.* Bloomington: Indiana University Press and the Feminist Press.
Ross, Elizabeth P.
1976   *The Kindergarten Crusade: The Establishment of Pre-School Education in the United States.* Athens: Ohio University Press.
Rossi, Alice S., ed.
1973   *The Feminist Papers: From Adams to de Beauvoir.* New York: Columbia University Press.
Rothman, Sheila M.
1978   *Woman's Proper Place: A History of Changing Ideals and Practices, 1870 to the Present.* New York: Basic Books.
Rubin, Jerome, and Cynthia Rubin
1972   *Comprehensive Guide to Boston.* Newton, Mass.: Emporium Publications.
Ryan, Mary P.
1990   *Women in Public: Between Banners and Ballots, 1825–1880.* Baltimore: Johns Hopkins University Press.
1981   *Cradle of the Middle Class: The Family in Oneida County, N.Y., 1790–1865.* Cambridge: Cambridge University Press, 1981.
Schindler, Solomon
1889   *Israelites in Boston: A Tale Describing the Development of Judaism in Boston.* Boston: Berwick and Smith.
Scott, Anne F.
1990   Women's Voluntary Associations: From Charity to Reform. In *Lady Bountiful Revisited*, ed. Kathleen D. McCarthy, 35–54. New Brunswick, N.J.: Rutgers University Press.
1991   *Natural Allies: Women's Associations in American History.* Urbana: University of Illinois Press.
1971   *The American Woman: Who Was She?* Englewood Cliffs, N.J.: Prentice-Hall.
Scott, Joan W.
1988   *Gender and the Politics of History.* New York: Columbia University Press.
Shaw, Stephanie J.
1991   Black Club Women and the Creation of the National Association of Colored Women. *Journal of Women's History* 3 (2): 10–25.
Snyder, Agnes
1972   *Dauntless Women in Childhood Education 1856–1931.* Washington, D.C.: Association for Childhood Education International.

Solomon, Mrs. Maida Herman

1977   Oral Memoir. 3 vols. William E. Weiner Oral History Library of the American Jewish Committee. Schlesinger Library, Radcliffe College, Cambridge, Mass.

South, Stanley

1977   *Method and Theory in Historical Archeology.* New York: Academic Press.

South End House.

1910   *South End House 1910: Democracy Domesticated.* SEH, Schlesinger Library, Radcliff College, Cambridge, Mass.

Spencer-Wood, Suzanne M.

1971   A Feminist Critique of Eggan's Social Organization of Western Pueblos. Paper for graduate course in Social Organization, Northwestern University. Manuscript in author's possession.

1984   A Survey of Sites and Activities Generated by Boston's Material Feminists. Paper presented at the annual meeting of the Council for Northeast Historical Archaeology, Binghamton, N.Y., October 20.

1987   A Survey of Domestic Reform Movement Sites in Boston and Cambridge, ca. 1865-1905. *Historical Archaeology* 21 (2): 7-36

1989   Feminist Archaeology and the Pro-active Roles of Women in Transforming Gender Concepts, Roles, and Relationships in Nineteenth Century America. Paper presented in the session "Making Women Visible Through Historical Archaeology" at the 1989 Society for Historical Archaeology Conference, Baltimore, January 8.

1991a   Feminist Empiricism: A More Holistic Theoretical Approach. Paper presented in the mini-plenary "Shaken, Not Stirred: Current Gender Issues in Historical Archaeology" at the 1991 Conference on Historical and Underwater Archaeology, Richmond, January 10.

1991b   Feminist Historical Archaeology and Domestic Reform. Paper presented at the Winterthur Conference on Historical Archaeology and the Study of American Culture, Winterthur Museum, Wintherthur, Del., October 3-5. Published proceedings forthcoming.

1991c   Toward an Historical Archaeology of Domestic Reform. In *The Archaeology of Inequality*, ed. R. McGuire and R. Paynter, 231-86. Oxford: Basil Blackwell.

1991d   Towards an Historical Archaeology of the Construction of Gender. In *The Archaeology of Gender, Proceedings of the 22nd [1989] Annual Chacmool Conference*, ed. D. Walde and N. E. Willows, 234-44. Calgary: University of Calgary Archaeological Association.

1992a   A Feminist Program for a Non-sexist Archaeology. In *Quandaries and Quests: Visions of Archaeology's Future*, ed. LuAnn Wandsnider, 98-114. Center for Archaeological Investigations, Occasional Paper 20. Carbondale: Southern Illinois University Center for Archaeological Investigations.

1992b   Class and Ethnicity in Domestic Reform. Paper presented at the 1992 Society for Historical Archaeology Conference on Historical and Underwater Archaeology, Kingston, January 10.

1992c   Introduction to Critiques in Historical Archaeology Symposium. Paper presented at the 1992 Society for Historical Archaeology Conference on Historical and Underwater Archaeology, Kingston, January 9.

1992d   Towards a Feminist Urban Archaeology. Paper presented in the Urban Historical Archaeology session of the annual meetings of the Society for American Archaeology, Pittsburgh, April 11.

1993   How Reform Women Transformed Nineteenth Century American Culture. Invited presentation at the Peabody Museum, Harvard University, Cambridge, Mass., December 1.

Stansell, Christine
1986   *City of Women: Sex and Class in New York, 1789–1860.* New York: Knopf.

Stanton, Laura, ed.
1985   *North Bennet Street School: A Short History 1885–1985.* Boston: Chadis Printing.

Starbuck, David R.
1984   The Shaker Concept of Household. *Man in the Northeast* 28: 73–86.

Stein, Robert
1898   Girls' Cooperative Boarding Homes. *The Arena* March 1898: 397–417.

Stilgoe, John R.
1988   *Borderland: Origins of the American Suburb, 1820–1939.* New Haven, Conn.: Yale University Press.

Strasser, Susan
1982   *Never Done: A History of American Housework.* New York: Pantheon.

Tanner, Nancy, and Adrienne Zihlman
1976   Women in Evolution. Part I: Innovation and Selection in Human Origins. *Signs* 1 (3): 585–608.

Weber, Evelyn
1969   *The Kindergarten: Its Encounter with Educational Thought in America.* New York: Teachers College Press.

Welter, Barbara
1966   The Cult of True Womanhood: 1820–1860. *American Quarterly* 18: 151–74.

Wertheimer, Barbara M.
1977   *We Were There: The Story of Working Women in America.* New York: Pantheon.

Woman's Education Association Records (WEA). Schlesinger Library, Radcliffe College, Cambridge, Mass.
1924   *Ruggles Street Nursery School and Training Centre, Cambridge Nursery School Under the Auspices of the Woman's Education Association of Boston.* Boston: WEA.

Women's Educational and Industrial Union (WEIU) (Boston, Mass.) Records. Schlesinger Library, Radcliffe College, Cambridge, Mass.

n.d.a   History of the WEIU: Origin of the WEIU. Reminiscences of Dr. Harriet Clisby. Handwritten.

n.d.b   The Law of Employer and Domestic Employee. Pamphlet. Boston: Todd. Box 1, Folder 5.

1898   Report of the Employment Committee. Pages from *Report of the Women's Educational and Industrial Union, 264 Boylston, Boston, Massachusetts, for the Year Ending May 1, 1898*. Boston: WEIU. Box 1, Folder 6.

1903   History of the Domestic Reform League: Organized by the Women's Educational and Industrial Union of Boston, Massachusetts, and Under the Special Supervision of the Employment Department of the Union. Box 1, Folder 5.

Woods, Robert A., ed.

1898   *The City Wilderness: A Settlement Study by Residents and Associates of the South End House*. New York: Houghton Mifflin; reprint, New York: Garrett Press, 1970.

Woods, Robert A., and Albert J. Kennedy, eds.

1911   *Handbook of Settlements*. New York: Charities Publications Committee.

Wright, Gwendolyn

1980   Moralism and the Model Home: Domestic Architecture and Cultural Conflict in Chicago, 1873-1913. Chicago: University of Chicago Press.

Wylie, Alison

1991   Feminist Critiques and Archaeological Challenges. In *The Archaeology of Gender, Proceedings of the 22nd [1989] Annual Chacmool Conference*, ed. D. Walde and N. E. Willows, 17-23. Calgary: University of Calgary Archaeological Association.

Young Women's Christian Association of Cambridge (Mass.) Records (YWCAC). Schlesinger Library, Radcliffe College, Cambridge, Mass.

1902   *The Reminder.* May.

Index

lationships in, 187–97; description of, 178–80; feminist approaches to, 176–78; historical archaeology of, 180–87; Jewish women's, 189–90; kindergartens, 190–191; Latin American women's, 177; negotiations within, 191–97. *See also* reform movements, women's

domesticity, 176, 178. *See also* Cult of Domesticity

domination, 92. *See also* domination and resistance

domination and resistance: among African Americans, 81–92, 177, 188–89; among Apaches, 60–75; in domestic reform movements, 191–98; feminist scholarship of, 7; historical archaeology of, 6–7; in mining towns, 134; among Native Alaskans, 35–49

DuBois Boyhood Homesite: description of, 82–83; historical archaeology of, 86–87

DuBois, W.E.B., biographical sketch of, 81–82. *See also* Black Burghardts; Burghardt relatives of W.E.B. DuBois

Edmonds, H.M.W., 41
Eggan, Frederick R., 175
Elliott, Henry, 40–41
Elliott, Russell R., 141
Etholén, Adolf, 40

feminist materialist approach, 181
feminist scholarship: in archaeology, 4–6, 55, 102, 175–76; on colonialism, 7; on domestic reform, 176–78; on domination and resistance, 7; on gender, 10–11; on gender, race, ethnicity, and class, 7–9; on race, 12–13;

in related fields, 4–5, 16n, 175–76; on sexuality, 12–13

feminist theories, Western, 11–13, 56
Ferguson, Leland, 14
Fisher, Charles, 125
Fitch, Jabez, 120
Fort Edward, New York, 118, 120
Fort Stanwix, 124–25
Foucault, Michel, 112n. 2
Freeman, Caesar, 88
Freeman, James, 90
Froebelian toys, 191–93

Garrow, Patrick H., 168n. 4
gender: approaches to historical archaeology of, 5; archaeology of, previous, 4, 101–102, 111, 125–26; as cultural construction, 10–11, 97–99, 101; in frontier societies, historians' models of, 129–130; interrelated with race, ethnicity, and class, 7–9, 13–15, 91–92, 101–102, 131–35, 141–42, 177–78; interrelated with religion, 177–78; interrelated with status and age, 101–102; and sexuality, 9–11

gender inequality, 4, 92
gender roles: construction of masculinity, 102, 112n. 2; nineteenth-century, 102–103; nineteenth-century, in the mining West, 132–35, 139, 141; nineteenth-century, in Washington, D.C., 152–53, 163–66

Gero, Joan, and Margaret Conkey, 4
Gibb, James G., and Julia King, 137
Gordon, Linda, 7, 13
gota, 60, 67–74
gowa, 60, 67–74
Graniger, Caroline, 150, 152
Great Barrington, Massachusetts, description of, 84

Handsman, Russell, 14

About the Editor

ELIZABETH M. SCOTT received an M.A. from the University of Florida in 1984 and a Ph.D. from the University of Minnesota in 1991, both in anthropology. She is an independent consultant (Zooarch Research) and a Research Associate with the Illinois State Museum. Her publications include "A Feminist Approach to Historical Archaeology: Eighteenth-Century Fur Trade Society at Michilimackinac," *Historical Archaeology* (1991); "Gender in Complex Colonial Society: The Material Goods of Everyday Life in a Late Eighteenth-Century Fur-Trading Community" in *The Archaeology of Gender;* and *French Subsistence at Fort Michilimackinac, 1715–1781: The Clergy and the Traders.* Her research interests include the use of feminist and historical materialist approaches to historical archaeology, particularly the archaeology of colonial and postcolonial societies in North America and Central America, and the use of subsistence to examine social and economic relations in past societies.